Debates in Economic History

Edited by Peter Mathias

The Price Revolution in Sixteenth-Century England

The Price Revolution in Sixteenth-Century England

edited with an introduction by
PETER H. RAMSEY

METHUEN & CO LTD

11 NEW FETTER LANE LONDON EC4

First published *1971* by Methuen & Co Ltd
Introduction © *1971* Peter H. Ramsey
Printed in Great Britain by
Richard Clay (The Chaucer Press), Ltd,
Bungay, Suffolk

SBN (hard bound) 416 12180 2
SBN (paperback) 416 29830 3

Distributed in the U.S.A.
by Barnes & Noble Inc.

Contents

Preface

The label 'price revolution' has been firmly attached to the European experience of the sixteenth century by historians, although this was neither the first nor the last great inflationary episode in the economic development of western Europe. The thirteenth and the twentieth centuries share this distinction with the sixteenth. Despite all the complications of establishing normative measures for calculating price indexes and comparing their significance over long distances in time, the broad shapes of the curve are not in doubt: prices (more particularly food prices) tripled between the mid-twelfth and the early fourteenth century; food prices rose between four- and fivefold (although non-agricultural prices much less) between the late fifteenth and the mid-seventeenth century; price indexes have risen about sixfold – so far – during the present century.

As yet little mention has been made of possible monetary influences behind the thirteenth-century price rise; and contemporaries, it seems, did not broach the matter. Some present-day historians have suggested that the decline in prices during the fifteenth century may have been associated with the economy of western Europe running short of precious metals. But, from this point on, contemporaries and later historians have been arguing over the monetary aspects of price movements, and the debate grows more vigorous as it becomes sustained by greater knowledge and newer theorizing. Inflationary times, it seems, have proved more fruitful for such theoretical arguments than deflationary times. In the sixteenth century contemporaries fumbled towards a link between rising prices and the New World silver flooding into Europe through Spain. The financial emergencies of the Napoleonic wars, with the Bank of England off gold, stimulated much important monetary theory and urgent public enquiry, with an unconvertible paper currency widely blamed for the inflation. In the last quarter of the nineteenth century a more sophisticated debate took place over the responsibility which varying quantities of precious metals (plus bimetallism) coming into the world economy had in the upswing of prices in the third quarter of the century and their decline thereafter. At the present time, in very different circumstances, when virtually all countries possess managed currencies and powerful central banks, still more esoteric debate ranges over the 'new monetarism' – the causal relationships between movements in total money supply and incomes.

This revival of monetary theorizing, as an instrument of policy, comes paradoxically at a time when monetary explanations for price movements in the sixteenth century and before have been challenged by analyses based upon 'real' causes, particularly population movements. In all these confrontations between real and monetary causes of price movements famous names have been deployed on opposite sides, from Tooke versus Ricardo to Kaldor versus Friedman. Debate has thus flourished amongst contemporaries arguing over current issues, while economic historians, with the benefit of hindsight, have transferred such theorizing into their interpretations of past sequences. More facts and better theories have not resolved the conflicts of interpretation; nor should mere historians be surprised at this when the current debate still rages amongst economists, with more sophisticated analytical tools and more complete data than historians will ever be able to deploy effectively. Indeed, the progress of these historical debates, as other volumes in this series have exemplified, has reflected swings in intellectual fashions (allowing for a certain time-lag for these to get translated between disciplines) as much as access to new evidence. So often facts have been tributary to theory or – if that dignifies a methodology too much – to hypothesis and hunch.

The latest chapter in the monetary debate (which conceives of limitations in the money supply as a possible restraint upon inflation, rather than an increase in the money supply being itself the sole motive force of inflation) may yet invite a new twist to the interpretation of the price revolution of the sixteenth century. Of course, modern theory has to be transmuted into a very different institutional context, where monetary constraints were so much greater than in our own financially more permissive society – to a context without a permanent public debt, without a central bank or a banking system (or bank money); above all without paper currency and with few of the credit instruments of a modern society. The motive forces behind inflation may have been primarily real, rather than monetary (and these provide the important explanatory hypotheses for changes in the structure of prices and wages). But rising population, increasing public and military spending, or rising private extravagance, as propulsive forces, may have needed an increasing money supply as an agency for activating their impact on the price level. To ask where the money came from is to be led inexorably into another debate – if from abroad, then what does this imply for the balance of payments or the balance of trade; if from within, then what must we infer about stocks of precious metals or the growth of credit and 'money substitutes'? For the sixteenth century, as for any other, a full understanding of price movements perforce requires an understanding of the whole dynamics of economic change at the time.

PETER MATHIAS

Acknowledgements

The editor and publishers wish to thank the following for permission to reproduce the articles listed below:

Professor Y. S. Brenner for 'The Inflation of Prices in Early Sixteenth-Century England' (*Economic History Review*, vol. XIV, 1961–2); *Economica* and the authors for 'Seven Centuries of the Prices of Consumables, Compared with Builders' Wage Rates', by E. H. Phelps Brown and Sheila V. Hopkins (*Economica*, No. 92, November 1956, N.S. vol. XXIII); Professor J. D. Gould for 'The Price Revolution Reconsidered' (*Economic History Review*, vol. XVII, 1964–5); Harvard University Press for 'American Treasure and Andalusian Prices', by Earl J. Hamilton (*Journal of Economic and Business History*, vol. I, No. I, November 1928); *The Scandinavian Economic History Review* and the author for 'The Price Revolution of the Sixteenth Century', by Ingrid Hammarström (vol. V, 1957).

Editor's Introduction

The great price rise in Tudor and early Stuart England has been almost as puzzling to modern economic historians as to worried contemporaries. Those who lived through it lacked the statistical techniques and grasp of economic theory that would have enabled them to interpret their painful experience, and to establish chains of cause and effect. Today we lack the basic evidence on which to build more sophisticated explanations, and it seems unlikely that the gaps in our knowledge will ever be satisfactorily filled. Hence, then and now, there has been a welter of conflicting theories, amply illustrated in the articles collected here, and no wholly convincing account has emerged or seems likely to emerge. Advances in knowledge and technique have deepened our understanding, but have done so chiefly by underlining the complexities of the problem and demolishing some oversimplified explanations offered. The debate remains open, and none of the contributors to this volume would claim to have spoken a final word.

It is in the first place impossible to establish with any certainty how far prices did rise in England during the sixteenth century. For only a few commodities have we reliable and continuous series, where we can be reasonably sure that we are dealing with the same product over a long period of time. The evidence for grain prices is the most abundant, but these are the prices most subject to violent fluctuation with the accidents of seasonal fluctuations or the fate of the harvest. Wool prices, thanks to the labours of P. J. Bowden,[1] are now much better known; these are less volatile than grain prices, though still not immune from the hazards of weather and disease, and of commercial boom and slump. Unavoidable dependence upon institutional records may also produce distorting effects.

[1] P. J. Bowden, *The Wool Trade in Tudor and Stuart England* (1962). See also his valuable article 'Agricultural prices, farm profits, and rents' in *The Agrarian History of England and Wales, Vol. IV, 1500–1640*, ed. Joan Thirsk (1967).

Almshouses and hospitals were able to negotiate long-term bulk contracts with their suppliers, and their records may be insensitive to short-term price changes and understate the extent of price increases. Since, too, such institutions would normally do their own baking and brewing, they record the price paid for wheat, malt and hops, not that of the bread and beer that the townsman bought in the market-place. We are very ill informed about even the most basic commodities, whenever labour costs formed an important constituent of the price. Major industries, such as leather, escape us almost entirely. Services of all kinds are almost entirely undocumented, and ignorance of house rents leaves a formidable gap in our knowledge of the costs of urban living.

Industrial goods raise almost insuperable problems of comparability. While successive statutes laid down official dimensions for woollen cloths, these established minimum rather than normal standards, and might not be rigidly followed. Contemporary descriptions of cloths as 'long' or 'short' are too vague for the historian of prices, and qualitative terms such as 'fine' or 'coarse' are equally baffling and unhelpful. Now and then a merchant's private accounts, such as those of Sir Thomas Kitson in the 1530s or Sir Thomas Gresham in the 1540s,[1] provide details of a series of transactions with a particular clothier, and it is plausible to assume that the cloths are a uniform product. But the series are very short, and the assumption not entirely safe, so the basic difficulty remains. And if England's major industry remains so obscure, there is still less hope of finding good price series for the nascent minor industries of Elizabethan England or for the profusion of imported manufactures – the Italian velvets, Netherlands linens or German copperware – that entered into the cost of living of the wealthier classes.

The problems are multiplied and aggravated when an attempt is made to constitute a general price index or anything approximating to a cost of living index. The most valiant and

[1] Accounts of Sir Thomas Kitson in the Hengrave Hall Deposit 78 (1–4) in Cambridge University Library. The Day Book of Sir Thomas Gresham in Mercers' Hall, London.

successful effort is that of E. H. Phelps Brown and Sheila V. Hopkins, widely used by all historians of the period ever since its appearance in 1956.[1] Since its use has sometimes been uncritical and indiscriminate, it is perhaps worth re-emphasizing the warnings that the authors themselves make. The index is based on a composite unit of consumables, in which foodstuffs are given a heavy weighting and rent omitted. It reflects, therefore, the expenses of the poorer household, not those of the well-to-do. It is necessarily assumed that the weighting remained unchanged over long periods, and that the Tudor family persisted in buying the same goods, year in year out, regardless of variations in their price. This is clearly unrealistic and supposes total rigidity in the housewife's spending habits, not merely in face of temporary changes in the price of bread, meat and butter, but also longer-term changes in price shifts and spending patterns. The index is over-sensitive to harvest fluctuations, as in the late 1550s or 1590s. It is a good approximate guide to the cost of living of an urban wage-labourer (for which purpose it was constructed). It cannot be used as a guide to the cost of living of the squire, merchant or peer, and only with very great caution as a general guide to the movements of prices in Tudor England at large.

The 'equivalent of wage rate of a building craftsman' must be used with similar caution. It is based on recorded wage rates, not earnings, of Oxford building craftsmen. It does not and cannot reflect seasonal and occupational unemployment or payments in kind (such as board and lodging) which may have raised or lowered the labourer's actual earnings at any time. It does not reflect the situation of those agrarian labourers who were able to produce at least some of their own food, and were thus to some extent cushioned against inflation. It represents the extreme and not the typical case.

With these warnings in mind, the figures and graphs may give us a fair impression of the general course of basic commodity prices in Tudor England. The price rise came after a long period of relative stability in the fifteenth century,

[1] See below, pp. 38–41.

interrupted only by two brief rises in the 1440s and 1480s. A sustained upward movement did not begin before 1510, and is clear only in the 1520s, and the use of a composite index tends to conceal the fact that prices of manufactures did not move up as soon or as fast as those of foodstuffs, and perhaps did not rise very appreciably till the 1540s. By the 1550s prices have rather more than doubled, though the exceptionally high figures for 1556 and 1557 clearly reflect the catastrophic harvests of the preceding years. The rate of increase slows in the 1560s, though by the late 1570s and 1580s prices are three times what they had been in 1500, and during this period industrial prices kept pace with agricultural ones. A sharp upswing of food prices in the 1590s meant at least a quadrupling of prices by the turn of the century; this is followed by a slower climb until the 1630s, when another violent leap brought prices to six times the level of 1500. A heavier weighting of industrial products in the index would have the effect of flattening out the sharp peaks of the 1590s and 1630s, and also of prolonging the great inflation into the later seventeenth century (when agricultural prices tend to level off). In some ways this might give a truer overall conspectus of the price rise, though at the cost of masking the very urgent problems of the poor in Elizabethan and early Stuart England.

From the perspective of the twentieth century a sixfold increase in prices over a period of 120 years does not seem so dramatic as to warrant the term 'price revolution'. But to contemporaries, coming as it did after so long a period of price stability, it seemed harsh and unprecedented in its severity, and their institutions were less adaptable and more vulnerable than our own. Understandably there was much discussion of the great 'dearth', though this was concentrated mainly in the two periods of greatest distress, at the middle and at the end of the century, and concerned chiefly with the high price of food, which prompted the most acute social unrest.

Most of the explanations offered by modern historians can be found at the time, albeit in a confused form, though today we would tend to discount the complaints of enclosure in the early part of the century and of the iniquities of middlemen throughout it. The *Discourse of the Common Weal* (1549) offers an early example of a monetary explanation of inflation, since the Doctor (clearly representing the author's views) singles out debasement of the coinage as the mainspring of recent price increases.[1] The revised text of 1581 contains an interesting extension of the theme: faced with the need to explain why prices have not fallen after the deflationary measures of 1551 and the recoinage of 1561 the writer adduces rack-renting and the import of American silver as the main reasons, possibly under the influence of Jean Bodin's treatise of 1568.[2] Debasement and American silver were certainly more plausible explanations than a suggestion of 1551 that exchange depreciation was the 'father of all dearth of almost all things', and even the unrevised text of 1549 showed an intelligent appreciation of the way in which rising prices compelled landlords to raise rents, which in their turn contributed to the inflationary spiral. But no orthodox and accepted explanation emerged by 1600, and much of the discussion bears the marks of mutual recrimination rather than dispassionate analysis. The two favourite themes of twentieth-century historians – American silver and population pressure – had certainly not won general acceptance, though a letter of 1576 made the connection between rising population and the high price of victuals.[3]

Until comparatively recently modern historians concentrated their attention on monetary explanations of the great Tudor price rise. This was due partly to the work of Irving Fisher and his elaboration of the quantity theory of money, and partly to the researches of Earl J. Hamilton who appeared to have established a clear correlation between imports of silver from the New World and rising prices in Andalusia, backed by impressive

[1] Edited by E. Lamond, 1893. The most likely author would appear to be Sir Thomas Smith, though the case against John Hales's authorship has not been conclusively made out.

[2] *La Response de Jean Bodin à M. de Malestroit*, ed. H. Hauser (1932).

[3] A good brief summary of contemporary reactions to the price rise is in pp. 15–23 of R. B. Outhwaite, *Inflation in Tudor and Early Stuart England* (1969), which also contains much valuable and lucid discussion of modern interpretations.

statistics.[1] It seemed plausible to extend this explanation to England and other countries, and it appeared to provide a convincing working example of Fisher's hypnotic formula $MV = PT$. The preoccupation with monetary factors was reinforced by a number of works of the early 1930s on the English mint and coinage, which inevitably focused fresh attention on the great debasement of the 1540s. Serious criticism of this dominant orthodoxy has been developed only in the last fifteen years.

The difficulties in using the celebrated Fisher formula, and the doubtful nature of some of Hamilton's assumptions are cogently developed in I. Hammarström's article of 1957. The formula $MV = PT$ is a tautology, and therefore strictly speaking unexceptionable, though Fisher's assumption that changes in M (the total amount of money, including credit instruments, in circulation) would have relatively little effect on T (the total number of transactions), and therefore affect mainly P (the general price level), is more open to question. Its usefulness in the Tudor context is a lot more dubious. It is difficult enough to reach any reliable estimate of the coin in circulation at any moment, though C. E. Challis has produced a well-documented assessment that is unlikely to be far wide of the mark. It is impossible to estimate the volume of bills of exchange or obligations in limited circulation, though it is arguable that their lack of free negotiability at discount makes them ineligible to be considered as a part of M. A vague assertion that their number probably increased in the sixteenth century does not help very much. There is no conceivable way of measuring V (the velocity of circulation) in the Tudor economy. T likewise escapes accurate quantification, since we have moderately reliable figures only for exports of some commodities (notably woollen cloth), and for a few industrial products (e.g. coal and tin) of minor importance in the economy. The great bulk of transactions on the home market completely eludes us. So, too, does much of the information required to compile a meaningful index to represent P. The Phelps Brown/Hopkins index, compiled for a limited specific purpose, does not pretend to portray

[1] See below, pp. 147–79.

P in the way required by the Fisher formula. Thus all four terms of that formula are more or less incapable of being filled, and its usefulness as a tool of historical analysis is minimal.

Even if the formula $MV = PT$ is incapable of exact application, it might still remain true that the quantity theory of money was broadly applicable – that debasement and American silver were the main causes of inflation, even if we cannot demonstrate this with statistical precision. But there are serious difficulties about the theory even in such an attenuated and imprecise form. Even in Spain prices were rising rapidly before precious metals from the New World arrived there in any substantial quantities, and a recent reworking of the Spanish price material actually suggests that they rose faster in the first half of the century than in the second (when silver imports reached their peak). In England prices of basic consumables had at least doubled by the middle of the century, before the silver of Potosi and Zacatecas had begun to flood into Spain. American bullion can hardly account for this. For the second half of the century there remains a serious gap in the causal chain – how did the silver get from Spain to England? Favourable trade balances would be a possible answer, but in the present state of knowledge it is one that cannot be proved or disproved. The rise of the New Draperies at the end of the century may have compensated for the stagnation of the traditional woollen export trade, but it is impossible to say how far this was offset by rising imports, on whose volume contemporaries commented adversely. It seems on the whole unlikely that the balance of trade can have been so consistently favourable as to produce an inflow of bullion big enough to account for the rapid inflation that took place. Mary Tudor's dowry and the lucky strikes of some Elizabethan privateers did a little to siphon off the flow of Spanish silver to England, but once again it is improbable that they can bear the full weight of explanation.

The great debasement of 1544–51 seems at first sight to offer rather better support for the quantity theory of money. Figures for the total coin in circulation during the period of debase-

ment and of deflation and recoinage down to 1561, both those
of J. D. Gould and the more fully documented ones of C. E.
Challis, suggest a rough correlation between coin and the level
of prices.[1] But it is only rough, and looks plausible only if we
take the period as a whole and do not look too closely at the
detailed course of either coin production or price increases.[2]
Prices did not increase in proportion to the reduction of silver
in the silver coin (which was not to be expected), nor in proportion to the increase in face value of the coinage in circulation. This remains true even if we discount the distorting effects
on the Phelps Brown/Hopkins index of unusually good or bad
harvests. Prices, moreover, rise very unevenly, with food prices
rising a good deal more sharply than those of woollen cloth.
Dr Outhwaite rightly warns us that it would be naïve to expect
price increases to remain exactly constant while the supply of
money increased greatly,[3] but the discrepancies are too large
to be easily dismissed. Moreover, the calling down of the currency in 1551 failed to produce the fall in prices which the
government of the day did expect and a quantity theorist might
expect. Nor did the more modest deflation of 1561. The privy
council's inept handling of the 1551 deflation – announcing the
calling down of the silver coins before it became effective, thus
causing a flight from money and abiding suspicion of government intentions – was no doubt partly responsible. Individuals
and institutions could not be expected to react instantaneously
to the new situation, and some time-lag was inevitable. The fiat
of the government, supported by the law courts, would also
help to ensure throughout the period that coins could circulate
at values well above their content of precious metal. There is
also Dr Challis's interesting suggestion that the mid-century
increase in the circulating medium helped to make good a long-

---

[1] See below, pp. 117–46. See also the same author's 'The debasement of the
coinage, 1542–1551' in *Economic History Review*, 2nd ser., xx (1967), pp. 441–66.
It should be stressed that the article here printed for the first time was written
prior to and independently of J. D. Gould's *The Great Debasement* (1970).

[2] Gould, op. cit. pp. 71–86, where he concludes that the discrepancies are too
great for the monetary theory to be regarded as a helpful explanation even in this
period.

[3] Outhwaite, op. cit., pp. 45–6.

standing shortage of specie, and therefore had the effect of allowing prices to adjust to appropriate levels rather than of forcing a general increase.[1] So while it seems difficult to deny that the debasement had any effect on prices, the precise connection seems impossible to establish. At least some other important factors were at work.

The difficulties of relating currency debasement to inflation in the mid-century years recur when we try to apply the quantity theory to the price rise as a whole. Once again we are faced with the unevenness of the increases for different commodities, and for the marked tendency of wage rates to lag behind prices. The quantity theory alone will not explain all this. It is possibly true that unproductive government spending at different times had an inflationary effect. The early wars of Henry VIII, the Scottish and French campaigns of the 1540s, the Spanish war and Irish troubles at the end of the century might seem to be reflected in part by contemporaneous price movements. But by French and Spanish standards the expenditure of successive English governments was modest indeed, and can only have played a minor contributory role. It is moreover impossible to say in our present state of knowledge how much of the £622,000 that went on military expenditure in 1513 or the £2,134,000 in 1537–47, was spent in England, and how much overseas. In the last ten years of Henry VIII's reign more than £1,125,000 was spent on the acquisition of Boulogne and its defence along with Calais, but clearly not all this money crossed the Channel. The general effect of increased taxation in wartime would clearly be to accelerate dehoarding and was likely to have an inflationary impact, but this cannot be measured at all accurately. In any case it seems clear that neither the scale nor the nature of the great Tudor price rise is adequately explained in terms of American silver, debasement and government spending.

Faced with these difficulties and inconsistencies in the orthodox explanation of Tudor inflation, historians have in recent years sought 'real' causes of it. Since Dr Brenner's first article[2] appeared in 1961 the main emphasis has been put on an alleged

---

[1] See below, pp. 144–5.   [2] See below, pp. 69–90.

rise in population that bore increasingly hard on limited natural resources, though this theory was not wholly new in 1961 and owed a good deal to the pioneering researches of Professor Phelps Brown and Miss Sheila Hopkins. The main argument is that English population expanded substantially during the sixteenth century, while agricultural production failed to match this growth. Inevitably food prices rose, the increase being accelerated in bad harvest years like those of the 1550s and 1590s. A corollary might be that neither agriculture nor industry expanded its labour force enough to absorb the increasing number of workers available. Extension of the amount of land under cultivation was offset by enclosure, engrossment and more rational farming methods, and perhaps some conversion of arable to pasture. Industrial advance, though striking in some new industries, the most notable being coal-mining, was not remarkable in the older-established woollen and leather manufactures which employed a far greater proportion of the Tudor labour force. The result was growing unemployment and underemployment, reflected both in the falling real wages of the labourer and in the substantial (if unmeasurable) growth of vagabondage, which caused so much concern to Tudor philanthropists, municipalities and parliament.

This theory, based on expanding population and relatively inelastic food supplies and job opportunity, has a good deal to recommend it. It would go far to explain why prices rose before the monetary supply was affected by either American silver or debasement, why food prices rose faster than others, and why wages lagged behind prices – just those features which monetary theory left unexplained. If its main premise could be firmly substantiated, it would command wide acceptance.[1]

The difficulty lies precisely in the substantiation. Up till recently there have been no satisfactory figures for English population movements in the early modern period. In his *British Medieval Population* (1948) J. C. Russell estimates that after the demographic collapse of the mid- and late fourteenth century, there was an increasingly rapid recovery from the low

[1] Brenner carries his arguments further in 'The inflation of prices in England, 1551–1650, *Economic History Review*, 2nd ser., xv (1962–3), pp. 266–84.

point of 2·1 million about 1430 to 3·22 million in 1545. But this estimate is based on an assumed rate of growth between the two remote points of 1377 and 1690, with only some very fragmentary and dubious support from the chantry certificates of 1547. Such a vague and hypothetical estimate is little help in explaining the exact chronology and nature of the Tudor price rise, and in the absence of more solidly based statistics the whole argument from population pressure is conjectural and circular – a population increase is adduced to explain certain features of the Tudor economy, those features being themselves the main evidence for the increase.

A critical study of Russell's figures and some new evidence from military surveys and subsidy rolls of the 1520s has now enabled Mr Julian Cornwall to present more reliable estimates.[1] While accepting (with reservations) Russell's figure of 2·1 million in 1430, he argues that population remained low until well into the sixteenth century, reaching only 2·3 million by 1522–5. There followed a rapid rise to 2·8 million in 1545, and a further rise (possibly interrupted by a brief recession in the 1550s) to 3·75 million in 1603, an increase of 63 per cent in eighty years. This pattern of development has the advantage of being more solidly based on contemporary evidence, and also of fitting in (much better than Russell's conjectures) with what is known about price history. It would help to explain why prices began to rise markedly only from about 1520, and not earlier, and why food prices continued to shoot up until the end of the century. A great deal of further research is needed before the demographic picture is complete, though we may expect further valuable information from the work of the Cambridge Group for the History of Population and Social Structure. It seems unlikely that we shall ever have enough details to establish a precise correlation between population increase and the graph of price rises, and even less likely that we shall ever be able to assess accurately the agricultural output of Tudor England and plot it against both population and price increases. But it can be said that Mr Cornwall's researches have given

[1] 'English population in the early sixteenth century', *Economic History Review*, 2nd ser., XXIII (1970), pp. 32–44.

added weight to the principal 'real' explanation of the inflationary process and provided it with a measure of statistical respect-
ability.

Rises in agrarian rents were clearly in part a reflection of
growing food shortage and land hunger. They may well have
been also a major contributory cause of rising food prices. Dr
Eric Kerridge has demonstrated how on a number of Seymour
and Pembroke estates the increases in rents and fines actually
ran ahead of prices, and it seems likely that further evidence
will confirm this initial finding.[1] If this is so, then the complaints
of the Husbandman in the *Discourse of the Common Weal* would
gain added support, while the claim of the Knight that landowners raised rents only under pressure of their own rising
expenses would seem less plausible. It remains true, of course,
that the profitability of food production sets an upper limit on
rent increases, and that though price and rent increases are
closely interdependent the former might be regarded as a prior
condition of the latter. It is difficult to see how rent increases
can be claimed as the *main* cause of Tudor inflation.

Further researches into the price history of particular commodities and services may deepen and refine our knowledge of
that inflation and reinforce 'real' explanations of it. They may
also make possible the construction of a more comprehensive
and sophisticated general price index than has hitherto been
possible, and this of itself might modify our view of both the
nature and the causes of the process. In our present state of
knowledge the period must still be counted among 'the Dark
Ages in English economic history',[2] and it is doubtful whether
we shall ever have enough light to see our way quite clearly. At
the moment it seems plausible to attribute Tudor inflation
mainly to pressure of population on resources, while admitting
that debasement of the currency and growing credit facilities,
along with heavy government expenditure at certain times, had
an aggravating effect. The role of American silver remains

---

[1] 'The movement of rents, 1540–1640', *Economic History Review*, 2nd ser., VI
(1953), pp. 16–34.
[2] F. J. Fisher, 'The sixteenth and seventeenth centuries: the Dark Ages in
English economic history', *Economica*, Vol. XXIV (1957), pp. 1–18.

obscure and conjectural until more is known about trade balances and the gains of the privateers, and should probably be relegated to a subordinate place.

It was suggested earlier that the price rise was revolutionary in its impact rather than its scale, especially if viewed from a twentieth-century perspective. An attempt to discuss the effects of the price rise, however, raises certain difficulties of principle, and involves a prior decision on its causes. Only if one opts for a monetary explanation is it really appropriate to speak of the price rise as though it were an independent entity with an identifiable impact on the economy and society of Tudor England. If, on the other hand, one gives greater weight to the 'real' causes, which are essentially 'disaggregative' and give money a passive role,[1] then the price rise is simply an index of multifarious changes in the Tudor economy and its impact on society has to be explained by reference to those changes. Since population increase has become the favoured explanation of the price rise, indeed, perhaps one should nowadays discuss the effects of the Tudor 'population explosion' and not those of the 'price revolution'. Contemporaries, however, thought it not inappropriate to discuss the effects of the universal 'dearth', especially in the mid-century years and in the 1590s. And today, since the extent of at least some price and wage increases is better established than their complex causes, it is not wholly unreasonable to discuss the immediate effects of these changes upon the people of the time.

It has been argued that the differential movement of prices and wages gave manufacturers an advantage by lowering their costs of production relative to the selling price of their goods. This gain (a modest one if we compare wages with *industrial* prices), however, must have been largely offset by the rising price of raw materials, especially of fuel prices in areas where the iron industry was making heavy inroads on timber supplies, and the net gain was probably not great. A population that was facing ever-mounting food bills could not provide a mass market for English industrial products, and Tudor England did not produce much in the way of luxury goods for the wealthier

[1] Cf. Outhwaite, op. cit., p. 40.

sections of the population. The failure of the main Tudor industries to expand fast enough to absorb a growing labour supply
may have been partly due to this. More particularly, it has been
held that in the period of the great debasement the cost price of
woollen cloth rose more slowly than the exchange rate between
London and Antwerp deteriorated, thus giving the English
merchant a competitive advantage when selling his goods on
the Antwerp market. The recent study of J. D. Gould has cast
considerable doubt on this theory,[1] since he points out that
only from the end of 1548 was the actual fall in the exchange
rate sufficient to have this effect, and that even in 1548–9 the
more likely result was enhanced profits for the merchant than
lowered prices and expanded sales in Antwerp. The drastic fall
in the exchange rate in 1551 may likewise have served to maintain merchant profits even during the drastic slump of cloth
exports, and thus explain the apparent paradox of falling exports
and declining exchange rate combined with rising wool and
cloth prices in England. But only briefly did the exchange rate
exercise the influence attributed to it by some contemporaries,
and then not in quite the way that the orthodox account of these
years has held.

In the later years of the sixteenth century it is possible that
English woollen manufacturers had an advantage over their
Mediterranean competitors, since the production costs of the
former rose less rapidly than those of the latter, who were more
affected by the flow of Spanish silver that entered the country
via Genoa. But the advantage was shared with England's other
northern competitors, and in the event was exploited more
successfully by the Dutch. Once again, no clear long-term gain
can be attributed to relative price movements, though the prosperity of the New Draperies was doubtless partly due to them.

Within England the main victim of price changes was undoubtedly the urban labourer, producing none of his own food
and perhaps suffering a fall in real wages of more than 50 per
cent. Studies of urban communities in the late sixteenth and
early seventeenth century suggest that perhaps half their populations lived in direst poverty and squalor, on the edge of total

[1] J. D. Gould, op. cit., Chapter 6, 'Exports and the debasement'.

destitution and starvation.[1] The agrarian worker was cushioned against inflation to the extent that he was able to grow some of his own food, but in the same plight as the urban worker if he was totally landless. The national poor law of Elizabeth I's reign did little or nothing to mitigate their extreme poverty, since it catered for the unemployed rather than for the under-paid, and was activated only in times of quite unusual distress. And while the face value of private charitable donations cer-tainly increased, inflation produced a sharp drop in their actual purchasing power. In 1600 there was less relief available for a larger population than in 1500, and a greater proportion of them were poorer than ever before.[2]

The small tenant farmer benefited from rising food prices if he was fortunate enough to have security of tenure, and if the terms of his lease or copyhold protected him against ferocious rack-renting and eviction. Otherwise he would fall victim to the rise in rents that was both cause and result of the general inflation, and find himself reduced to the ranks of the landless labourer. His surplus for the market was likely to be small, and he was clearly more vulnerable than the wealthy landowner to the hazards of crop failure and pestilence. But essentially it was the nature of his tenure, not price changes as such, that decided whether he prospered or went under.

The more substantial landowners – yeomen, gentry and magnates – profited likewise in proportion to their efficiency and to the extent they farmed for the market. The big man was favoured by his ability to buy the most expert advice and assist-ance, and to ride out temporary periods of difficulty that would wipe out his lesser rival. The relative movements of wool and grain prices should in theory have made it profitable to convert pasture to arable by the end of the century, and the absence of any large-scale conversion or reconversion seems at first sight strange – more especially if an inverse movement of prices is used to explain conversion to pasture at the beginning of the

[1] e.g. W. T. MacCaffrey, *Exeter, 1540–1640* (1958).
[2] Notwithstanding W. K. Jordan, *Philanthropy in England, 1480–1660* (1959). In this and subsequent studies the author obstinately declines to allow for the effects of inflation in his estimates of charitable giving.

period. It is possible, however, that contemporaries found it hard to discern the long-term trend of grain prices behind the violent fluctuations of such periods as the 1590s, and a catastrophic harvest was not in itself an incentive to put more land under the plough. The problems of the rentier landlord were, self-evidently, the converse of the tenant's: how far was he willing or able to rack-rent to the limit? In a broad sense that limit was itself determined by the price of grain or wool, but in the short run the landlord's solvency depended on the text of the leases. The recovery of some peers' incomes at the turn of the century reflects both the substitution of long for short leases and a growing willingness of lords to tap the pockets rather than the loyalty of their tenants. The 25 per cent fall in the real incomes of the peerage during Elizabeth I's reign, which made such a recovery desirable, was due to lack of adaptability and to habits of extravagance, not to inexorable economic forces.[1] The fall was not as serious as that suffered by the urban labourer, and recovery was possible. The peer's fate was in his own hands; the labourer's was not.

The fortunes of the urban upper classes are hard to assess, and the involvement of many great landlords in trade and industry makes it hard to establish a clear division. How are we to classify George Talbot, Earl of Shrewsbury, the greatest entrepreneur of the age? Contemporaries were impressed by a number of great fortunes quickly won, but these were probably few, and the more impressive because of that. The opening of new markets and the development of new industries offered great opportunities to the enterprising and adaptable. Privateering in the 1580s and 1590s made great profits for the merchant investor who could spread his risks, but could mean total disaster for the man who put all his eggs into one basket. The studies of J. W. Gough do not suggest that fortunes were commonly made by even the most bold and ingenious undertakers and promoters, and that success depended at least as much on luck or a grant of monopoly as on enterprise and energy.[2] In trade and industry, much more than on the land,

[1] L. Stone, *The Crisis of the Aristocracy, 1558–1641* (1965), Part 2.
[2] J. W. Gough, *The Rise of the Entrepreneur* (1969).

success depended on individual circumstances and ability. The general movement of prices, favourable to farmers rather than to merchants or manufacturers, does not go far to explain it.

There were no dramatic changes in the social structure of Tudor England, at least in its upper strata. The losses of the peerage were largely to be made good in the early Stuart period. Some merchants and lawyers waxed rich, but they did not yet constitute a commercial or professional class. Though their status was improving, a majority still hankered after landed gentility and used their new wealth to found gentry families. If, as is usually held, the middling ranks of landed society improved their economic position during the sixteenth century, it was not so much at the expense of their betters or of each other as of the poor. The real victims of economic forces in this age were the evicted agrarian smallholder and the landless labourer of both town and country. They lost comfort and status in both real and absolute terms. Their diet deteriorated, with bread bulking significantly larger in their purchases, and it would be two centuries and more before they began to recover the position they had enjoyed in the golden days of the fifteenth century. Their plight can be expressed in terms of rising food prices and lagging wage rates, but it seems doubtful if they can be regarded simply as the victims of a 'price revolution'. If there were too many empty bellies and idle hands in the England of 1600 it was because productivity had failed to match population growth. Only an agrarian and industrial revolution could put this right.

1 Seven Centuries of the Prices of Consumables, Compared with Builders' Wage Rates

E. H. PHELPS BROWN and SHEILA V. HOPKINS[1]

This article was first published in *Economica*, No. 92 (November 1956), N.S. vol. XXIII

In an earlier paper[2] we gave an account of builders' wages in southern England from 1264 to 1954, and now we shall try to relate these to the prices of some of the main articles of consumption. In 1901 Steffen[3] displayed the movements of two wage rates in comparison with those of the prices of wheat and meat through the preceding six centuries and more: it was his Tafel II that first displayed the striking evidence for a great rise and fall in the real income of the wage-earner between 1300 and 1600, the level reached in 1450–1500 apparently not being regained until after 1860. We shall test these indications by bringing a wider range of prices to bear.

I

Nowadays, real wages are commonly estimated by comparing money earnings with an index of the cost of living, but there are several reasons why we cannot do that here. On the side of income, all we have is the rate of pay for a day, and we do not

[1] We owe to Mr S. Ahmed, Dr Gethyn Davies and Mr J. Veverka much valued help in computing, and are further indebted to our colleagues Professors Carus-Wilson and Fisher and Dr A. H. John for commenting on our work in galley.

[2] 'Seven centuries of building wages', *Economica*, XXII, 87 (August 1955).

[3] G. F. Steffen, *Studien zur Geschichte der englischen Lohnarbeiter*, vol. I (Stuttgart, 1901), esp. Tafel I and II, at p. 112. Most of the materials of these two graphs are reproduced in App. I of H. O. Meredith, *Economic History of England*, 5th ed. (1949).

know how many days' work the builder was getting in the year from time to time, nor what other resources he had. On the side of outlay, we know little or nothing about some important costs, notably rent, and the prices we do have are more wholesale than retail. These things apart, we still could not attach much meaning to 'the cost of maintaining a constant standard of living' through seven centuries of social change.

So we have not tried to construct any measure of real wages in the modern sense. Yet when we find the craftsmen who have been building Nuffield College in Oxford in our own day earning a hundred and fifty pennies in the time it took their forebears building Merton to earn one, the impulse to break through the veil of money becomes powerful: we are bound to ask, what sort of command over the things builders buy did these pennies give from time to time? It is this question we try to answer here.

Our answer takes the form of an aggregate price year by year for a composite commodity, made up always of the same amounts of some of the main heads of consumption: we can think of it as a package always containing the same sized bagfuls of bread-stuffs, meat, cloth, and so on. The contents of each bag have been made up variously from time to time: in our bread-stuffs, for instance, we give a greater place to wheat, and correspondingly less to rye and barley, as the eighteenth century wears on. But we have kept the bags themselves of the same size throughout, so that the package they make up should provide what is in the main a common composite physical unit, in which to express the purchasing powers of sums of money at different dates throughout our long period. Whenever the costs of the bagfuls move differently from one another, the changes in the cost of our composite unit will indicate those of the wage-earner's cost of living only to the extent that the make-up of our unit resembles that of his actual basketful. But this will certainly have varied from time to time, particularly when his purchasing power changed as much as this inquiry proves to suggest it did; and the evidence by which we chose the make-up of our unit is in any case fragmentary.

This evidence is set out in Table 1. William Savernak's

TABLE 1 *Distribution of outlay between certain heads of household expenditure*

		W. Savernak 1453–60	Davies & Eden 1790s	Board of Trade 1904–13	Weights taken here
		%	%	%	%
1	Farinaceous	20	53	16	20
2	Meat, fish	35	12	$21\frac{1}{2}$	25
3	Butter, cheese	2	7	16	$12\frac{1}{2}$
4	Drink (malt, hops, sugar, tea)	23	9	24	$22\frac{1}{2}$
Subtotal, Food		80	81	$77\frac{1}{2}$	80
5	Fuel and light	$7\frac{1}{2}$	$7\frac{1}{2}$	9	$7\frac{1}{2}$
6	Textiles	n.a.	$11\frac{1}{2}$	$13\frac{1}{2}$	$12\frac{1}{2}$
Total		$87\frac{1}{2}$	100	100	100

account book[1] records seven years of the weekly expenditure of a small household – two priests and a servant – at Bridport in Dorset, in the 1450s: within our scope here fall the entries for thirteen articles of food, and for candles and fuel, to the amount of some forty pence a week, or getting on for seven days' pay of a building craftsman at that time. But there is not sufficient record of outlay on clothes, and in showing the distribution of the outlay included in Table 1 over its first five heads, we have allowed them only the $87\frac{1}{2}$ percentage points in all that they get in the last column. The second column summarizes the accounts of nearly sixty households in the villages or small towns of southern England, that two students of poverty recorded in the 1790s.[2] The third column rests on the estimate made, when the old Cost of Living Index was set up during the First World War, of the distribution of 'average pre-war working-class expenditure', and so its detail for food derives mainly from the '1,944 urban working-class budgets collected by the Board of Trade in 1904',[3] but we have raised the weight of the fourth head and of food as a whole by adding outlay on beer, which

[1] K. L. Wood-Legh, *A Small Household of the Fifteenth Century* (Manchester University Press, 1956).

[2] David Davies, Rector of Barkham, Berks, *The Case of Labourers in Husbandry* (1795). Sir Frederic Morton Eden, Bart., *The State of the Poor* (1797).

[3] *The Cost of Living Index Number: Method of Compilation* (Ministry of Labour, June 1934).

we took to be a slightly greater part of all outlay in 1904–13 than in 1938.[1]

The most striking feature of the Table is the similarity between Savernak's budget and that of the wage-earners four and a half centuries later: Savernak, it is true, spent much more on meat and fish and less on butter and cheese, but the combined weight of these two heads is almost the same in both columns. Davies and Eden portray poor people in hard times, and it is not surprising that they show so great a part of the outlay on food as spent on bread-stuffs: what again is striking is that the distribution of the recorded outlay over food and the two remaining heads should differ so little from the budgets of 1904–13. So it seemed not unreasonable at the outset to adopt the figures of the last column as weights with which to combine the price indexes of the six heads, all through the centuries: though, since this amounts to following the total cost of a package of unchanged physical make-up, it does imply changes from time to time in the proportionate distribution of *outlay*, to the extent that those price-indexes diverged from one another.

But the components under each of those six heads change their own sub-weights not a little from time to time. Sometimes we made these changes deliberately, to take account of shifting habits of consumption, or the entry of new products; more often our hand was forced by lack of materials. In general, we arranged the sub-weighting of such series as we selected or were all we had from time to time, according to the detail in the budgets already cited, and failing that, in the half-light of general knowledge: such were our only grounds, for instance, for giving beef and mutton equal weights, and meat of all kinds about five times the weight of fish.

The upshot is illustrated by Table 2, which takes as the unit of our composite commodity what a hundred pence would buy in 1451–75, and shows the articles that made up this unit about the beginning and end of our period and at two equidistant points between. There is continuity between one year and another in two ways: the weights of the six heads remain the

[1] Para. 12 of Supplement No. 2 (January 1948) to the *Industrial Relations Handbook* (Ministry of Labour, 1944).

same; when one article takes over outlay from another under the same head, the place of each pennyworth withdrawn is taken by so much of the new article as a penny would buy at its own

TABLE 2 *Approximate quantities of articles making up the composite unit of consumables, around four dates*

		1275	*1500*	*1725*	*1950*
1	Farinaceous	1¼ bush wheat 1 bush rye ½ bush barley ¾ bush peas	1¼ bush wheat 1 bush rye ½ bush barley ⅔ bush peas	1½ bush wheat ¾ bush rye ⅓ bush barley ½ bush peas	2 bush wheat 1 cwt potatoes
2	Meat, fish	The meat of ½ pig ½ sheep 40 herrings	The meat of 1½ sheep 15 white herrings 25 red herrings	The meat of ½ sheep 33 lb beef 1¼ salt cod	The meat of ⅔ sheep 28 lb beef 1½ lb cod 3 lb herrings
3	Butter, cheese	10 lb butter 10 lb cheese	nil	10 lb butter 10 lb cheese	10 lb butter 10 lb cheese
4	Drink	4½ bush malt	4½ bush malt	3¼ bush malt 3 lb hops 1½ lb sugar	2⅓ bush malt 2¼ lb hops 5 lb sugar 4½ lb tea
5	Fuel, light	nil	4¼ bush charcoal 2¾ lb candles ½ pt oil	1½ bush charcoal 1 cwt coal 2½ lb candles ½ pt oil	2 cwt coal 5½ pints paraffin 400 cu ft coal gas
6	Textiles	3¼ yd canvas	⅔ yd canvas ½ yd shirting ⅓ yd woollen cloth	½ yd woollen cloth	¾ lb wool yarn 3 yds printer's cotton cloth

price, or the price of its lineal forbear, in the base period. It is in this limited sense that we can regard our changing package as providing a common unit in different years: and even say, for instance, that in the 1930s the craftsman's rate would cover five of these units for every one it covered around 1300. This is far

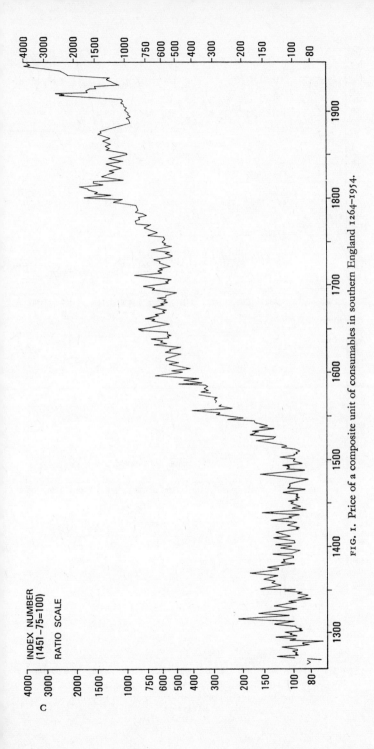

FIG. I. Price of a composite unit of consumables in southern England 1264–1954.

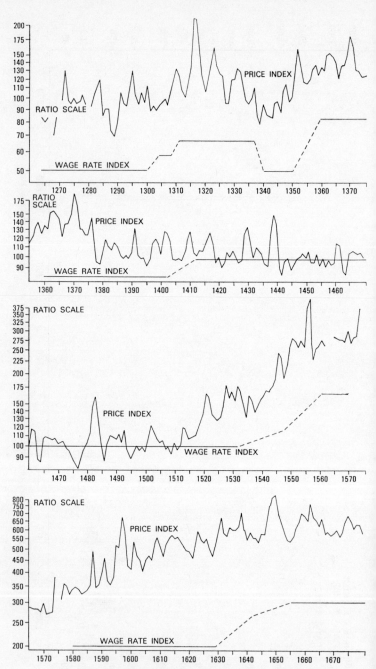

FIG. 2. Indexes of wage rate of building craftsman and price of composite unit of consumables in southern England 1264-1954 (1451-75 = 100).

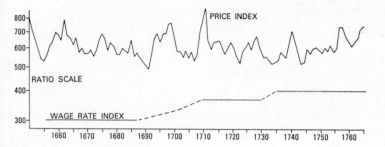

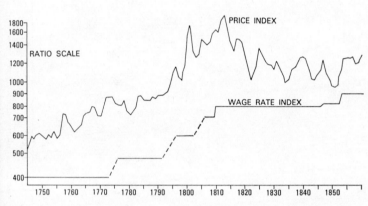

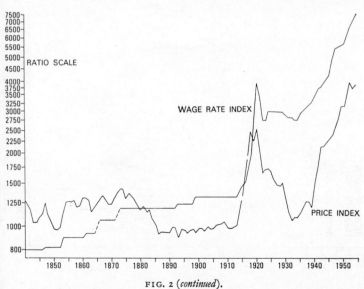

FIG. 2 (*continued*).

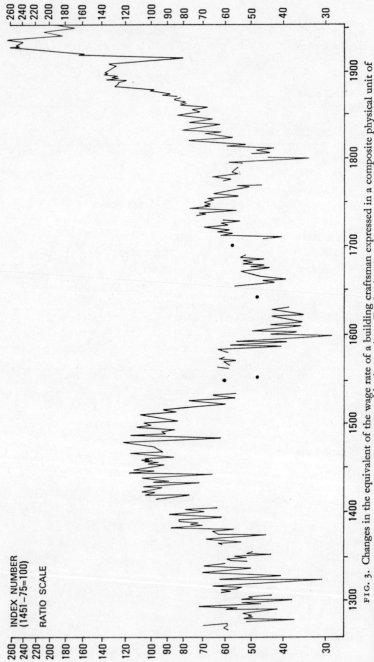

FIG. 3. Changes in the equivalent of the wage rate of a building craftsman expressed in a composite physical unit of consumables in southern England 1264–1954.

from measuring changes in the standard of living, but it tells us something about them. Yet the very size of the changes it suggests brings out one of its limitations: for it takes the relative quantities of the main heads as constant, whereas in such a fall, for instance, in the purchasing power of the wage as the sixteenth century brought, the proportion of meat to bread must surely have fallen.

II

The sources we have drawn on for our prices are set out in Appendix A. Two of them are outstanding. We are reaping where other men have sown, and for any interest this study may afford, the credit belongs to Thorold Rogers and Beveridge.

Until early in the nineteenth century, most of our prices record what was paid by buyers in a local market or annual fair, or what a local purveyor charged for supplies delivered to the consumer's door. Rogers's prices come mostly from the accounts of the manors of Oxford colleges, and the provisioning of Oxford and Cambridge colleges themselves, with the similar household accounts of some great lay and monastic landlords. Most of the prices we have taken from Beveridge come from the accounts of colleges and hospitals, and from the Navy Victualling service. In sum, these prices give the terms on which raw or partially processed materials were available to consumers who bought locally in some bulk. But after Beveridge's records end, in the early nineteenth century, we have gone on with prices that are wholesale in the modern sense – quotations from the organized produce markets, and average values of imports or exports. We know how these show more and bigger movements than the prices paid for small quantities at retail. It is a further limitation that we have been able to include few fabricated articles. So our prices are not those at which the craftsman's wage was spent with the butcher, the baker, the candlestick maker; they do measure changes in the command of money over some of the main materials of consumption, at points where these are bought in some bulk, and when such changes were substantial and sustained they would come through to the craftsman; but even so, our index is still not responsive enough to changes in the costs of fabrication.

There are other respects in which these materials fall short. For one thing, they make no allowance for changes in quality: how like or unlike were the three quarters of wheat that were sold at Easington near Thame and helped make up our index for 1264, to the Manitoba No. 1 that is the subject of our last quotations? Changes in quantity as well as quality may have crept in, when provisioning went on, as it often did, for a long run of years at an unchanging price; or other adjustments, not recorded in the price, would have been made in the payment from time to time: our only remedy was to avoid all such constant series as far as possible, though sometimes they will have meant what they said. The worst shortcoming is the absence of some annual records altogether: especially for fuel and light in the earliest years, butter and cheese in the fifteenth and sixteenth centuries, and fish in the eighteenth. There are also many gaps, here and there, of a year or two at a time. It has been a matter of judgement, place by place, which of three possible courses to follow: simply accept the gap and carry the index on with the remaining series; transfer the weight of the missing series to some other that is close akin to it; fill the gap by interpolation.

To give our price series their place in the index for the composite commodity, we had to express each as a relative to its own average in a common base-period. This is 1451–75, chosen because it lies within a long period of stability in the trend of prices – though it turns out to have been a time of exceptional prosperity. But of course many series do not run through it, and these we have had to set in their right relation to those that do. Often this raised no problem: if a new series differed from an old only by giving the price of another grade or region, and the two moved together through a number of years of overlap, then splicing was straightforward. But if either of these conditions was absent, we had to be wary of falsifying the whole later course of the new index by including some abnormality in the splice, or misplacing a turning-point by choosing the wrong place at which to join two series of divergent trends. Again, when the new series was not merely a variant of some old one, but brought a new commodity in – when hops appeared in the sixteenth century, for example, or potatoes in the eighteenth – we had to select the old series that seemed most akin to it, to joint it to: so we joined hops to malt, and potatoes to peas. This involved the absurdity, if you will, of saying that potatoes cost four times as much in 1785 as in 1451–75, when there were none: but we can give an intelligible cast to this if we take potatoes and peas as two spokesmen, so to speak, for the one class of vegetables, and think of the one being brought in to supplement or take over from the other, just as when a series for beef becomes available we bring it in to supplement the price of mutton and fill out the index for meat.

III

Our findings are summarized in Appendix B and displayed in the three figures. Many of them will be familiar to the economic historian. It is to his knowledge, and to the more detailed study of our present materials period by period, that we must look for answers to the questions they seem to raise.

The index of prices has two periods, each of about 130 years, 1380–1510, and 1630–1760, throughout which there is constancy in the general level, and this surprising stability, as it seems to us, was maintained through fluctuations of two or three years' span, due no doubt mostly to the harvest, whose violence seems no less extraordinary: what was the secret of this stability, and how was it held through such vibration? There are also two periods, about 1270–1380, and 1815–1914, when a trend that is fairly level from end to end is modulated by 'secondary secular movements', as we call them now: what makes the difference between the two sorts of period? The most marked feature of Fig. 1 is the extent, and persistence, of the Tudor inflation: what carried it on so far, and why did it end when it did? For a century and more, it seems, prices will obey one all-powerful law; it changes, and a new law prevails; a war that would have cast the trend up to new heights in one dispensation is powerless to deflect it in another. Do we yet know what are the factors that set this stamp on an age; and why, after they have held on so long through such shakings, at last they give way, quickly and completely, to others?

The simplest impression of the physical equivalent of the wage rate, that Fig. 3 displays, is of a level much the same throughout, broken through only by a time of much greater prosperity from 1380 to 1510, and a rise that sets in at the last, from 1820 onwards, and carries us up to a new region altogether. We can go on to notice some differences in the level: the depths, for instance, to which it fell at the ends of the sixteenth century and the eighteenth, and the substantial rise from the Civil War to the 1740s. In considering all these things we want to know how far our building craftsman was representative of working men generally, whether wage-earners or not, and it is relevant here that the building labourer's rate did change in the same proportion as the craftsman's with great consistency from the Black Death to the First World War. If the movements of Fig. 3 were indeed not confined to certain crafts but were of some generality, then their size and shape mark deep-going economic changes. Was it an advance in productivity, deserving the title of revolution, that about doubled the commodity equivalent between the Black Death and Agincourt, and held it at its new level for nearly a century? A drastic fall set in about 1510: the level enjoyed at the accession of Henry VIII was not to be reached again until 1880; the lowest point we record in seven centuries was in 1597, the year of the *Midsummer Night's Dream*. Do we not see here a Malthusian crisis, the effect of a rapid growth of population impinging on an insufficiently expansive economy; such as perhaps we see also in the fall that set in again around 1750, until this time a commercial and industrial revolution came to save Britain from the fate of Ireland?

APPENDIX A

Abbreviations

AS: Annual Statements of the Trade of the U.K.

B: Sir Wm. Beveridge and others: *Prices and Wages in England from the Twelfth to the Nineteenth Century*, vol. 1.

BPP: British Parliamentary Papers.

JRSS: *Journal of the Royal Statistical Society*, annual reports on wholesale prices by the Editor of *The Statist*.

PWH: Price and Wage History Research, manuscript materials, collected under the direction of Sir Wm. Beveridge, in the Institute of Historical Research, University of London.

R: J. E. Thorold Rogers: *A History of Agriculture and Prices in England*.

TN: Tooke and Newmarch: *A History of Prices and of the State of the Circulation from 1792 to 1856*.

WRP: *Report on Wholesale and Retail Prices in the U.K.*, BPP 1903, LXVIII, 321.

Dates

Dates given for series record the length used here, either as a component of the final index or for splicing; the original is sometimes longer. We have entered the average price for a harvest year against the calendar year beginning during that harvest year, e.g. against Mich. 1400–Mich. 1401 we put the calendar year 1401.

Series

(01) *Wheat 1264–1703:* average of prices recorded, mostly in manorial and college accounts, in Southern England. R, I. 226–34; IV, 282–90; V, 268–74.

(02) *Wheat 1583–1770:* mean of prices at Lady Day and Michaelmas, found in Oxford college accounts of payments of rent in kind. TN, VI, 427–36, from W. F. Lloyd, 1830.

(03) *Wheat 1595–1826:* mean of prices at Lady Day and Michaelmas, taken by Eton College from the Windsor market, for the purpose of rent audit. 1595–1770, TN, VI, 352. 1646–1826, TN, II, 387–9.

(04) *Wheat 1631–1818:* annual averages of prices paid by Winchester College: B, 18, 81–4.

(05) *Wheat 1771–1954:* Gazette Average prices, England and

Wales, weekly since 24 Nov 1770 in the London Gazette, here from: 1771–1841, 'Porter's Tables', XI, 69 (BPP 1843, LVI); 1842–1902, WRP, 70–1; 1903–54, Statistical Abstract of the U.K.

(06) *Wheat 1854–1907* average value of wheat imported into the U.K.: 1854–70, 'computed real values'; 1871+, 'declared values'. WRP, 80; and AS.

(07) *Wheat 1905–52:* market quotations for Northern Manitoba Wheat, No. 1 except 1924–38, when No. 2. Price at 1 Jan 1906–12; thereafter at 'end year'; price at 1 Jan 1906 taken here as for end year 1905, and so on. *The Economist*, Annual Commercial History and Review, through 1953, then British Wholesale Prices.

(08) *Barley 1264–1833:* average of prices recorded, mainly in manorial, college and church accounts, and in southern and eastern counties, but Durham included 1341–1541, and some northern counties 1771–1822. Entries sparse 1542–1728. PWH.

(09) *Rye 1264–1540, 1688–1782:* same origins as (08); mainly Winchester manors and eastern counties down to 1454; 1455–1540 Dorset and Durham only; from 1688 Kent and Middlesex. PWH.

(10) *Peas 1264–1685:* same origins as (01). R, I, 227–35; IV, 283–91; V, 269–75.

(11) *Peas 1686–1790:* average price at which Navy Victualling bought peas under short-period contracts. B, 538–9, 567–9.

(12) *Peas 1791–1809:* presumably for England and Wales; from 'An Account of the Average Price of all sorts of Grain in each Year', 1791–1821, BPP 1821, XVII, 11.

(13) *Peas 1810–1833:* London Gazette Average prices, England and Wales, taken here from 'Porter's Tables', XI, 69 (BPP, 1843, LVI).

(14) *Potatoes 1762–1830:* average price of old potatoes bought by the Lord Steward's department. B, 374–6, 427.

(15) *Potatoes 1832–45:* 1832–36, middlings and middling whites from Borough and Spitalfields markets; 1837–45 Yorkshire reds, 1846–50 Yorkshire Regents, at Southwark Waterside. Averages of weekly quotations for October in each year, given in *The Christian Advocate* and *Mark Lane Express*.

(16) *Potatoes 1846–84:* average of prices in Jan–April and Sept–Dec annually, of good English, mostly Kent Regents. A. Sauerbeck, 'Prices of commodities and the precious metals', JRSS, XLIX (1886), 636.

(17) *Potatoes 1885–1954:* London wholesale prices, grade A or good English. *The Economist*.

(18) *Porci 1264–1460:* same origins as (01). 1264–1401, annual

averages from R, I, 342–50. 1402–60, median or mean of entries from southern and eastern counties, in R, III, 122–202.

(19) *Muttons 1265–1582:* same origins as (01). 1265–1401, median of entries from southern and eastern counties, in R, II, 184–269. 1402–1582, 3-year moving average of highest price found in each year, reduced by a quarter throughout; a few exceptionally high entries omitted. R, IV, 346–54.

(20) *Beef 1584–1659:* purchases by King's College, Cambridge; apparently annual averages. R, V, 347–51.

(21) *Beef 1587–1767:* purchases by St Bartholomew's Hospital, Sandwich, in August of each year. B, 219–21, 236–7.

(22) *Beef 1602–21:* purchases by estate of Theydon Gernon, Essex; apparently annual average. R. V, 356.

(23) *Mutton 1602–1700:* purchases of mutton by Eton College from the college butcher; annual averages. B, 112, 144–6.

(24) *Mixed beef and mutton 1613–87:* purchases by Winchester College; weighted average of prices for the two kinds including *ex gratia* to the butcher to compensate for losses. B, 33–5, 81–3.

(25) *Beef 1683–1797:* Beef for salting bought by Navy Victualling, London. 1683–1747, from Arthur Young, *Political Arithmetic*, pp. 139–41, apparently annual averages; 1748–97, annual average of varying number of monthly entries in B, 548–53, 568–72.

(26) *Beef 1688–1833:* purchases by St Thomas's Hospital, Southwark; average of prices at Lady Day and Michaelmas. 'Porter's Tables', BPP, 1835, XLIX, 390.

(27) *Mutton 1701–1831:* market prices used to fix the money payments due from tenants of Eton College farms in lieu of rent sheep; average of prices at Lady Day and Michaelmas. B, 112, 146–7.

(28) *Mutton 1725–1833:* as for (26).

(29) *Beef 1789–1865:* annual average of monthly price (from 1792 mean of highest and lowest price on a day near end of month) at Smithfield market, London; extracted by Dr A. H. John from contemporary sources (from 1796 onwards, the *Gentleman's Magazine*).

(30) *Mutton 1796–1865:* as for (29) from 1796 onwards.

(31) *Beef 1858–1954:* 1858–1914, mean of highest and lowest prices of inferior middling butcher's meat, Newgate or Smithfield, at beginning of each year; 1913–27, mean of prices of middling and prime at end of year; 1924–47, imported chilled hindquarters (Argentine 1924–38, New Zealand 1939–47); 1948 onwards, 'beef imported'. *The Economist*, Annual Commercial History and Review through 1953, then British Wholesale Prices.

(32) *Mutton 1858–1954:* 1858–90, mean of highest and lowest prices for middling butcher's meat, Newgate or Smithfield, and 1891–1914, price of middling, at beginning of year throughout; 1913–27, mean of middling and prime at end of year; 1924–54, imported (1924–38 New Zealand frozen wethers) at end of year. *The Economist*, Annual Commercial History and Review through 1953, then British Wholesale Prices.

(33) *Herrings 1264–1400:* kind not specified; most of earlier entries from E. Anglia, and of later from monastic accounts esp. Wolrichston in Warwickshire. R, I, 635–40.

(34) *White Herrings 1404–1590:* generally bought at Stourbridge fair. Through 1583, R, IV, 540–4; 1584–90, from entries in R, VI, 392–4.

(35) *Red Herrings 1405–1561:* generally bought at Stourbridge fair. R, IV, 540–4.

(36) *Haberden (salt cod) 1584–1703:* mostly from King's College, Cambridge, and probably mostly bought at Stourbridge fair. R, V, 427–8.

(37) *Crimped (dried) cod 1783–1830:* Lord Steward's dept. B, 369–71, 370.

(38) *Fresh cod 1783–1830:* Lord Steward's dept. B, 369–71, 420–1.

(39) *Herrings 1827–1902:* average declared value per barrel exported, 1827–39, from 'Porter's Tables' in various BPP, 1836–43; 1840–1902, WRP, 158.

(40) *Herrings 1898–1938, 1945–54:* average value per cwt of British takings landed. Annual Reports on Sea Fisheries, later Sea Fisheries Statistical Tables, of Board, later Ministry, of Agriculture.

(41) *Cod 1898–1938, 1945–54:* as for (40).

(42) *Cheese 1264–1429:* same origins as (01); numerous gaps in 14th century; 1401–29, Hornchurch (Essex) only. R, I, 430–5; III, 209–12.

(43) *Cheese 1573–1752:* Suffolk cheese bought by St Bartholomew's Hospital, Sandwich. Numerous gaps. B, 223–5, 238–40.

(44) *Cheese 1684–1758:* Suffolk cheese bought by Navy Victualling, London. B, 555–6, 576.

(45) *Cheese 1703–96:* Gloucester cheese bought by Chelsea Hospital, London, B, 308, 313.

(46) *Cheese 1713–1824:* Gloucester cheese bought by Greenwich Hospital. B, 261, 293, 295.

(47) *Cheese 1756–1827:* Cheshire cheese bought by Navy Victualling, London. B, 555–6, 576.

(48) *Cheese 1815–1902:* cheese (unspecified) bought by Bethlem Royal Hospital, London. Contract price 1815–71, thereafter open market. WRP, 150.

(49) *Cheese 1854–1954:* average value per cwt of cheese imported into U.K. AS.

(50) *Butter 1264–1379:* same origins as (01). R, I, 430–4.

(51) *Butter 1561–1702:* 1561–83, Oxford city accounts; 1584–1702, average of prices recorded mostly by New College, Oxford, King's College, Cambridge, and Winchester. R. III, 217–18; V, 372–8.

(52) *Butter 1659–1767:* fresh butter bought by St Bartholomew's Hospital, Sandwich. B, 222–3, 236.

(53) *Butter 1684–1827:* purchases by Navy Victualling, London. B, 555, 576.

(54) *Butter 1805–1902:* contract prices paid by Royal Hospital, Greenwich. WRP, 139.

(55) *Butter 1815–1902:* contract prices 1815–71, market prices 1872–1902, paid by Bethlem Royal Hospital, London. WRP, 140.

(56) *Butter 1886–1954:* average value of butter imported into the U.K. AS.

(57) *Malt 1266–1703:* specified as 'first quality' through 1401, unspecified afterwards; same origins as (01). R, I, 227–35; IV, 238–91; V, 268–74.

(58) *Malt 1596–1832:* Windsor market prices, average of Michaelmas and Lady Day, recorded by Eton College for assessing money due in lieu of malt rents. B, 111, 144–7.

(59) *Malt 1684–1827:* price paid by Navy Victualling, London. B, 547–8, 574–5.

(60) *Malt 1805–65:* contract price paid by Royal Hospital, Greenwich. J. R. McCulloch, Dictionary of Commerce (1882 edn), 1138–40.

(61) *Malt 1863–1954:* average declared value of exports. AS.

(62) *Hops 1559–1594:* mainly Flemish; price paid by Eton College. B, 108, 143–4.

(63) *Hops 1584–1703:* English mainly Eton and King's College, Cambridge, with Winchester coming in from 1644. R, V, 289–301.

(64) *Hops 1684–1827:* kind unspecified; bought by Navy Victualling, London. B, 539–40, 567–9. Some gaps filled according to movement of Greenwich Hospital price, B, 254–5, 292, 294.

(65) *Hops 1805–64:* average contract price paid by Royal Hospital, Greenwich. WRP, 88.

(66) *Hops 1854–1914:* average declared value of imports. AS.

(67) *Hops 1906–54:* index no. of average price of home-grown hops. Ministry of Agriculture: Agricultural Statistics.

(68) *Sugar 1689–1771:* brown, bought, by Navy Victualling, London. Gaps after 1750 filled by reference to Navy Victualling, Plymouth. B, 557–8, 565.

(69) *Sugar 1765–1831:* powder or Lisbon, bought by Lord Steward's dept. B, 383–5, 429–31.

(70) *Sugar 1820–1954:* average declared export value. 1820–1902, WRP, 165; 1903–54, AS.

(71) *Tea 1801–71:* average price in bond. WRP, 176–7.

(72) *Tea 1854–1954:* average declared value of imports.1854–1902, WRP, 173; 1903–54, AS.

(73) *Charcoal 1441–1583:* mostly at Oxford and Cambridge. R, IV, 383–7.

(74) *Charcoal 1442–1583:* as for (73). R, IV, 383–7.

(75) *Charcoal 1551–1785:* price paid by Eton College. B, 119–22, 143–7.

(76) *Charcoal 1584–1703:* at Oxford or Winchester. R, V, 398–405.

(77) *Charcoal 1584–1703:* at Cambridge, mainly King's College. R, V, 398–405.

(78) *Charcoal 1609–47:* at Oxford. R, V, 398–401.

(79) *Charcoal 1576–1785:* price paid by Westminster (School and Abbey). B, 177–8, 193–5.

(80) *Coal 1584–1703:* usually Newcastle coal, bought at Cambridge, mostly by King's College. R, V, 398–404.

(81) *Coal 1586–1831:* bought for Westminster (School and Abbey) brewery 1586–1619, College 1620–1831. B, 173–7, 193–6.

(82) *Coal 1654–1832:* bought for Eton College brewery. B, 116–19, 145–7.

(83) *Coal 1717–1902:* Newcastle coal delivered Royal Naval Hospital, Greenwich. B, 264–7, 294–5.

(84) *Coal 1846–1954:* price in London of Wallsend Hetton, 1846–1916, best Yorkshire house coal after 1916: JRSS.

(85) *Candles 1321–1703:* same origins as (01). R, I, 439–44; IV, 376–80; V, 398–404.

(86) *Candles 1645–1831:* price paid by Eton College, less tax. B, 128–9, 145–7.

(87) *Candles 1703–1811:* price paid by Chelsea Hospital, less tax. B, 311–12, 313.

(88) *Candles 1713–1868:* price paid by Greenwich Hospital, less

tax. B, 271, 293–5. J. R. McCulloch, Dictionary of Commerce, 1138–40.

(89) *Tallow 1846–1910:* town. JRSS.

(90) *Oil 1402–1535:* olive and rape oil, mainly at Oxford and Cambridge. R, IV, 376–9.

(91) *Oil 1567–1783:* train-oil bought for Naval Stores. B, 633–4, 670–4, 680.

(92) *Oil 1783–1853:* Northern (1783–1839), Southern (1840–53), oil, without casks. TN, II, 394–5, 407; III, 297; IV, 430; VI, 504.

(93) *Oil 1854–1880:* price exclusive of duty of train or blubber oil, from the Northern whale fishery and British North America: AS.

(94) *Oil 1856–1912:* average import value of petroleum, illuminating and lubricating: AS.

(95) *Oil 1903–54:* average import value of petroleum, lamp oil, later called Kerosene (burning oil): AS.

(96) *Gas 1876–1954:* price paid by domestic consumers: 1876–1937, mean of prices of three London gas companies. Report from the Select Committee on Gas Undertakings, BPP, 1918, III, app. 4. 1949–54, price of North Thames Gas Board, from Annual Reports; rise 1937–49 distributed by years according to rise in price of coal.

(97) *Canvas 1265–1583:* same origins as (01). R, I, 587–92; IV, 583–8.

(98) *Shirting 1402–1583, Sheeting or Shirting 1584–1701:* same origins as (01). R, IV, 583–8; V, 561–4.

(99) *Linen and Canvas 1506–1673:* price paid by Eton College. B, 131–2, 143–5.

(100) *Cloth 1394–1624:* bought by Winchester College for scholars and servants. B, 45–6, 85–9, 90.

(101) *Cloth 1394–1554:* bought by Winchester College for fellows, stewards and others. B, 46–7, 85–7.

(102) *Cloth 1402–1583:* average of three qualities of cloth, bought mainly by New College, Oxford and King's College, Cambridge. R. IV, 583–8.

(103) *Cloth 1576–1757:* broad cloth bought for scholars of Westminster School. B, 182, 193–6.

(104) *Cloth 1615–1757:* bought for scholars and choristers of Eton College. B, 130–1, 144–7.

(105) *Cloth 1748–1829:* blue cloth bought by Greenwich Hospital. B, 273, 293, 295.

(106) *Yarn, woollen and worsted, 1831–1954:* average declared value of exports. 1831–9, 'Porter's Tables' in BPP; then AS.

(107) *Cotton cloth 1812–60:* average price paid by printers per piece of 7/8–72 reed printing cloth. JRSS, 1861, 491–7.

(108) *Cotton cloth 1858–1954:* 1858–1906, mean of 26 in 66 reed printer's cloth and 40 in 66 reed shirting; 1897–1950, 38 in or 39 in shirting; 1949–54, a printer's cloth. *The Economist*, Annual Commercial History and Review.

APPENDIX B

INDEXES (1451–75 = 100) OF: (1) PRICE OF COMPOSITE UNIT OF CONSUMABLES; (2) EQUIVALENT OF WAGE RATE OF BUILDING CRAFTSMAN, EXPRESSED IN THE ABOVE COMPOSITE PHYSICAL UNIT; IN SOUTHERN ENGLAND, 1264–1954

	(1)	(2)		(1)	(2)		(1)	(2)		(1)	(2)
1260	—	—	1290	80	63	1320	106	63	1350	102	49
1261	—	—	1291	106	47	1321	121	55	1351	134	—
1262	—	—	1292	96	52	1322	141	48	1352	160	—
1263	—	—	1293	93	54	1323	165	41	1353	138	—
1264	83	60	1294	110	45	1324	137	49	1354	117	—
1265	80	63	1295	131	38	1325	127	53	1355	115	—
1266	83	60	1296	104	48	1326	124	54	1356	121	—
1267	—	—	1297	93	54	1327	96	70	1357	133	—
1268	70	71	1298	106	47	1328	96	70	1358	139	—
1269	83	60	1299	96	52	1329	119	56	1359	126	—
1270	—	—	1300	113	44	1330	120	56	1360	135	61
1271	98	51	1301	89	—	1331	134	50	1361	131	63
1272	130	38	1302	93	—	1332	131	51	1362	153	54
1273	98	51	1303	89	—	1333	111	60	1363	155	54
1274	95	53	1304	94	62	1334	99	68	1364	151	55
1275	100	50	1305	97	60	1335	96	70	1365	143	58
1276	96	52	1306	100	58	1336	101	66	1366	121	69
1277	97	52	1307	94	62	1337	111	60	1367	137	61
1278	103	49	1308	105	55	1338	85	—	1368	139	60
1279	94	53	1309	119	—	1339	79	—	1369	150	55
1280	94	53	1310	135	—	1340	96	52	1370	184	45
1281	93	54	1311	123	54	1341	86	58	1371	164	51
1282	104	48	1312	108	62	1342	85	59	1372	132	63
1283	111	45	1313	101	66	1343	84	60	1373	131	63
1284	120	42	1314	112	60	1344	97	52	1374	125	66
1285	83	60	1315	132	51	1345	98	51	1375	125	66
1286	91	55	1316	216	31	1346	88	57	1376	146	57
1287	91	55	1317	215	31	1347	109	46	1377	112	74
1288	72	69	1318	154	44	1348	116	43	1378	95	87
1289	69	72	1319	119	56	1349	97	52	1379	94	88

APPENDIX B—*continued*

	(1)	(2)		(1)	(2)		(1)	(2)		(1)	(2)
1380	106	78	1430	138	72	1480	103	97	1530	169	59
1381	119	70	1431	115	87	1481	115	87	1531	154	65
1382	111	75	1432	102	98	1482	145	69	1532	179	56
1383	108	77	1433	112	89	1483	162	62	1533	169	—
1384	116	72	1434	109	92	1484	128	78	1534	145	—
1385	112	74	1435	105	95	1485	99	101	1535	131	—
1386	104	80	1436	95	105	1486	86	116	1536	164	—
1387	100	83	1437	93	108	1487	103	97	1537	155	—
1388	102	81	1438	128	78	1488	110	90	1538	138	—
1389	100	83	1439	154	65	1489	109	92	1539	147	—
1390	106	78	1440	140	71	1490	106	94	1540	158	—
1391	133	62	1441	93	108	1491	112	89	1541	165	—
1392	104	80	1442	85	118	1492	103	97	1542	172	—
1393	100	83	1443	97	103	1493	117	85	1543	171	—
1394	101	82	1444	102	98	1494	96	104	1544	178	—
1395	93	89	1445	87	115	1495	89	112	1545	191	—
1396	99	84	1446	95	105	1496	94	106	1546	248	—
1397	116	72	1447	100	100	1497	101	99	1547	231	—
1398	121	69	1448	102	98	1498	96	104	1548	193	61
1399	113	73	1449	106	94	1499	99	101	1549	214	—
1400	104	80	1450	102	98	1500	94	106	1550	262	—
1401	130	64	1451	109	92	1501	107	93	1551	285	—
1402	127	65	1452	97	103	1502	122	82	1552	276	48
1403	119	—	1453	97	103	1503	114	88	1553	259	—
1404	99	—	1454	105	95	1504	107	93	1554	276	—
1405	99	—	1455	94	106	1505	103	97	1555	270	—
1406	100	—	1456	101	99	1506	106	94	1556	370	—
1407	99	—	1457	93	108	1507	98	102	1557	409	—
1408	107	—	1458	99	101	1508	100	100	1558	230	—
1409	120	—	1459	95	105	1509	92	109	1559	255	—
1410	130	—	1460	97	103	1510	103	97	1560	265	—
1411	106	—	1461	117	85	1511	97	103	1561	283	59
1412	103	97	1462	115	87	1512	101	99	1562	266	63
1413	108	93	1463	88	114	1513	120	83	1563	—	—
1414	108	93	1464	86	116	1514	118	85	1564	—	—
1415	115	87	1465	108	93	1515	107	93	1565	290	58
1416	124	81	1466	109	92	1516	110	90	1566	287	58
1417	129	78	1467	108	93	1517	111	90	1567	282	59
1418	114	88	1468	106	94	1518	116	86	1568	281	59
1419	95	105	1469	107	93	1519	129	78	1569	276	61
1420	102	98	1470	102	98	1520	137	73	1570	300	56
1421	93	108	1471	103	97	1521	167	60	1571	265	63
1422	97	103	1472	104	96	1522	160	63	1572	270	62
1423	108	93	1473	97	103	1523	136	74	1573	274	61
1424	103	97	1474	95	105	1524	133	75	1574	374	—
1425	109	92	1475	90	111	1525	129	78	1575	—	—
1426	103	97	1476	85	118	1526	133	75	1576	309	—
1427	96	104	1477	81	123	1527	147	68	1577	363	—
1428	99	101	1478	89	112	1528	179	56	1578	351	—
1429	127	79	1479	97	103	1529	159	63	1579	326	—

D

APPENDIX B—*continued*

	(1)	(2)		(1)	(2)		(1)	(2)		(1)	(2)
1580	342	58	1630	595	—	1680	568	53	1730	599	61
1581	347	58	1631	682	—	1681	567	53	1731	553	—
1582	343	58	1632	580	—	1682	600	50	1732	557	—
1583	324	62	1633	565	—	1683	587	51	1733	544	—
1584	333	60	1634	611	—	1684	570	53	1734	518	—
1585	338	59	1635	597	—	1685	651	46	1735	529	—
1586	352	57	1636	593	—	1686	559	54	1736	539	74
1587	491	41	1637	621	—	1687	580	52	1737	581	69
1588	346	58	1638	707	—	1688	551	—	1738	563	71
1589	354	56	1639	607	—	1689	535	—	1739	547	73
1590	396	51	1640	546	—	1690	513	—	1740	644	62
1591	459	44	1641	586	—	1691	493	—	1741	712	56
1592	370	54	1642	557	48	1692	542	—	1742	631	63
1593	356	56	1643	553	—	1693	652	—	1743	579	69
1594	381	52	1644	531	—	1694	693	—	1744	518	77
1595	515	39	1645	574	—	1695	645	—	1745	528	76
1596	505	40	1646	569	—	1696	697	—	1746	594	67
1597	685	29	1647	667	—	1697	693	—	1747	574	70
1598	579	35	1648	770	—	1698	767	—	1748	599	67
1599	474	42	1649	821	—	1699	773	—	1749	609	66
1600	459	44	1650	839	—	1700	671	—	1750	590	68
1601	536	37	1651	704	—	1701	586	57	1751	574	70
1602	471	42	1652	648	—	1702	582	—	1752	601	67
1603	448	45	1653	579	—	1703	551	—	1753	585	68
1604	404	50	1654	543	—	1704	587	—	1754	615	65
1605	448	45	1655	531	56	1705	548	—	1755	578	69
1606	468	43	1656	559	54	1706	583	—	1756	602	66
1607	449	45	1657	612	49	1707	531	—	1757	733	55
1608	507	39	1658	646	46	1708	571	—	1758	731	55
1609	559	36	1659	700	43	1709	697	—	1759	673	59
1610	503	40	1660	684	44	1710	798	46	1760	643	62
1611	463	43	1661	648	46	1711	889	41	1761	614	65
1612	524	38	1662	769	39	1712	638	58	1762	638	63
1613	549	36	1663	675	44	1713	594	62	1763	655	61
1614	567	35	1664	657	46	1714	635	58	1764	713	56
1615	561	36	1665	616	49	1715	646	57	1765	738	54
1616	562	36	1666	664	45	1716	645	57	1766	747	54
1617	537	37	1667	577	52	1717	602	61	1767	790	51
1618	524	38	1668	602	50	1718	575	64	1768	781	51
1619	494	40	1669	572	52	1719	609	60	1769	717	56
1620	485	41	1670	577	52	1720	635	58	1770	714	56
1621	461	43	1671	595	50	1721	604	61	1771	775	52
1622	523	38	1672	557	44	1722	554	66	1772	858	47
1623	588	34	1673	585	51	1723	525	70	1773	855	47
1624	543	37	1674	650	46	1724	589	62	1774	863	—
1625	534	37	1675	691	43	1725	610	60	1775	815	—
1626	552	36	1676	652	46	1726	637	58	1776	797	61
1627	496	40	1677	592	51	1727	596	62	1777	794	61
1628	466	43	1678	633	47	1728	649	57	1778	826	58
1629	510	39	1679	614	49	1729	681	54	1779	756	64

APPENDIX B—*continued*

	(1)	(2)		(1)	(2)		(1)	(2)		(1)	(2)
1780	730	66	1830	1146	70	1880	1174	102	1930	1275	229
1781	760	64	1831	1260	63	1881	1213	99	1931	1146	247
1782	776	62	1832	1167	69	1882	1140	105	1932	1065	266
1783	869	56	1833	1096	73	1883	1182	102	1933	1107	248
1784	874	55	1834	1011	79	1884	1071	112	1934	1097	251
1785	839	58	1835	1028	78	1885	1026	117	1935	1149	254
1786	839	58	1836	1141	70	1886	931	129	1936	1211	248
1787	834	58	1837	1169	68	1887	955	126	1937	1275	242
1788	867	56	1838	1177	68	1888	950	126	1938	1274	249
1789	856	56	1839	1263	63	1889	948	127	1939	1209	269
1790	871	55	1840	1286	62	1890	947	127	1940	1574	222
1791	870	55	1841	1256	64	1891	998	120	1941	1784	206
1792	883	—	1842	1161	69	1892	996	120	1942	2130	176
1793	908	—	1843	1030	78	1893	914	137	1943	2145	183
1794	978	—	1844	1029	78	1894	982	127	1944	2216	184
1795	1091	—	1845	1079	74	1895	968	129	1945	2282	186
1796	1161	52	1846	1122	71	1896	947	132	1946	2364	208
1797	1045	57	1847	1257	65	1897	963	130	1947	2580	210
1798	1022	59	1848	1105	74	1898	982	127	1948	2781	198
1799	1148	52	1849	1035	79	1899	950	140	1949	3145	178
1800	1567	38	1850	969	84	1900	994	134	1950	3155	180
1801	1751	34	1851	961	85	1901	986	135	1951	3656	170
1802	1348	45	1852	978	84	1902	963	138	1952	3987	167
1803	1268	—	1853	1135	79	1903	1004	133	1953	3735	187
1804	1309	—	1854	1265	71	1904	985	135	1954	3825	194
1805	1521	—	1855	1274	71	1905	989	135			
1806	1454	49	1856	1264	71	1906	1016	131			
1807	1427	50	1857	1287	70	1907	1031	129			
1808	1476	49	1858	1190	76	1908	1043	128			
1809	1619	44	1859	1214	74	1909	1058	126			
1810	1670	48	1860	1314	68	1910	994	134			
1811	1622	49	1861	1302	72	1911	984	135			
1812	1836	44	1862	1290	72	1912	999	133			
1813	1881	43	1863	1144	82	1913	1021	131			
1814	1642	49	1864	1200	78	1914	1147	124			
1815	1467	55	1865	1238	—	1915	1317	114			
1816	1344	60	1866	1296	82	1916	1652	94			
1817	1526	52	1867	1346	79	1917	1965	87			
1818	1530	52	1868	1291	82	1918	2497	80			
1819	1492	54	1869	1244	86	1919	2254	126			
1820	1353	59	1870	1241	86	1920	2591	154			
1821	1190	67	1871	1320	81	1921	2048	167			
1822	1029	78	1872	1378	—	1922	1672	164			
1823	1099	73	1873	1437	84	1923	1726	159			
1824	1193	67	1874	1423	84	1924	1740	172			
1825	1400	57	1875	1310	92	1925	1708	176			
1826	1323	60	1876	1370	88	1926	1577	190			
1827	1237	65	1877	1330	90	1927	1496	201			
1828	1201	67	1878	1281	94	1928	1485	202			
1829	1189	67	1879	1210	99	1929	1511	199			

2 The Price Revolution of the Sixteenth Century: Some Swedish Evidence[1]

INGRID HAMMARSTRÖM

This article was first published in *The Scandinavian Economic History Review*, vol. V (1957)[2]

I

Since the publication in 1895 of George Wiebe's work, *Zur Geschichte der Preisrevolution des XVI und XVII Jahrhunderts*,[3] the 'price revolution' has been a generally accepted concept found in most historical textbooks. By the 'price revolution', Wiebe meant the general rise in commodity prices which occurred in western Europe during the sixteenth century, the primary cause of which according to him was the influx of silver from the new Spanish possessions in America. His explanation also came to be generally accepted, but perhaps an even more significant contribution to the influence which this book has wielded is the fact that he synthesized in readily usable form the price analyses in existence when he wrote, i.e. at the end of the nineteenth century. In the 1930s his tables still formed the basis of sweeping conclusions and generalizations.

On the other hand it was clear by about 1930 that grave methodological objections could be raised against the collection of price data used by Wiebe. When the International Scientific

[1] This article is based on a paper delivered to the Scandinavian Historical Conference at Aarhus in August 1957. The introductory survey of the works on European price trends in the sixteenth century has been made somewhat fuller than in the paper; it still does not pretend, however, to give a complete bibliographical account but only to indicate some of what I consider to be the main themes of the debate.

[2] The concluding section of this article, which is of purely Swedish interest, is not reprinted here.

[3] *Staats- und socialwissenschaftliche Beiträge*, ed. A. von Miaskowski (Leipzig, 1895), II, 2.

Committee on Price History was formed in 1930, it drew up a list of rules for dealing with these problems, that had often been ignored by earlier price historians. Data on wages and prices should not be collected from different regions of a country but only from a single city or a definite, limited area; each commodity series should, if possible, be drawn from the same set of records for the whole of the period under review; price data should be published in a form as close as possible to that of the sources, so as to facilitate their use by other research workers.

The studies made by the Committee were intended to embrace the *ancien régime* in Europe's economic life – i.e. the Middle Ages if possible, and the period from then until the beginning of the nineteenth century. However, partly as a result of the requirement that continuous price series should be constructed from the same source, the sixteenth century is less adequately represented than later periods in those works which have been published under the auspices of the Committee. One of the best works from the point of view of methodology, *Nederlandsche Prijsgeschiedenis*,[1] by W. Posthumus, begins at 1585 because the weekly price currents issued by the Amsterdam stock exchange, which the author used, began in that year. Of the price and wage material for England collected under the direction of Lord Beveridge, price series for the period 1550–1830 have been published: the earlier material is still unpublished.[2]

If one wishes to obtain a complete picture of sixteenth-century price movements beginning at the transition from the price level of the late Middle Ages to the new upward tendency of prices, there is only a limited number of works that are of use. The German member of the Committee, M. J. Elsas, has published price series for six German cities, some of them starting as early as the fourteenth century.[3] During the 1930s a number of works were also published outside the aegis of the Commit-

---

[1] Vol. I (Leiden, 1943).

[2] W. H. Beveridge, *Prices and Wages in England from the 12th to the 19th Century* (London, 1939), I.

[3] M. J. Elsas, *Umriss einer Geschichte der Preise und Löhne in Deutschland vom ausgehenden Mittelalter bis zum Beginn des neunzehnten Jahrhunderts* (Leiden, 1936–49), I–II.

tee, for instance by a research group in Poland which presented price data for the city of Kraków for the period 1369–1600.[1] An Italian study published in 1939 gives prices for Florence in the years 1520–1620.[2] When we add to this list Professor E. J. Hamilton's two studies of price trends in Spain, for 1351–1500 and 1501–60 respectively,[3] all those most important modern works have been mentioned which consider the beginnings of the rise in prices as well as its subsequent course.

How complete is the picture of sixteenth-century price trends that can be composed from these studies? One finding is common to all these studies, that the sixteenth century was a time of rising prices: so far Wiebe was right. Further, the price rise seems as a rule to have been more pronounced in the second half of the century.

On the other hand, it is obvious that important regions and trade centres are still missing.[4] There are not many regions for which the start of the upswing of prices can be fixed with any accuracy. In Germany and Poland, the prices of certain commodities had already begun to rise as early as the later decades of the fifteenth century; in Spain a gentle upward movement can be discerned from the beginning of the sixteenth century.

[1] J. Pelc, *Ceny w Krakowie w latach 1369–1600, Badania z dziejow spolecznych i gospodarczych* (Lwow, 1935), XIV. Similar publications for Lwow, Warsaw and Danzig start with the sixteenth century, too late, however, to be of use in this particular context.

[2] G. Parenti, *Prime richerche sulla rivoluzione dei prezzi in Firenze*, Pubblicazioni della R. Università degli Studi di Firenze, Facolta di Economia e commercio (Florence, 1939), XVI.

[3] E. J. Hamilton, 'Money, prices and wages in Valencia, Aragon and Navarre, 1351–1500', *Harvard Economic Studies* LI (1936), and 'American treasure and the price revolution in Spain, 1501–1560', *Harvard Economic Studies*, XLIII (1934), hereafter cited as *American Treasure*.

[4] The study of French prices published by H. Hauser in 1936 received severe criticism for its methodological shortcomings and should only be used with great caution. Further studies of the history of prices are at present under way in several countries. Preliminary findings of two of these are presented in *Annales* (1955), viz., C. Verlinden *et al.*, 'Mouvements des prix et des salaires en Belgique au XVI siècle', pp. 173–98, and C. M. Cipolla, 'La prétendue "révolution des prix". Réflexions sur l'expérience italienne', pp. 513–16. E. Waschinski gives certain of the results of a study of prices and money (but not the price tables themselves) in 'Währung, Preisentwicklung und Kaufkraft des Geldes in Schleswig-Holstein von 1226–1864', *Quellen und Forschungen zur Geschichte Schleswig-Holstein* (1952), XXVII.

In these countries the rise in prices continued through the first half of the sixteenth century. In Italy, by contrast, it does not seem possible to find any significant rise before the middle of the century.

Nor is it easy to resolve the question of the size of the total price rise in the various regions of Europe over the century as a whole. Professor Hamilton estimates that the average price level in Spain around the year 1600 was about four times as high as in 1501.[1] The general price index for Kraków in Poland shows a figure about two and half times as high in 1600 as in 1500.[2] Here again, the indexes computed for Italy lag behind. On the whole, prices seem to have risen less in Italy than in any other country so far studied, with the possible exception of Sweden. In all these computations prices are reckoned in silver, not in the nominal coin.

II

If the compilation and study of price data for the sixteenth century thus flourished in the 1930s, the same is also true of the general debate about the rise in prices. The compilers of price data were, naturally enough, not inclined to wait until such time as a statistically satisfactory number of further studies should have been completed for the whole of Europe before discussing the causes and effects of the 'price revolution'. The chief question at issue was: what was the cause of the price rise which seems to have been a general phenomenon in western Europe during the sixteenth century? Since questions of principle and method are very much involved, the controversy has flared up over and over again, and the 'price revolution' is still the subject of conflicting views and varying methodological approaches.

It is possible to discern in retrospect different stages in this debate. The first stage may be characterized as the period of the quantity theory of money, or the 'bullion explanation'. It is not so easy to say when this period ended, especially since not a

---

[1] Hamilton, *American Treasure*, p. 202.
[2] Pelc, op. cit., p. 136.

few price historians still adhere to the theory and the history textbooks still unanimously claim that the price revolution was 'caused by' the flow of gold and silver from the Spanish possessions in America.

The ancestry of the quantity theory is usually traced back to Jean Bodin, who in the 1560s saw in the increased volume of coin the explanation of the general rise in prices which his generation had experienced. The theoretical approach of the 1930s to the problems presented by the sixteenth-century rise in prices was not much more elaborate. In accordance with Irving Fisher's simple exchange equation formulated some twenty years earlier, four factors were considered: the general level of prices, P; the volume of transactions, or 'trade', T; the quantity of money, M; and the velocity of circulation, V. Fisher's equation states that $PT = MV$ and the quantity theory of money claims that changes in P are as a rule caused by and are proportionate to changes in M.

All this is no doubt well known to readers of this journal. Nevertheless I would like to repeat it with somewhat greater precision. P is defined as the average of all prices paid in money for goods and services during a given period; T is the total volume of transactions (i.e. quantities of goods and services traded for money) during the same period; M is the total sum of money, including credit money, used in these transactions; and V is the average velocity of circulation, a concept which is introduced because each individual money unit is used more than once during the period in question.

With proper definitions the equation simply represents two ways of expressing the sum of transactions: it is valid because it is a truism.

There is no need to relate here how the quantity equation has fared since 1930 at the hands of economists, how it has been modified and elaborated by some and subjected to severe criticism by others. Its concepts, especially that of the velocity of circulation, have been shown to be summary averages of economic phenomena of widely different origins and therefore of limited value as a means of explaining strategic changes within the economy. The growing preoccupation of economists with other than monetary problems, with factors determining real income, output and employment, has also made them turn to other modes of analysis.

As often happens in the relationship between economics and economic history, it was the historians who gave the original theory a shelter and a longer span of life. But historians had no practical use for the necessarily valid, because tautologically defined, Fisher equation. They had to transform P into an average of such price series as could be constructed from the available sources and to see changes in T in the fluctuations they observed (or assumed) in the general economic activity of the societies they were studying. Changes in M were represented by what one knew about the minting of coin during various periods or, in the sixteenth century, by figures of imports of precious metals from America.

It was not always kept in mind that under these conditions the equation does not express any formally valid relation between money and prices. Further, to assume that changes in M produced proportionate effects on P meant that changes in T and V were disregarded and that these factors were presumed to be constant during the period in question. The assumption, tacit or explicit, was that in the sixteenth century these factors were capable of much smaller fluctuations than in our present-day society, making the quantity theory of money more useful for historians than for economists. Whether this should be regarded as another instance of the tendency to overrate the stability of former times, may be left an open question.

We may agree that the quantity theory as used by price historians is not a formally valid hypothesis. But there is another test we can apply, the test of practical usefulness. Has it been a useful theory, a better approach to the problems of the 'price revolution' than the more varied and possibly more pragmatic interpretations that might have taken its place, had it not been so widely accepted?

The quantity equation is sometimes defended as a useful summary of important factors to look for in the economy. Is this true of the debate on sixteenth-century prices? Has the quantity theory brought historians into contact with strategic factors which would otherwise have been neglected? Has it helped to explain the rise in prices as a historical phenomenon – not only the overall rise but also the temporary falls, not only the general trend but also the divergencies between countries or, within a country, between various groups of commodities?

It is not the present purpose to try to give definitive answers to these questions, but only to throw light on some aspects of the quantity theory approach which I regard as shortcomings, and to draw attention to some recent attempts to analyse the price rise of the sixteenth century through different approaches.

The best known and most widely cited of modern works on the price revolution is at the same time a good example of the impact of the quantity theory on the historical thinking of the 1930s, namely, Earl J. Hamilton's *American Treasure and the Price Revolution in Spain* which appeared in 1934 (cited above, p. 44).

To Professor Hamilton it seemed evident that the activating forces behind the rise in prices were to be found on the side of money – i.e. in American silver. We are told that the main aim of his index numbers of prices is 'to measure changes in the purchasing power of money'.[1] In an earlier study of Spanish prices we find, in the same general context, another formula: 'to measure the impact on prices of the influx of precious metals'.[2] Both aims amount to the same thing: to construct a general price index, a rise in which will reflect a proportionate fall in 'the purchasing power of money', and then to compare this index with changes in the supply of money, or bullion. Thus, attention is concentrated right from the start upon the monetary factor which, on the assumptions of the quantity theory, must be supposed to affect all prices alike. Relative price movements are of no significance to the final result since they are balanced out to form a 'general price level'.

In the final chapter of *American Treasure*, entitled 'Why prices rose', the centre of interest is a chart for the period 1501–1650, showing the amount of bullion imported annually into Seville

[1] Hamilton, *American Treasure*, p. 149.
[2] Hamilton, 'American treasure and Andalusian prices, 1503–1660'. See pp. 147–81 of this volume.

from America, and the movement of the price level as represented by an average commodity index.[1] The two curves rise
in about the same fashion, with the closest correlation in the
period 1535–90. This is interpreted as confirmation that
'the abundant mines of America were the principal cause of the
price revolution in Spain'. Only at the beginning and the end
of the century, when the curves diverge, 'did other factors play
important parts in the price upheaval'.

We may agree with Professor Hamilton that this chart shows
a correlation between imports of precious metals and the rise
of prices. And yet we may feel that we have not been given the
whole explanation, or at least not a full discussion of all possible explanations. Why should the level of prices be correlated
to the yearly imports of bullion? Does not the quantity theory
require that changes in the price level should be compared with
changes in the existing *total* amount of bullion (or money)?
Furthermore, bullion had to be not only imported but also
coined, and not only coined but also spent by someone, before
having a general impact on prices. Professor Hamilton is content to leave the gold and silver once it has been weighed and
stored in the House of Trade at Seville. His general assumption
is of course that the recipients of bullion did not allow it to stay
idle for long but used it, after coining, as means of payment for
commodities and services. This seems to me to illustrate one
of the weaknesses of the quantity theory as a tool of historical
analysis: it is not concerned with the *process* through which an
increase in bullion may create new incomes and new demand
and thus force prices up, but only with the *final* changes in the
amount of money.

The American bullion is sometimes likened to manna falling
from heaven on a country that had done nothing (nothing, that
is, in the way of economic exertions) to deserve it. This is a
simile fully compatible with the quantity theory, since it enables us to picture all prices, wages, rents, etc., rising in

[1] Hamilton, *American Treasure*, p. 301. In reality we have here two charts, one
superimposed on the other: one gives absolute figures of the quantities of gold
and silver imported into Seville from 1500 to 1650 (average annual figures for
each five-year period); the other gives yearly relative figures – index numbers –
of prices for the same period.

proportion to the influx of bullion. Also it becomes unnecessary, if not downright impudent, to enquire about the mechanism by which the amount of money was increased.

But the simile is, of course, misleading. Gold and silver did not rain from above, but flowed into the country in consequence of a favourable balance of trade. Most of the bullion constituted payment for commodities exported to the colonies. It must have influenced first the profit expectations, then the ultimate incomes of the Seville merchants. Next it would reach their contractors, and finally agricultural and industrial producers. There is no reason to assume that all groups of income-receivers, or all groups of prices, were affected in the same way by this process. On the whole, this influx of bullion seems to be worthy of study in its sixteenth-century setting as a phenomenon in itself. It was not the same as those modern phenomena which, when the quantity equation is applied to economic data, are concealed under changes in M.

These considerations are, of course, not a criticism of Professor Hamilton's manner of applying the quantity theory but rather of the theory itself. What we may question is the underlying assumption that relative price-changes may be balanced out and the resultant 'general change in prices' regarded as an automatic effect of changes in the supply of money.

III

The quantity theory is fundamentally a monetary theory, just as the Fisher equation represents two ways of expressing the sum of cash expenditure at a given time. But when we study the rise in prices of the sixteenth century, we are often forced to take into consideration economic facts which do not depend upon changes 'on the side of money' but represent 'real changes' within the economy.

Can these facts – of which any analysis of the price revolution must take account – be explained within the framework of the quantity theory? We may take as examples the two main difficulties which Professor Hamilton encounters when correlating the rise in prices with specie imports. The first one is that the rise in the price level was not equal for all types of commodities. On the whole, agricultural products show a steeper rise than non-agricultural during the first three-quarters of the sixteenth century. The second difficulty is that the rise in prices was much smaller than the increase in the available stock of precious metals (I have already suggested that prices should be compared not with the yearly additions to the stock of bullion but with the total volume of bullion available).

When discussing these facts Professor Hamilton still uses the concepts of the quantity equation, $PT = MV$. The first discrepancy is accounted for chiefly by assuming a decline in agriculture beginning as early as the first half of the sixteenth century.[1] If, as in this case, M and V must be regarded as constant (since they are related only to changes in the *general* price level), then T – output within agriculture – must diminish as P rises.

The second difficulty is met by enumerating factors alleged to have 'neutralized' a proportion of the bullion: the flow of specie to the East, the enhanced production and exchange of goods that presumably accompanied the general growth of population, an assumed increase in hoarding among the upper strata of Spanish society and an assumed contraction of credit, are among the most important factors which 'tended to counteract the rapid augmentation of gold and silver money' – i.e. to counteract the rise in prices.[2]

The problem here is that P rose less than proportionally to M. The lag is explained by reducing V (increase in hoarding, diminution of credit) and increasing T (increase in production and exchange of goods – which, however, if agriculture declined, must have occurred solely within trade and industry, a minor sector of the Spanish economy of the sixteenth century).[3]

---

[1] Hamilton, *American Treasure*, p. 261. He mentions as a contributory cause the fact that imports 'whose prices reflected the influx of American treasure less than did domestic goods' comprised a larger proportion of non-agricultural commodities than of agricultural products.

[2] Ibid., pp. 302 ff.

[3] In a recent application of the Fisher equation to the price revolution, we are told to discard altogether the notion of a diminishing V. F. Braudel and F. C. Spooner, 'Les métaux monétaires et l'économie du XVIème siècle', *Relazioni del*

In an earlier study of Spanish prices made in 1928, Professor Hamilton sought not counteracting forces but ancillary causes of the price rise, because he had not then taken into account the enormous increase in the *stock* of bullion. In this study he mentioned, as factors helping to raise prices, 'the decline in agriculture, the decay of industry, the heavy emigration to America'.[1] When he thought that P rose more than proportionally to M, it seemed natural to call in general economic decline and depopulation as causes of a decrease in T.

I am not relating all this in order to embark upon a discussion of the conflicting forces at work during the price upheaval in Spain. The point I want to make is merely that the quantity theory with its general average concepts does not seem to be of great help when we have to discuss real changes within the economy, i.e. changes dependent upon demographic fluctuations and fluctuations of output and demand, etc. Particularly when handling those factors which are lumped together under the headings T and V, we are led to hypothetical conclusions which not only do not seem self-evident, but in some cases even seem highly improbable (as for instance the assumption of a decline in agriculture from the first half of the sixteenth century).

Another debatable point is that the quantity theory, as illustrated above, logically leads to the conclusion that increases in economic activity, output and population, should militate against a rise in prices, while decreases should tend to force prices up (since changes in T are not supposed to induce changes in M, a rising T must mean relatively less money to go round – i.e. lower prices – whereas a diminishing T must lead accordingly to higher prices).

This is a simplified and one-sided way of describing the inter-

---

X Congresso Internazionale di Scienze Storiche, IV, in *Biblioteca Storica Sansoni*, Nuova Serie, XXV (1955), p. 244. According to these authors, trade and production rose in the sixteenth century in proportion to the increase in the supply of bullion, thus counteracting the rise in prices. The fact that prices nevertheless rose all over western Europe is attributed to a rise in 'the velocity of money'.

[1] Hamilton, 'American treasure and Andalusian prices, 1503–1660'. See p. 179 of this volume.

play between output and prices and is especially misleading during periods of economic change. Using the quantity theory we can easily forget that the amount of money employed in transactions is not an autonomous factor and is not independent of the general economic climate. Money – or bullion – may be available in greater volume but not used, because T is *not* rising and prospects are therefore looking bad; if so, a fall in T is more likely to bring about a fall in prices, thus apparently contradicting the assertion that PT equals MV.

On the other hand, it is a commonplace that an increase in economic activity usually leads to a rise in prices, whether this is due to rising marginal costs or to the new incomes created when agricultural producers and industrial entrepreneurs enlarge their expenditures on materials and wages. The monetary fuel for the expansion is secured by the activation of money which has been lying idle, or by the creation of additional money. We must assume that in earlier centuries, just as much as in our own, an upward economic trend would not only reduce idle savings, but would also create new money by stimulating the mining of precious metals and the coining of existing bullion or by causing an increase in credit-money. The supply of money in circulation may thus be regarded as a secondary factor and the quantity theory as not generally applicable but of use only for interpreting periods in which there are no 'real' changes in the economy to be taken into account.

IV

There are economic historians today who, when dealing with prices, are less interested in factors determining the available amount of money than in such factors as investment, output, incomes, which influence the actual level of spending. One notable exponent of this approach is W. W. Rostow, who in his work on the British economy in the nineteenth century manages to explain both secular and cyclical movements of prices without resort to those earlier monetary theories which saw in American and Australian gold the most important agent of change. He ventures the opinion that 'men in the past have, on the whole, and over a period of time, been sensible enough to adjust their monetary institutions to their requirements'.[1]

I may also mention the Italian scholar, C. M. Cipolla, who, in a short but penetrating study of 'the so-called price revolution' in Italy, has questioned the validity of the bullion interpretation and the quantity theory approach.[2] His argument is that the general rise in prices, which did not start in Italy until the middle of the sixteenth century, was in no way revolutionary. Prices doubled from 1552 to 1600, a yearly rise of about 2 per cent. The only inflationary rate of increase is found in the period 1552–60, when the annual rise averaged 5·2 per cent. During this period, however, the import of precious metals from abroad cannot have been very large, certainly not as large as in the decades after 1570 when the influx of Spanish silver increased rapidly. But in the early 1570s a twenty-year period of stagnant and even falling prices set in!

According to Professor Cipolla, what actually happened within the Italian economy was that, after the devastating wars of the first half of the century had come to an end, a period of reconstruction started about 1550. In the 1550s both the population and the volume of investment increased, two circumstances which brought about a rise in prices. He regards fluctuations in the volume of investment as the principal and primary cause of change. The role of bullion and of monetary institutions was secondary: the influx of new coining metal helped to keep the wheels of economic activity turning at greater speed during the booms, but on the other hand prevented prices from falling too much during depressions. It accentuated the booms and alleviated the depressions.

Professor Cipolla's re-assessment of the Italian price revolution has recently been challenged by a French scholar, A. Chabert, who at the same time defends the use of the quantity

---

[1] W. W. Rostow, *British Economy of the 19th Century* (Oxford, 1948). The quotation is from p. 22.

[2] *Annales* (1955), pp. 513–16. The historian who has made a study of the influx of Spanish silver into Italy after 1570 (and to whom Professor Cipolla refers) is F. Braudel, in his work *La Méditerranée et le monde méditerranéen à l'époque de Philippe II* (1949).

theory in its traditional form.[1] He claims that Italian conditions were exceptional. If prices rose in the 1550s without any considerable influx of bullion, this was because both the amount of money and its velocity of circulation increased in another way, through people drawing upon their savings for reconstruction purposes. If the import of bullion after 1570 did not prevent a fall in prices, this was because of, firstly, an increase in output when reconstruction had got under way and, secondly, the rise in population: these two factors caused an increase in T, which, so the quantity equation tells us, varies inversely to P.

It is obvious that when every allowance is made for changes in T and V, the difference between the quantity theory interpretation and that of Professor Cipolla is to some extent a difference of emphasis. Cipolla stresses the improved economic climate and the propensity to increase investment and consumption expenditure in the 1500s; Chabert stresses the secondary fact that in so doing people set money moving.

As a general rule, however, Chabert does not believe changes in 'trade' and 'velocity of money' to be of great importance in the development of prices in the sixteenth century. Even if an increase in economic activity did occur in some countries, he argues, the limits of expansion and a state of full employment must very quickly have been reached, after which an addition to the supply of money could only have meant higher prices and no further 'real' changes represented by changes in T and V. Thus, the low level of productivity and capital formation in the sixteenth century is taken by Chabert as proof that the price level was as a rule determined by the flow of money along the lines of the traditional quantity theory approach.

This debate will no doubt continue. Personally I am not convinced that one can, on general grounds, dismiss a methodological approach such as Professor Cipolla's as being too 'modern'. Obviously it is better suited than the traditional quantity theory to explain what happened in Italy in the latter half of the sixteenth century. We know too little about other countries to be able to proclaim the Italian example an exception.

[1] A. Chabert, 'Encore la révolution des prix au XVIe siècle', *Annales* (1957) pp. 269-74.

I find it difficult moreover to appreciate the neat legerdemain by which historians using the quantity theory contract or expand the T and V of the Fisher equation according to the requirements of the situation. We are entitled to demand that changes in 'trade', or the sum of transactions, be studied first of all as independent phenomena; only then should one be confronted with the price level, the velocity of circulation, and so on. This involves a study of output in different sectors of the economy as determined by the conditions of demand and supply, possibly in conjunction also with demographic changes.

As to the concept of the velocity of circulation, one may well begin by demanding a clearer definition. Under this one heading historians have included changes in hoarding habits, effects of monetary debasements (causing the silver to move at a greater 'velocity'), changes on the credit market, institutional as well as temporary, and changes in the relation between barter and money economy.

Perhaps it is now time that we gave to the factors summarized in the concepts of 'trade' and 'velocity of circulation' some of the attention which has hitherto been paid to American bullion. American silver was no doubt the medium of the price revolution, at any rate after 1550. But the question is: could the bullion have penetrated the European economies and exerted its influence on prices without an earlier transitory phase in which trade and economic activity expanded in both agriculture and industry? I have already mentioned that the import of American bullion into Spain was not wholly fortuitous since it consisted chiefly of payments for commodities. The same is also true where other countries were concerned.

The fundamental question, sounding perhaps a little ingenuous, seems to me to be: why did western Europe need the American bullion, not to be hoarded as treasure nor to be used for ornaments in the holy places (the use to which it was put in Asia and among the natives of America), but to form an important addition to its body of circulating coin – i.e. as a medium of payment? Why was the silver so eagerly awaited that the absence of the treasure fleet during its visits to America meant threatening bankruptcy for the trading houses of Seville ?[1] And why do we find in various parts of Europe heavy debasements and complaints about the scarcity of coin, both of which indicate a real or supposed scarcity of bullion, even in the later sixteenth century when the American silver is alleged to have flooded Europe? It seems to me that, when price historians using the quantity theory take as their starting point figures of bullion imports or production, they leave out important elements in the dynamic processes going on behind the façade of rising price trends.

V

Turning to price trends in countries other than Spain, we find again that it is the works of Wiebe and Hamilton that are responsible for the teaching of the textbooks that the price rise occurred later and on the whole was less extensive 'because of the time required for American treasure to make its way thither and the dilution it underwent in the process'.[2]

The picture of silver spreading itself over Europe and bringing about price rises on a scale varying inversely with the distance from Seville is readily acceptable as true because of its very simplicity. It must be kept in mind, however, that it is only a hypothesis. We cannot be content to regard it as proven by the price data which Professor Hamilton borrows from Wiebe, for countries other than Spain. Furthermore, recent price studies seem to complicate the problem. I have already

---

[1] F. Braudel and F. C. Spooner give a description of the lively speculation in Seville and of 'cette atmosphère quasi permanente de crise et de banqueroute'. Op. cit., pp. 251 ff.

[2] Hamilton, 'American treasure and Andalusian prices, 1503–1660'. See p. 178 of this volume. In 1952 the same theme recurs: 'It' – i.e. the Spanish bullion – 'flowed into Italy, Holland, France, England and Portugal. In England, France and Italy – the countries for which we have data – prices rose moderately in the first half of the 16th century, with the beginning and the magnitude of the up-swing largely depending upon the political and commercial relations with Spain, and very rapidly in the second half of the century.' Hamilton, 'Prices and progress', *The Journal of Economic History*, XII (1952), p. 331. The selection of countries – England, France and Italy – seems somewhat arbitrary. For England and France, Professor Hamilton still resorts to the price data assembled by Wiebe. Ibid., pp. 333 ff.

mentioned Italy where the price level moved in the opposite direction to the bullion import figures. It is not easy either to explain why Poland, for instance, should experience a greater and more rapid price rise than a West German city like Frankfurt.[1]

Just as when one considers the influx of the silver into the Spanish economy, concrete studies are required for other countries also of those international economic processes in which silver may have served as a medium. At present there are only two countries whose imports of gold and silver from abroad have been measured with any accuracy: Spain and Italy. In Spain Professor Hamilton finds a correlation between specie imports and prices; in Italy no such correlation is observable. Further research is required to show how the interplay between bullion and prices worked out in the rest of Europe.

The greatest need is for a study of west European balances of payments. Far too many authors have resorted to 'the influx of bullion' as an explanation of price trends in their respective countries, without realizing that they are making certain tacit assumptions about the balance of trade, without taking the trouble to prove that exports exceeded imports so that an influx of bullion became possible.

An example of the contradictions originating with the influx of American silver can be found by comparing different works on sixteenth-century English history. Authorities on monetary history have declared that Spanish-American silver began to flow into England as early as the 1540s[2] and later caused the steady rise in prices that characterized the reign of Elizabeth I.[3] But in a study by Lawrence Stone dealing with English foreign trade in the sixteenth century, we are told that England's overall balance of trade was either slightly adverse or at best in rough equilibrium.[4] This must mean that exports did not in fact exceed imports.

---

[1] Cf. below, pp. 59–60.

[2] A. E. Feavearyear, *The Pound Sterling. A History of English Money* (Oxford, 1931), p. 44.

[3] R. De Roover, *Gresham on Foreign Exchange* (Cambridge, Mass., 1949), p. 85.

[4] L. Stone, 'Elizabethan Overseas Trade', *Economic History Review*, 2nd ser., II (1949), pp. 36, 54.

Moreover, it may be taken as an established fact that the out-flow of bullion from Spain was slight before the middle of the sixteenth century. Nevertheless in several countries prices began to rise as early as the closing decades of the fifteenth century and continued to do so during the first half of the sixteenth. In this connection it is, of course, necessary to take into account the European production of coining metals. As Professor Nef has recently shown, the increase in silver production on the continent of Europe from the late fifteenth century was grossly underestimated by Soetbeer, who since 1879 has been regarded as the authority on the subject.[1] What is more, the peak of production occurred as early as the decade 1525–35, which is earlier than Soetbeer calculated. If we are looking for monetary explanations we must take German and Bohemian silver into account for the period before 1550.

VI

To put European silver in the place of American, however, does not eliminate the problems of method and principle to which I have referred above. A feature common to all interpret-ations based upon fluctuations in the quantity of bullion is that they are only applicable to changes in the *general* price level – i.e. changes in the price relationship between silver (or gold) on the one hand and all other goods and services on the other. The 'general price level' of the quantity theory is an abstraction which it is very difficult to study statistically, especially so far as sixteenth-century statistics are concerned. In actual fact some prices rose more, some less, in all countries.

In the Polish work which gives price series for Kraków, for instance, we find a table showing a general commodity price index (of prices in terms of silver). Around 1550 this reached a figure 35 per cent higher than that of 1500.[2] If the price move-ments of individual commodities are studied, however, it will be found that the figure of 35 per cent is an average of such

---

[1] J. U. Nef, 'Silver production in central Europe', *Journal of Political Economy*, XLIX (1941), pp. 584–6. Cf. Nef, *Cambridge Economic History*, II, 469 ff.

[2] Pelc, op. cit., p. 136.

disparate figures as, e.g., an increase of 144 per cent for wheat, 158 per cent for rye, 242 per cent for butter, 20 per cent for wax, and 3–20 per cent for certain types of cloth; and a fall of 17 per cent for bricks.[1] If the figures range from +242 per cent to −17 per cent, is a final figure of 35 per cent for the rise in the 'general' price level of any significance? The problem of weighting is also very difficult. What significance can we attach to a general price index which has been constructed by adding together index numbers of commodity prices and wages in the arbitrary proportion of two to one?[2]

The practical difficulties seem very great indeed. Since it is also difficult to see exactly what the changes in this general price level tell us about the economy we are studying – apart from showing fluctuations in the value of precious metals – it may be doubted whether the outcome represents anything worth while to show for our trouble.

It may well be that, from both the technical and theoretical point of view, the study of relative price movements is a better point of departure for the analysis of sixteenth-century price trends. Technically, our results are more reliable when we base our computations on averages for groups of commodities whose prices are broadly subject to the same set of economic factors. From the theoretical standpoint it is arguable that the study of relative changes in commodity prices and wages is more likely to bring us into contact with strategic changes in the economy. What has been said above concerning the unwieldiness of the general average concepts of the quantity theory may also be regarded as an argument for concentrating on strategic groupings of more easily defined variables.

The construction and comparison of price indexes for single commodities or groups of commodities is, of course, no methodological novelty. I have already mentioned that, in his work of 1934, Professor Hamilton compared the prices of various groups of commodities. The most obvious divergence

[1] Ibid., pp. 127–33. The figures compared are the averages for 1491-1505 and 1546–55 respectively.
[2] Professor Hamilton presents such 'indices of the general price level' for Spain, France and England, in *American Treasure*, pp. 206 ff.

emerging from his data is that between agricultural and non-agricultural commodities. Two years earlier, a French historian, F. Simiand, had demonstrated that all the studies of west European prices made up to that time indicated a greater rise during the sixteenth century in the prices of agricultural products than of manufactured goods, metals, colonial goods, etc.[1] This attracted little attention, however, in the discussion on the price revolution. Instead the debate centred on a different kind of price comparison, i.e. between commodities and wages.

The impact of the price revolution on industrial conditions became a special focus of interest as a result of the writings on the subject of Earl J. Hamilton and John Maynard Keynes.[2] The discussion revolved around Professor Hamilton's figures of prices and wages in Spain, and Wiebe's data on England and France. The conclusion reached was that the rise in prices, particularly in England but less markedly in France, also greatly encouraged the industrial entrepreneur and promoted the 'rise of capitalism', because commodity prices rose much more than wages in the latter half of the sixteenth century. This was taken as a proof of decreasing costs and radically widened profit margins in industry.

Later criticism by Professor Nef has shown that the value of both the price and the wage material was more limited than had been thought.[3] Since the composite commodity indexes used were dominated by agricultural products they tended to exaggerate the rise in prices. In fact wages generally seem to have risen more than the prices of the manufactured goods from which industrialists drew their earnings. And on closer examination the English wage material turns out to consist of wages in the building industries only.[4]

[1] F. Simiand, *Recherches anciennes et nouvelles sur le mouvement général des prix du XVIe au XIXe siècle* (Paris 1932), pp. 101, 114 f., 138 ff., 167 f.

[2] Hamilton, 'American treasure and the rise of capitalism', *Economica*, IX (1929), pp. 338–57. J. M. Keynes, *A Treatise on Money* (1930). The 'profit inflation' of the sixteenth century serves as one of the historical illustrations in II, pp. 152–63.

[3] J. U. Nef, 'Prices and industrial capitalism in France and England, 1540–1640', *Economic History Review*, VII (1937), pp. 155–85.

[4] Ibid., pp. 172, 164. Professor Nef also deploys an array of further objections centred upon the difficulties involved in calculating a true cost of living index for the sixteenth century.

If we draw the logical conclusions of these criticisms, the only safe inference from the comparisons based on Wiebe's tables of English prices and wages seems to be that agricultural producers could more easily afford hired labour for building activities or, if we allow the generalization that other wages rose in conformity with wages in the building crafts, that the period of the price revolution in England was a time of profit inflation not so much for the industrial entrepreneur as for the agricultural producer.[1]

The relation between wages and prices, i.e. the trend of real wages, in the sixteenth century is one of a whole array of problems the further study of which may yield interesting results, especially for England and France. In other countries where recent research has made such comparisons possible, wages in general seem to have risen less than the prices of foodstuffs. But nowhere is the gap so wide as would appear from the collections of price data for England and France summarized by Wiebe in the 1890s.

A study at present being made of prices and wages in Antwerp indicates, according to a recent article in *Annales*, that wages followed fairly closely the price of wheat, one of the commodities with the greatest price rise.[2] It is true that, compared with the situation at the end of the fifteenth century, the rise in the wages of certain labourers and artisans was rather smaller than the rise in the price of corn in the period 1521–56. But from about 1560 on the relationship was again about the same as in the closing decades of the fifteenth century. The authors feel that they can abandon what they call the 'tradi-

[1] In a recent study E. H. Phelps Brown and Sheila V. Hopkins have compared the changes in prices of foodstuffs and certain industrial commodities with the changes in the wage rates of building craftsmen for the period 1400 to 1700. As did Hamilton (and Wiebe) they use the price and wage material collected by J. E. Thorold Rogers. Their conclusions are, however, more in accordance with Nef's critical views. The really important phenomenon in the sixteenth century is stated to have been 'the shrinkage of the foodstuffs in the industrial wage earner's basketful' resulting from the fact that wage rates rose much less than prices of grain, meat, butter, etc. The authors also conclude that population pressure probably was at the root of the fall in the purchasing power of wages in the sixteenth century. *Economica*, XXIV (1957), pp. 289–306.

[2] C. Verlinden *et al.*, *Annales* (1955), pp. 191–8.

tional thesis' that there was a considerable lag between wages and prices; if that were correct, the wage-earner group would have been completely eliminated. Even the minor disparity which they discover between the rates of increase of wages and prices must have involved a heavy strain upon this section of the population, especially in years of crisis.

VII

It is somewhat surprising that the controversy around sixteenth century prices should now be concentrated so largely upon industrial conditions. In 1932 F. Simiand demonstrated that the prices of agricultural products, grain and other vegetable and animal products, rose much more than the prices of metals, building materials, textiles and other manufactures, and colonial goods (spices, etc.). This finding has been confirmed by all the later studies of sixteenth-century prices that have been published since then; the divergence appears as early as the beginning of the sixteenth century.[1] If only records of the prices of industrial and other non-agricultural products had been preserved in the archives, it might never have occurred to anyone to speak of a 'price revolution'. But this central fact – that the prices of foodstuffs, especially grain, were the only ones to change in a revolutionary manner – has still scarcely received the attention it merits.

In this respect the debate on the sixteenth century rise in prices can be compared with the controversy on economic trends in the late Middle Ages, a period of stagnant or falling prices. Historians such as M. M. Postan and W. Abel have emphasized the importance of relative price movements in the fourteenth and fifteenth centuries, when grain prices fell more

[1] In addition to the works mentioned above, the reader is referred to G. Mickwitz, 'Aus Revaler Handelsbüchern', *Societas Scientiarum Fennica. Commentationes Humanarum Literarum*, IX, 8 (1938), pp. 96–107, in which are presented prices extracted from the books of Reval merchants for the years 1500–1560. W. Koppe has published prices of grain, butter and other agricultural products in Holstein from 1500 to 1560, in 'Zur Preisrevolution des 16. Jahrhunderts in Holstein', *Zeitschrift der Gesellschaft für Schleswig-Holsteinische Geschichte*, LXXIX (1955), pp. 185–216.

than other commodity prices.[1] The latter fact is linked with
what is known of agrarian trends: depopulation and rapidly
increasing numbers of vacant holdings are signs of an agricultural depression over large areas of western Europe. The
inference is that less was produced and yet prices nevertheless
fell because, relative to demand, supplies of food were more
plentiful than before.[2] It will be observed that this theoretical
approach yields results quite different from those of the quantity theory. In giving demographic and agrarian trends a central
place it is supported by topographical evidence from different
parts of Europe.

The German price historian, M. J. Elsas, adopts the general
method of Abel and Postan when he compares the development of various commodity prices with figures of population
trends in those cities for which he has collected price data. His
study ranges over a very long period, from the late Middle Ages
to the beginning of the nineteenth century. The prices of foodstuffs, especially grain, are the ones which show the greatest
degree of conformity with population curves. When population
rose in the sixteenth century, grain prices rose too: when population fell during the first half of the seventeenth century, grain
prices did the same.[3]

Dr Elsas mentions a number of factors which may have
caused the simultaneous upward movement of grain prices and
population in the sixteenth century. A rising population enhanced the demand for goods, including foodstuffs. Agricultural producers were unable to respond with a rapid increase
in supplies of grain, since the technical prerequisites of more
intensive cultivation were lacking. Instead, new land was
brought into cultivation and this resulted in increased marginal
costs of grain production. From the fact that his data indicate a
reduction in the real wages of wage-earners in the sixteenth

[1] M. M. Postan, 'Some economic evidences of declining population in the later
Middle Ages', *Economic History Review* (1950), pp. 221–46; 'The trade of Medieval
Europe: the north', *Cambridge Economic History*, II; W. Abel, 'Wüstungen und
Preisfall im spätmittelalterlichen Europa', *Jahrbücher für Nationalökonomie und
Statistik*, CLXV (1953), pp. 380–427.

[2] Postan, *Cambridge Economic History*, II, 197 f., 208–16.

[3] M. J. Elsas, op. cit., II: B. 71–84.

century, Dr Elsas draws the inference that a relatively larger proportion of their demand must have been directed towards the necessities of life – i.e. grain and similar foodstuffs.[1]

This relatively large increase in the price of agricultural produce is a feature common to all countries of western Europe. To account for it in terms of monetary causes is clearly impossible. We ought instead to carry out further research along paths such as those followed by Abel, Postan and Elsas, studying the conditions of supply and demand in the sixteenth century.

If we leave colonial products aside as being influenced by the opening of new trade routes and study those commodities that were both produced and consumed inside Europe, we must account for such phenomena as the divergent price curves for industrial and agricultural commodities. The products of industry, or manufacture, did not as a rule fall in price, but they do show a considerable lag in relation to the steeply rising prices of agricultural products. We must ask whether the so-called 'industrial revolution' in sixteenth-century England and its counterpart on the continent half a century earlier may not have reduced industrial costs and passed the benefit on to the consumer.[2] We know that cost-reducing inventions and new forms of organization within, for instance, mining and cloth manufacturing were not counterbalanced by any similar developments in agriculture. On the contrary, the extension of the area under cultivation that we must assume to have taken place in sixteenth-century Europe must have led to the inclusion of 'marginal' land, necessitating heavier outlays and transport over greater distances. It was, too, a more time-consuming process for a farmer to find and break new land than, for instance, for a clothier to give out more wool to be spun, to hire more weavers and fullers, etc.

[1] Ibid., pp. 85–92.
[2] The expression 'the industrial revolution', which is perhaps too sweeping, originates with J. U. Nef, who in a number of studies emphasizes the technical and organizational innovations in sixteenth-century industry. J. U. Nef, 'The progress of technology and the growth of large-scale industry in Great Britain', *Economic History Review*, v (1934); 'A comparison of industrial growth in France and England from 1540 to 1640', *Journal of Political Economy*, XLIV (1936); and 'Industrial Europe at the time of the Reformation (*c.* 1515–1540)', *Journal of Political Economy* (1941).

If these factors caused what we may call 'inelasticity of supply' in agriculture, inelasticity of demand worked in the same direction. There was no substitute for bread in the diet of the masses; hence the price curves for grain can reach surprisingly high peaks in years of crop failure since a buyers' strike was impossible.[1]

When relative price movements are approached from the demand side, population trends and changes in the distribution of income are the important factors to be taken into account. Population changes have perhaps still not been allowed their due place as dynamic forces in economic history. The main difficulty is of course the lack of relevant sources for the centuries before the nineteenth.

The only sixteenth-century population figures that are at all reliable are those for towns. Estimates have been made for at any rate the larger towns of Spain, Italy, Germany, Poland and England; all these data show very considerable additions to population in the sixteenth century. Now mortality in the towns was higher than in the country. Constant new supplies of people were needed merely to keep numbers from falling. It is therefore difficult to imagine growing cities in an environment other than one where the reservoir of immigrants, the countryside, was itself experiencing an increase in numbers. In other words, the overall population must have been growing. Professor F. Braudel has shown how widespread this migration to the towns was in Mediterranean countries and that it was accompanied by a general increase in the population of this region during the period 1450–1600.[2] In other parts of Europe, there are indirect signs of a general increase in population, signs that there was a pressure of population on land, by contrast to

[1] Grain prices obviously ought to be studied with not only long-term movements but also short-term fluctuations in mind. What happened to consumers and producers in years of crop failure, when prices suddenly increased many times over? For whom did this represent a crisis; to whom did it bring the opportunity of profit? Interesting contributions to this line of research have been made by Professor Astrid Friis, 'The two crises in the Netherlands in 1597', *Scandinavian Economic History Review*, 1 (1953), 193–241, and by C. Verlinden *et al.*, *Annales* (1955), 174–90 (here the role of speculators, driving prices upwards during years of crop failure, is analysed).

[2] Braudel, op. cit., pp. 347–59.

the situation in the later Middle Ages when land was abundan
and people scarce.[1]

A relative growth of towns, perhaps also an increase in the
number of people industrially employed in the countryside, is
in itself a satisfactory, even if only partial, explanation of the
greater rise in agricultural prices. In view of the inelasticity of
supply of agricultural products, the impact on prices can be
assumed to have been far greater than the demographic changes
producing it.

The distribution of income among the various sections of the
community in the sixteenth century is, needless to say, very
imperfectly known. I have already mentioned that Dr Elsas has
suggested, on the basis of German price and wage material,
that wage-earners suffered a fall in real wages and in consequence had to curtail purchases of goods other than essentials –
i.e. other than foodstuffs. The hypothesis that this was the
decisive factor leading to the rise in the prices of foodstuffs may
be criticized on the ground that the wage-earner group must
have been much smaller than it is today, since the countries of
Europe were still overwhelmingly agrarian in character. But
of course the term wage-earner does not only mean industrial
employees. What we now call agricultural workers must have
been a very large category. Some were hired workers without
either house or land, others were cottagers holding a small strip
of land or perhaps merely having right of access to common
land to raise cattle or sheep. The larger the proportion of their
income that consisted of money payments, the harder they too
were hit by the divergent trends of prices and wages. If the
lower strata of the agricultural sector were thus pauperized,
partly by an increase in their number and partly through other
factors, we may infer the same effect upon their total demand as

[1] On the subject of the rise in population in Germany and other parts of central
Europe, see W. Abel, 'Wachstumsschwankungen mitteleuropäischer Völker seit
dem Mittelalter', *Jahrbücher für Nationalökonomie und Statistik*, CXLII (1935), pp.
682 ff. For Spain, see Hamilton, 'The Decline of Spain', *Economic History Review*,
VIII (1938), p. 169; and for England, J. C. Russell, *British Medieval Population*
(Albuquerque, 1948). Compare also G. Utterström's article (*Scandinavian Economic
History Review*, III (1955), pp. 24 f., 36 ff.), where climatic changes are discussed as
a possible explanation of the increase in the population of western Europe which
began in the later fifteenth century.

upon that of the industrial wage-earner – a concentration on foodstuffs, and moreover on the cheaper kinds of foodstuffs.

It is also clear that harvest failures must have turned many small grain producers into buyers of grain, and this would constitute an important contributory cause of the widely fluctuating curves of grain prices.

But, to return to industrial prices and the lag behind other prices, the question arises whether we may assume that the total decrease in the demand of wage-earners for industrial products was large enough to offset the increase that we must infer in the demand of agricultural producers arising from their increased purchasing power. The section of the community whose income grew most must have been those agricultural producers who had considerable surpluses for the market. But there is little doubt that this group was also the one with the highest propensity to save. Landlords and peasants alike undoubtedly engaged in long-term saving not only for the future enlargement of their holdings but also simply for the sake of hoarding. The new silver spoons in the peasants' houses of the later sixteenth century may have functioned as stores of value just as much as they indicated a greater refinement in taste. Thus, the considerable increase that we must assume to have occurred in the income of this group may not have been paralleled by a proportionate increase in demand; this fact in itself has a bearing upon the price lag of industrial goods behind agricultural produce.

Much of the above is, of course, conjecture which may be proven, or disproven, by further research. I am quite sure that further research into sixteenth-century prices will have to deal with such matters as demographic changes and changes in the distribution of income. It may be found that a general increase in population was the most important of the 'real', i.e. non-monetary, changes contributing to the rise in prices. The soaring prices of foodstuffs, especially grain, indicate a pressure of population upon food supplies. This is not an *effect* of the price revolution, but is part of the dynamic process which we call 'the price revolution of the sixteenth century'.

3 The Inflation of Prices in Early Sixteenth-Century England

Y. S. BRENNER

This article was first published in the *Economic History Review*, vol. XIV (1961–2)

Intense structural, social and economic changes took place in England during the sixteenth century. These were accompanied by an outstanding rise in prices. The simultaneous occurrence of far-reaching structural changes and rising prices in England and other countries during the same century impose upon the economic historian the following questions. First: whether prices rose because money had become relatively more abundant or commodities relatively scarce. Second: whether the cheaper money or dearer goods, or both, had substantially contributed to, set in motion, or been the result of, the social and economic changes of the period.

A price level is usually determined by the quantity (M) and velocity (V) of circulation and by the amount of goods and services (Q) available. These three factors stand in the following relation to the price level (P):

$$P = \frac{M \cdot V}{Q}.$$

Therefore the alteration of the price level may have been the result of a relative change of any one, or more, of three different factors.[1] By the end of the nineteenth and beginning of the present century historians were inclined to emphasize the increased supply of the circulating media as the major cause for the rising prices in the sixteenth century. Lately, however, more importance has often been attached to a relative diminution of available supplies of goods.

[1] This point has been discussed at some length by Ingrid Hammarström, 'The 'Price Revolution" of the sixteenth century'. See pp. 50–3 of this volume.

The adherents of the first theory, of increased money circulation and lower money appraisement, rested their case on the evidence of the arrival of great increments of precious metals in Europe and the occasional inflation of the money circulation with coins of a reduced gold or silver content. The adherents of the other theory argued that the equilibrium between the supply and demand of goods has been upset by population growth which expanded demand in excess of a less swiftly increasing production. Their case rested primarily, though not exclusively, on the consideration of the fact that victual prices rose more sharply than those of more elastic goods and wages. From this they inferred that victual prices had risen because of a relatively increased demand and wages had comparatively lagged behind because of a relative surplus of labour.

Neither of these theories can be dismissed off-hand. For this reason I have summarized both, pointing out their relative merits and inconsistencies. Both suffer primarily from lack of historical evidence. This weakness I have tried to avoid, as well as I was able, in my own thesis. I selected and combined some of the elements contained in both the earlier mentioned theories and rejected others. I gave more credence to some contemporary complaints which have hitherto often been dismissed too easily. I have also added some further elements, like migration and excessive exportation.

For the compilation of the necessary statistics I have mostly relied upon the information contained in the boxes of the International Price Committee which are lodged in the annex building of the Institute of Historical Research of London University, Lord Beveridge's book on prices and wages,[1] J. E. Thorold Rogers's books,[2] and several other price or wage collections. Unfortunately not many records have survived from which reliable price series can be extracted for the late fifteenth century and they become even more scanty by the middle of the sixteenth, because of the dissolution of the monasteries which

[1] Sir W. Beveridge and others, *Prices and Wages in England from the 12th to the 19th Century* (London, 1939).

[2] J. E. Thorold Rogers, *A History of Agriculture and Prices in England from the Year after the Oxford Parliament 1259 to the Commencement of the Continental War 1793* (Oxford, 1866–1902), and *Six Centuries of Work and Wages* (London, 1894).

supplied most of the statistically valuable price material up to that time.

Having statistically treated the available price and wage data one can make the following generalizations: in the later part of the fifteenth century prices began gradually to rise. By the middle of the sixteenth they rose sharply. Prior to this time prices had risen over prolonged periods during the thirteenth and the middle of the fourteenth centuries. Later they rose again by the end of the eighteenth. On each of these occasions they behaved similarly throughout western Europe. The same is true of the prolonged periods of falling prices or price stability in the second quarter of the fourteenth and first half of the fifteenth, the turn of the seventeenth and early eighteenth, and later nineteenth centuries.

In their efforts to explain these long-term trends in the behaviour of prices various historians and economists have indicated the changes in the metal content and the metallic value of the price-measuring standard, i.e. of the money. Assuming that coins were roughly worth their metal content, or at least that a constant relation existed between them, the originators of such ideas explained falling or low prices by a relative metal deficiency, and rising prices, either by a relatively increased supply of precious metals or by a diminished gold and silver content of the coins in circulation. Judging by the frequent contemporary complaints of metal and coin deficiency during the period of 'low commodity prices' in the fifteenth century and the subsequent increase in the supply of metal and coin in the period of 'rising commodity prices' during the sixteenth century, this theory appears to be well founded. In the late fifteenth century a successful solution to the technological problem of drainage of underground flood water in mines was found and a difficulty which had kept most European mines idle for centuries was overcome. In the sixteenth century great quantities of treasure, first in gold and later in silver, arrived in Europe from America.[1] During the first decade of this century a little over a quarter of a million pesos' worth of treasure

---

[1] See Earl J. Hamilton's articles in *Economica* (November 1929), and H. Haring's article in the *Quarterly Journal of Economics* (1914–1915).

F

reached Spain annually. In the second decade nearly half a million, in the third a quarter million, in the fourth one million worth of treasure, mostly in silver after 1545, arrived in Spain annually.[1] The metal weight of coins was also docked, and their fineness reduced, during the late fifteenth and first half of the sixteenth centuries on several occasions: in 1465 the quantity of silver in English coins of a given nominal value was cut by 20 per cent and in 1526 by 8 per cent, and during the period of the great coin scandal between 1542 and 1551, when at the lowest point the pure metal content of silver coins was reduced by three-quarters and of gold coins by about one quarter.[2]

In summary: a comparison of an index combining the prices of a composite unit of foodstuffs and those of a sample of industrial products,[3] with the available information about silver and gold production and the diminished silver and gold content in the currency,[4] gave what is taken to be good evidence of a causal connection between commodity prices, the supply of precious metals, and the state of the coinage.

Taking the period 1451–75 as an index basis it can be seen that the prices of the composite unit of foodstuffs and the industrial products' sample fluctuated between the years 1450 and 1510 within the limits of 5 per cent and were in fact gently stagnating until 1480. There were, however, two exceptions to this rule: the first during the sixties, when the quantity of silver in the coins was cut by 20 per cent, and prices rose by 7 per cent; the second during the eighties, when a combination of civil war, severe harvest failure, and perhaps exportation of grains,[5] wool and cloth[6] may have contributed to the rise in prices which amounted to 15 per cent.

---

[1] See Earl J. Hamilton's statistics in the *Quarterly Journal of Economics* (1929).

[2] See Sir John Craig, *The Mint* (Cambridge, 1953), pp. 74, 109, 111.

[3] See E. H. Phelps and S. V. Hopkins, in *Economica* (November 1957), p. 306 and November 1956, pp. 296–303.

[4] Georg Wiebe, *Zur Geschichte der Preisrevolution des XVI. und XVII. Jahrhunderts* (Leipzig, 1895), pp. 253–321, and E. J. Hamilton, *Quarterly Journal of Economics* (1929), pp. 463–4, and Sir John Craig, op. cit. pp. 74, 109, 111.

[5] N. S. B. Gras, *The Evolution of the English Corn Market* (Harvard, 1915), App. B and C.

[6] Peter Ramsey, *Economic History Review*, 2nd ser., vi (1953), 181; Georg Schanz, *Englische Handelspolitik* (Leipzig, 1881), pp. 46, 58, 72, 84.

After the year 1510 when the European stock of precious metals was rapidly increasing, and especially during the twenties, when the metal weight of coins was docked by 8 per cent, and during the period of the great debasements in the forties (when at the lowest point the metal content of the coins was reduced by 75 per cent for silver and by 25 per cent for gold), the price index rose remarkably. In the twenties prices rose, compared to the index basis 1451–75, by 39 per cent, in the thirties by 40 per cent, in the forties by 77 per cent and in the fifties by 158 per cent.

Table 1 shows that each of the debasements of the coinage (1465, 1526 and 1542–51) was followed by rising prices. The same Table also shows that as the influx of precious metals from

TABLE 1[1]

Years	Price index	Price rise in %	Metal import from America in pesos	Wool & cloth exports	Quality of coins
15th Fifties	99	2		17 000	
Cent. Sixties	104	7		16 680	Reduction of 1465
Seventies	97	0		19 695	
Eighties	112	15		22 422	
Nineties	99	2		21 845	
16th 1st decade	102	5	286 932·5	25 532	
Cent. 2nd ,,	109	12	437 749·9	29 821	
3rd ,,	135	39	234 521·2	28 041	Reduction of 1526
4th ,,	136	40	1 117 624·9	28 333	
5th ,,	172	77	2 092 543·2	35 897	Debasement period.
6th ,,	251	158	3 572 905·9		

America into Europe progressed it was accompanied by a rising English price level.[2] A study of the price movements in other European countries shows very similar trends during the same period,[3] with the exception of Spanish prices which rose more

[1] Price index compiled from data in E. H. Phelps Brown, etc. article, op. cit. Metal Imports from Earl J. Hamilton's article, op. cit. Wool and cloth (4 cloth equal 1 sack, Export given in sacks) from P. Ramsey and G. Schanz, op. cit. Quality of coins, from J. Craig, op. cit.

[2] and [3] F. Simiand, Conférences d'Histoire et Statisque Economiques 1930–1932, Recherches Anciennes et Nouvelles sur le Mouvement Général des Prix du 16e au 19e Siècle (1932), Dia. XV and Dia. I. See also St Hoszowski, *Les Prix à Lwow* and an article in *Economic History Review*, 2nd ser., XI (1956), 1–10, on prices in Hainault, Flanders.

sharply than those of any other country in the sixteenth century.[1] Seeing this evidence it can hardly be surprising that historians and economists came to the conclusion that the rise in commodity prices, which undoubtedly took place, was mainly caused by the fall in the value of the precious metals as their stock in Europe increased, especially in the years following 1545.

It should however be noted that the adherents of this theory of 'lower money appraisement' disagree themselves about the importance which should be attributed to debasements and reductions of the coinage in comparison with the importance which ought to be given to the influx of new metals from America.

A careful examination of this theory of 'lower money appraisement', however, leaves room for a considerable amount of doubt as to its validity. Although it stands to reason that a great quantity of American treasure could have reached England by trade during the first half of the sixteenth century, there is little proof that this did actually happen. Undoubtedly the English export trade expanded considerably in this period but this 'growth of exports brought with it a corresponding growth of imports'.[2] Moreover, the expansion of English commerce was accompanied, and most probably stimulated, by an exchange depreciation. In other words, even the boom in English cloth exports in the forties can hardly account for a considerable influx of precious metals.

Furthermore, assuming that great quantities of precious metals did indeed arrive in England and did cause a 'lower money appraisement', a fall in gold and silver prices would have followed. This would have been especially notable in the twenties for gold and in the thirties and forties for silver. This did not happen. Both the price of gold and of silver, as expressed in money of account, continued to rise throughout the whole period and by more than can be accounted for by the debasements. Time after time when metal was to be attracted

---

[1] Earl J. Hamilton, *Journal of Economics and Business* (1928–29), p. 1 ff.

[2] F. J. Fisher, *Economic History Review*, x (1940), 98. See also G. Schanz, op. cit., II, 62, 63, 146–8.

to the Mint its rating in terms of money had to be raised.[1] On two occasions, in 1526 and in 1545, the reduction caused a rush to the Mint of people who wanted their metals coined. On other occasions, in 1542, 1544, 1547 and 1549, nothing very spectacular happened.[2] Even after the great influx of silver into Europe from America was well on its way the price of silver on the open market continued to rise rapidly. It must therefore be concluded that an increased flow of precious metals to the Mint was the result of higher nominal money returns rather than of falling metal prices. This indicates, unless one maintains that payments in gold and silver were made by weight, that the relatively low commodity price level during the fifteenth century was most likely the result of the unrealistic relation between the prices of metal and money. Contemporary evidence suggests that this was actually so. The complaints are that 'poor common retailers of victuals could neither sell ... nor liege people buy the same for lack of halfpence ...', etc.; that the London crafts had to sell their plate to meet the King's demands; that the Norwich clothiers would be unable to pay their workpeople if the King wouldn't accept their plate instead of coin, etc.;[3] but not that they had no silver or gold. It appears therefore possible that the market for money behaved with a large degree of independence from the market in precious metals. Professor Postan,[4] talking of the end of the thirteenth century, says that the 'total stock of silver in Europe, in relation to annual output, must have been truly enormous'. The amount of silver *per capita* must have been increased considerably by the Black Death. At the same time the various reductions of the silver content of the coinage could not have much exceeded the natural loss of coin by wear, because on an average for the whole period they amounted to no more than one fifth of one per cent a year. This leads to but one conclusion: the changes in

[1] See Sir John Craig, *The Mint*, Appendix, List of gold and silver contents of coins and their prices.

[2] See quantities of silver coined annually, Sir John Craig, op. cit., pp. 412–14.

[3] *Political Poems* (Rolls Series), *Rolls of Parliament* and *Statues of the Realm* (1464–5).

[4] Professor M. M. Postan, *The Cambridge Economic History*, Vol. ii, and *Rapports*, IX, Congrès International des Sciences Historiques, I (1950).

the commodity price level during the fifteenth and early six-teenth centuries resulted less from an increase, or lack of in-crease, in the European stock of metal, than from the manner in which this stock was employed. Indeed, one may well ask with Dr Hammarström,[1] 'Why did western Europe need the American bullion not to be hoarded as treasure, etc . . . but to form an important addition to its body of circulating coin? . . .' and, 'Could the bullion have penetrated the European econ-omies and exerted its influence on prices without an earlier tran-sitory phase in which trade and economic activity expanded in both agriculture and industry? . . . the import of American bullion into Spain was not wholly fortuitous since it consisted chiefly of payments for commodities. The same is also true where other countries were concerned.'

It remains, however, necessary to point out that it is also in-correct to attribute the rise in prices to mere debasement of the currency. Wiebe[2] made this absolutely clear when he translated all his money-of-account prices into silver prices. From his tables it becomes altogether evident that the rise in prices during the sixteenth century was far higher than can be allowed for by the reductions and debasements of the currency. Further-more, a study of the movements of the prices of individual goods, and even of whole groups of goods, does not illustrate the degree of similarity in the upward trend of prices which would have become visible if caused by a mere change in the standard of price measurement, i.e. of money. Until 1480 there was no upward movement of prices which demands an expla-nation. When after 1480 prices begin to rise they do not rise equally. They did not rise to the same extent nor did they rise simultaneously. The prices of some commodities (wheat) rose sharply, others (pewter) rose less, and some hardly rose at all or even fell (wax). Some started rising late in the fifteenth cen-tury (cloth, wine), and others only in the late sixteenth (paper). If 'relative price-changes between different groups of commodi-ties, with a greater rise especially for grain, butter and other animal products, could occur even in a country which, like

[1] I. Hammarström, op. cit. See p. 56 of this volume.
[2] G. Wiebe, op. cit. App. pp. 374-7, 354-62.

Sweden, was untouched during the period under review by the general fall in the value of silver, this makes it reasonable to suppose that the relative price-changes in Europe as a whole cannot be regarded as an indirect consequence of increased silver production, but must have had other independent causes'.[1] If the value of money alone had declined, all commodity prices, with only a few explicable exceptions, would have risen to the same relative extent. This was not so. Prices of consumables rose more sharply than the prices of industrial products, and prices of industrial products rose more sharply than wages. This fact was already noticed by Wiebe.[2] Although a reasonable explanation for the less striking increase of the price of labour than of victuals can be found in population growth and surplus labour, and the discrepancy between the prices of foodstuffs and the commodities in the production of which labour was involved is accounted for in consequence, the behaviour of the prices of individual commodities proves that this by itself does not suffice. Wiebe, who also felt this, tried by giving some explanatory examples to show that his theory of 'lower money appraisement' was all the same compatible with the facts. Unfortunately, in the light of new and better evidence, his examples were, to say the least, ill chosen. To give one example, Wiebe explains the relative stability of paper prices, or comparative fall of paper prices, by the introduction of technical improvements in its manufacture. This can however hardly account for the stability of paper prices before 1588, the year in which such improvements were introduced into England.

The place which Wiebe gives to population growth, in his explanation of the discrepancy between the rise in victual and industrial prices, deserves a more careful examination. He rejects the possibility of population growth being at the root of the developing discrepancy, and indeed of the whole process of rising prices, on the following grounds: first, that wages did not fall, but rose: second, that population growth in England

---

[1] I. Hammarström, op. cit., *Scandinavian Economic History Review*, vol. v, No. 1 (1957), p. 152.

[2] G. Wiebe, op. cit., pp. 228 and 151, 155.

only set in by the end of the sixteenth century; third, that grain prices during the forties did not rise in excess of what should be expected as a result of the debasements of the currency.

He was mistaken on all three points. There is no doubt that from the second decade of the sixteenth century wages continuously lagged behind the prices of victuals and industrial products, with the possible, though unlikely, exception of the thirties and forties when some wages might have temporarily caught up with industrial goods.[1] If Wiebe was wrong about the relation between wages and prices then his assumption was also incorrect that English population growth set in markedly only by the end of the sixteenth century, because it was based on his misapprehension of the wage–price relation in the early part of the century. Finally, his analysis of the relative behaviour of wheat and other commodity prices when compared to each other, during the forties, was based on erroneous evidence, which led him to underrate the rise in victual prices.[2]

In conclusion it can therefore be said that English prices were occasionally slightly increased, either temporarily, or with more lasting results,[3] by currency debasements. These debasements were, however, not the major cause of the general rise in sixteenth-century prices. Prices rose more sharply than can be explained by debasement, continued to rise after debasement had ceased, and did not rise equally for all goods. The influx of gold and silver into Europe from America had also little direct effect on English prices. The prices of many commodities rose before the arrival in Europe of American treasure. No evidence exists that the stock of metal in England increased, and a comparison of a price index from Spain, where 'lower money appraisement' was most probably influencing prices, with an English price index, shows that, contrary to those in England, Spanish prices rose steadily, simultaneously, more parallel one with another and far more sharply.

Attention must, however, be drawn to one further circum-

[1] E. H. Phelps Brown, etc. *Economica* (August 1955), p. 205 (wages); *Economica* (November 1957), p. 306 (prices) and *Economica* (November 1956), p. 311.

[2] G. Wiebe, op. cit. p. 218, footnotes 2 and 4.

[3] For example – occasionally in 1465. See W. Gregory, *Chronicle of London*, more lasting between the years 1542 and 1551.

stance. The study of the movements of grain prices year by year shows that while grain prices continued to rise gradually as the sixteenth century progressed, their yearly fluctuations became more severe.

TABLE 2[1] *Wheat prices (s. per qtr). S.D. standard deviations, A.M. arithmetic mean*

Decade	A.M.	S.D.	Decade:	A.M.	S.D.
1451–60	5·75	0·9215	1501–10	6·04	1·3932
1461–70	5·53	1·3168	1511–20	7·40	1·6093
1471–80	5·43	0·9609	1521–30	8·07	2·3941
1481–90	6·48	1·6087	1531–40	8·31	1·7493
1491–1500	5·37	0·9707	1541–50	11·38	4·0162
			(1541–48)	(9·98)	(3·1376)

The rising grain prices and their substantially increasing seasonal fluctuations are consistent with the price behaviour which is to be expected if a market's equilibrium between supply and demand is upset. Such a disturbance could have been caused in the sixteenth century either by a relatively diminished supply or by a relatively increased demand for victuals. The first possibility could have been caused by substitution of tillage by pasture or by soil exhaustion; the second, by population growth or urbanization. Indeed, 'It may be found that a general increase in population was the most important of the "real", i.e. non-monetary, changes contributing to the rise in prices. The soaring prices of foodstuffs, especially grain, indicate a pressure of population upon food supplies. This is not an effect of the price revolution but is part of the dynamic process. . . .'[2]

Turning to the theory which links the behaviour of prices with demographic changes, one must admit that the perception of at least three periods of secular population increase in medieval and modern European history which can be tolerably well identified with periods of rising prices strongly support this conception. The first extended from about the middle of the eleventh to the end of the thirteenth century, the second from

---

[1] $\bar{x} = 1/n \sum \times$ for each decade (A.M.); $\sigma^2 = 1/n \sum (x - x)^2$ (S.D.).

[2] I. Hammarström, op. cit. See p. 68 of this volume. See pp. 64–8 for fuller discussion of population pressure, and p. 66, in particular, for migration to towns.

the late fifteenth century to the end of the sixteenth, and the third following the middle of the eighteenth century.[1] The study of periods of price stability, or of falling price levels, again sustains the theory of the causal population–price relation. For each period of falling prices some evidence of declining population could be found.[2] Thus the argument in favour of the theory which links demographic changes with price behaviour was basically founded on the following observations: first, that in periods of rising prices those goods with an inelastic supply or demand rose in price more sharply than wages and those goods which were in more elastic supply and demand; secondly, that in periods of falling prices this relation was reversed, i.e. that prices of goods with an elastic supply and demand fell relatively less. The first observation led to the logical speculation that if population had indeed become more numerous in the late fifteenth and the sixteenth centuries, the following sequence of economic developments, which is in agreement with the phenomena observed in price behaviour, would have taken place. 'In some districts and by various methods, the outputs of food and wool (would have been) increased . . .' but as agriculture cannot be expected to have the necessary capacity for expansion, extensively or intensively, that could have raised either its labour force or its product proportionately to the rise in population, the overspill of labour would have had to go into what industrial employments it could find; '. . . the output of industrial products would (have been) raised, and the extra labour would have (had) its share in that output to offer in exchange for the available supplies of food',[3] which would not have increased to the same extent. As a result of this, food prices would have gone up sharply while the 'overspill of job-hungry labour' competing for the available employment would have prevented an equivalently

[1] K. F. Helleiner, *Canadian Journal of Economics and Political Science* (February 1957).

[2] M. M. Postan, *Economic History Review*, IX (1939); D. C. Coleman, *Economic History Review*, 2nd ser., VIII (1956). J. Cox Russell, *British Medieval Population* (1948).

[3] Sir J. Clapham, quoted by Phelps Brown, *Economica* (November 1957), p. 296.

sharp rise in wages from following. At the same time the less restricted expansibility of industrial production, and the relatively reduced production costs which would have been the result of the comparatively diminished capital outlay would have, subject to certain limitations, increased the supply of goods. The relatively smaller amount of money left over from the labourers' wage packets for the purchase of 'non-essential' industrial products after payment of higher victual prices would have relatively reduced the demand for industrial products and thus also contributed to the development of the discrepancy between the rise in the prices of agricultural products and the less essential industrial goods.

The second observation, that in periods of falling prices the above noted trend was reversed, i.e. that prices of goods in inelastic demand or supply fell relatively less than did those of elastic commodities, led to the logical speculation that if depopulation had indeed been considerable during the century preceding 1485, the following sequence of economic developments, which is also in agreement with the phenomena observed in price behaviour, would have taken place: 'when population fell, some marginal lands would in all probability be abandoned and food would be produced on better land. Relative to the amount of land and labour engaged in food production and relative to the demand for food, supplies would then be more plentiful and therefore cheaper.'[1] Land would also be obtainable on easier terms and part of the wage-earning labour force would become self-employed. As a result wages and prices of industrial goods would be high in comparison with agricultural products. As over-production in agriculture cannot explain the relatively low grain prices in view of the fact that wages were comparatively high and rising, and as the relative rise in agricultural wages followed very closely the rise in industrial wages, migration must be ruled out as an explanation for the discrepancy between the movement of the prices of different groups of commodities.[2] The abandonment of

---

[1] M. M. Postan, *Cambridge Economic History*, II, 213.

[2] M. M. Postan, *Economic History Review*, 2nd ser., II (1950); Tables III and IV show the rise in wages for various kinds of work in terms of wheat.

marginal lands in consequence of depopulation appears to be the logical interpretation of the price behaviour.

How then do these speculations compare with the available historical facts? The population of England was undoubtedly sadly reduced by the Black Death in the middle of the fourteenth century. The consequences of this decrease in population were further prolonged by the succeeding outbreaks of plague in 1361 and 1369, and depopulation was still complained of by contemporaries by the end of the following century.[1] Then by the year 1500 population seems to have started to increase rapidly, almost doubling itself before the end of the century when a redundancy of population was generally acknowledged. This accretion has sometimes been related by historians to the less frequent recurrence of great plagues,[2] and sometimes to higher rate of survival and earlier marriages which were the result of the relatively higher wages, or low cost of food, in the preceding period.[3] The fact that the population had become much more numerous during the sixteenth century than it had been during the fifteenth has, however, not been questioned.

A relative scarcity of people who made their living by working for wages in the fifteenth century, and a relative redundancy of the same in the sixteenth, appears to be evident in view of the following observations: during the greater part of the fourteenth and fifteenth centuries agricultural and industrial wages increased considerably and grew closer to each other. During the fifteenth century unskilled labourers' wages, which as a rule react more sensitively to the conditions of the labour market, rose more sharply than those of skilled labour.[4] In the sixteenth century all wages, if expressed in terms of purchasing power, fell markedly, and those of unskilled labour most of all.[5] Nominal wages of skilled labour began to rise only in 1532 and those of unskilled labour not before 1545. It is possible that a

[1] See J. Cox Russell, op. cit., Sir J. Clapham. *A Concise Economic History of Britain*, pp. 78, 186; D. V. Glass, *Population Studies* (1949–50), pp. 338 ff.

[2] C. Creighton, *A History of Epidemics in Britain*, vol. 1 (Cambridge, 1891).

[3] Malthus, *Principles of Political Economy*.

[4] M. M. Postan, *Economic History Review*, 2nd ser., 11 (1950), Table IV.

[5] E. H. Phelps Brown, *Economica* (August 1955), p. 205, and (November 1956), p. 311.

relative redundancy of industrial labour, at least temporarily, was already felt in the later part of the fifteenth century when legislation against labour-saving devices was introduced,[1] and the attacks on the exclusiveness of the guilds became more frequent; and when the Poor Law was based upon new principles which acknowledged the existence of involuntary unemployment.[2] It may therefore be concluded that the relative deficiency of people who made their living by working for wages during the fifteenth century gave way to a relative surplus in the sixteenth.

The conditions of the land market also changed by the turn of the fifteenth century in a way consistent with the theory of 'population growth'. The demand for land rose decidedly and this was revealed in the enhancement of rents, especially in the form of higher entry fines,[3] in the intensification of exploitation of agricultural holdings, by enclosure for better utilization of the land,[4] and in the diminution of the size of the individual holdings.[5] Similarly the mounting 'land hunger' reflected itself in the deterioration of the relations between landlords and their tenants,[6] and in the general outcry against the substitution of tillage by pasturage.[7]

Yet a relative scarcity of victuals and increased demand for land does not necessarily have to be explained by 'population pressure'. Extensive soil exhaustion or the encroachment of graziers on arable land would have caused the same results. Harriet Bradley,[8] for example, believed that soil exhaustion was the cause 'of the enclosure and conversion to pasture of arable land in the fifteenth and sixteenth and seventeenth centuries . . .' because the 'strips kept under cultivation gave a bare return for seed. . . .' Her argument was, however, disputed

---

[1] *Rotuli Parliamentorum*, pp. 187–90; Statutes of the Realm, II, 457–70.

[2] G. R. Elton, *Economic History Review*, 2nd ser., VI (1953), 55–6.

[3] E. Kerridge, *Economic History Review*, 2nd ser., VI (1953), pp. 16–34, Tables II, V, VII.

[4] Y. S. Brenner, Thesis (Hebrew University, Jerusalem, 1955).

[5] E. Kerridge, op. cit.

[6] R. H. Tawney and E. Poser, *Tudor Economic Documents*, II, 304.

[7] R. H. Tawney, *Agrarian Problem in the sixteenth Century* (London, 1912); M. Beresford, *The Lost Villages of England* (London, 1954).

[8] Harriet Bradley, *The Enclosures in England* (New York, 1918), pp. 106–7.

by Reginald Lennard,[1] and 'is hardly compatible with the fact that the complaints concerning sheep did not come from the traditionally most exploited grain-producing areas where at the time production, far from receding, almost certainly increased,[2] or with the observation that the number of years of harvest failure neither recurred more often nor became less evenly spread throughout the first half of the sixteenth century. The consideration that increased pasturage at the expense of food production was at the bottom of the sharp rise in victual prices is also hardly applicable. Had it been the cause the rise would have remained almost entirely an English phenomenon; in fact, grain prices were rising similarly all over Europe.[3] Furthermore, if land had competing uses, and could have been used alternatively for arable and pasture, it would have shifted from one application to another and made the price equilibrium follow a gradual, continual and almost parallel upward course. Finally, it must also be noted that when, because of the depreciation of the currency, cloth exports increased appreciably in the early twenties,[4] corn prices did not rise though they had risen some years earlier. And although pasturage must have expanded in England between 1525 and 1530 and between 1544 and 1550, wheat prices did not rise more sharply in England than, for example, in Hainault, as would have to be expected had the invasion of sheep on arable land caused a relative shortage of corn. Pasture and tillage must be regarded as two almost separate sectors of economy in the sixteenth century with only a very thin marginal interdependence.

In summary, increased demand, rather than relatively diminished supply of goods, disturbed in the sixteenth century the previously prevalent price equilibrium. The way in which this derangement was reflected in the prices, and the structure of the newly emerging price pattern, must suggest that it was caused

---

[1] Reginald Lennard, 'The alleged exhaustion of the soil in Medieval England', *Economic Journal*, vol. 32 (1922). (I am grateful to Professor Postan for drawing my attention to the fact that the argument of Lennard which is based on the Rothamsted experiment is far from satisfactory.)

[2] N. S. B. Gras, *The Evolution of the English Corn Market*, p. 220.

[3] F. Simiand, op. cit. Dia. No. I.

[4] F. J. Fisher, *Economic History Review*, x (1940), 99.

by population growth. The demographic disaster in the four-teenth century produced a relative surplus of land. Tenements became available on easy terms and those of only marginal fertility were abandoned. As a result a relative scarcity of wage workers was reflected in the high cost of labour, while the great productivity of the cultivated land was reflected in the low grain prices. While high wages and low grain prices restricted tillage to the better land, it encouraged pasturage especially in areas of marginal fertility and sparse population. At the same time the European metal stock failed to receive further increments, the relation between money of account and precious metals be-came unrealistic, as a result of which a shortage of coins developed which was reflected in a slight depression of the general price level during the first half of the fifteenth century. The low cost of victuals and high wages also permitted early marriages, the sustenance of large families, and a high survival rate. Hence, when the great epidemics ceased to recur, popu-lation growth set in again. When this happened land became scanty, rents were raised in one form or another, family hold-ings had to be shared by a greater number of people and less fertile land was again brought under the plough. Yet agri-culture could neither expand enough to raise its labour force nor increase its production proportionately to the rise in popu-lation. All who could do so added to the family earnings by any available sort of by-employment, spinning, nail-making or whatever it might have been; others went to the towns and into what industrial employment they could find at whatever wages they could get. Some took to the roads and to crime. As a result of all this victual prices rose sharply.

There is, however, one other observation, namely the grow-ing amplification of the difference between grain prices in good and in bad harvest years, which needs an explanation. This trend, which is well illustrated by the Price Standard Deviation Table 2 and by any comparison of price fluctuations on a log-arithmic scale, can be attributed to a rising money-demand for victuals which was probably due to rapid urbanization. In earlier times agriculture and industry had been very close to each other. Most of the towns were supplied with food by their own citizens and the distinction between labour employed in agriculture and in industry was very vague. In the sixteenth century, when the overspill of agricultural labour inflated the towns, and these were no longer able to produce their necessary food supplies themselves, the gap between agriculture and industry widened. Townspeople ceased to be producers as well as consumers of victuals and remained solely consumers. Not only land but the labour force employed in agriculture was thus further curtailed relatively to the increased demand for its produce. Supplies had to be brought from increasingly greater distances and transportation costs rose while towns became more and more dependent on the surplus production of the more fertile rural areas. How this might be reflected in the increasing fluctuations of grain prices from good to bad crops may be explained by the following theoretical model: if a rural society predominantly engaged in agriculture produces 200 units of grain for its subsistence and a crop failure reduces production by, say, 25 per cent, supplies would be 25 per cent short. If the same agricultural producing population could produce not only 200 units of grain but an additional 100 units for the supply of an urban market, the same crop failure would reduce the supply of grain for the subsistence of the producers to 150 units, and of the urban market to 75 units. As a result of this the quantity of grain needed to satisfy the home supply would be made up out of the part which would otherwise be sold to the town. By making up the 200 units for the rural producers' subsistence supply, 50 units would be taken out of the town's supply. Consequently the supply of the urban market would not only be reduced by 25 per cent but by 75 per cent. It would not be supplied with 75 units of grain but only with 25 units, and the difference (50 units) would remain for the supply of the producers' needs. Hence the reflection of a reduced agricultural supply in the urban market in years of dearth would grow, in the form of tightness of supply, relative to the growth of the towns. This increasing tightness of supplies is reflected in the greater fluctuations of prices between good and bad harvests.

How far then is this model applicable to sixteenth-century market conditions? A clear answer to this question would necessitate a greater knowledge of the money-demand for victuals in this period than is available. There are, however, indications that some movement of the nature described in the model took place. If one compares the relative trends in price movements in various regions of the country one may detect, for example, that London City prices were similar to those of the immediate neighbourhood of London until 1514; then between 1514 and 1571 they were higher; and after 1571 they were lower. Similarly, Cambridge wheat prices, which usually were lower than those of London, rose sharply during the twenties, and in years of dearth in this decade caught up with London prices. The rise in London wheat prices during the forties was out of line, i.e. much sharper, than in the rest of the country. Hampshire prices were lower than Durham prices during most of the period 1450–1550 but in the first and second decades of the sixteenth century they drew close to each other, and in years of plenitude Hampshire prices rose above Durham prices. Yet in the thirties the old relation was once again restored. There was, however, one difference: in years of dearth Durham prices did not rise as far as Hampshire prices.

TABLE 3[1] *Lowest and highest yearly wheat price averages* (*s.* per qtr)

Decade	Cambridge	Hampshire	Westminster	London	Durham	Exeter
1450–60	3·27 (–)	3·61 (–)	4·67 (8·14)			4·90 (8·13)
1460–70	2·55 (9·14)	2·70 (8·08)	3·50 (9·78)		4·57 (–)	
1470–80	3·44 (6·71)	4·00 (8·17)			4·00 (8·00)	5·12 (7·57)
1480–90	3·58 (8·80)	4·00 (9·83)	5·93 (8·49)		4·00 (13·24)	5·44 (9·00)
1490–1500	3·05 (6·07)	3·88 (–)	4·52 (8·67)		3·67 (8·00)	4·34 (9·38)
1500–10	2·59 (7·61)	5·00 (8·09)	4·15 (9·58)		4·00 (8·28)	5·02 (7·98)
1510–20	3·82 (10·06)	4·67 (8·00)	6·41 (10·17)	8·00 (10·00)	4·00 (8·00)	5·08 (9·14)
1520–30	4·30 (16·19)	4·89 (12·00)	6·59 (11·45)	5·33 (16·00)		5·52 (12·94)
1530–40	4·76 (12·84)	5·33 (12·00)	6·84 (9·23)	7·00 (14·00)	5·51 (9·74)	6·58 (10·00)
1540–50	4·13 (13·26)	4·67 (16·00)		6·25 (20·06)		6·46 (19·10)

A likely explanation for these trends in comparative local price behaviour can perhaps be given as follows: taking London, for example, and granted that our knowledge of the growth of London population is defective, it may still be true that prices behaved as indicated as a result of the city's relatively faster growth compared to the population of the rest of the country.

[1] Each entry is for the year with the highest/lowest yearly average price. Where no price is given no clear-cut average could be found.

In contrast the relative fall in London wheat prices after 1571 can perhaps be attributed to the improvements in the organization of the city's supply and its transport facilities which permitted the importation of corn from more distant fertile regions. The most outstanding rise in London corn prices during the years of dearth in the forties coincided with the industrial boom in which London greatly participated. Taking another example: the relative change in the level of Cambridge grain prices during the twenties. This relative rise coincided with the doubling of corn exports via Lynn. Giving one more example to illustrate this point of increasing money-demand for victuals, i.e. a higher rate of circulation velocity (V) as well as a tightening of demand, it can be seen that Hampshire prices rose relatively to the prices of the rest of the country when exports from there increased by 100 per cent, and fluctuations became relatively sharper in Henry VII's time when Southampton was expanding. In Henry VIII's reign, however, when the expansion of Southampton ceased to continue at the rate of Henry VII's time, the old relation with the other areas' prices was restored for most years except those of great dearth when the tightness of demand must have continued.

Finally it must also be noted that the rising amplitude of the price fluctuations was neither due to a higher standard average in the later years, which can be seen from the standard deviation table, nor to a deterioration of climatic conditions. In the second half of the fifteenth century twenty-one years with high grain prices can be counted, in the first half of the sixteenth only eighteen. The grouping of the years of dearth in the second half of the fifteenth century can be divided into six groups of two to three years of relative dearth following one upon the other; the same is true for the first half of the sixteenth century.[1]

The explanations of the enhancement of grain prices during the first half of the sixteenth century must then include: the effects of greater overall and money demand with a relatively reduced supply, which may have become particularly tight in years of dearth as a result of the diminishing fertility of the

[1] Y. S. Brenner, thesis – *Prices and Wages in England*, London University, 1960.

additional newly cultivated areas; the tighter nature of money demand in comparison with overall demand; the persistence of the legislation against the hoarding of victuals which prevented the laying up of stocks for years of dearth; some excessive exportation, and the cumulative effect of the increasing volume and velocity of circulation of money; the rise in price of imported goods due to the debasements and in the price of exportable goods due to the incentive to exports given by the rate of exchange; the nervous reactions of the markets to the psychological effect the debased coinage had on the people and the state of mind which accompanied the disposal of the monastic lands on a speculators' market.

In conclusion, the rise in prices during the first half of the sixteenth century was due to a combination of an increased velocity and volume of currency circulation with a relatively decreased supply of, and intensified tightness of demand for, agricultural products. Or, using Dr Hammarström's more carefully chosen words,[1] 'that the motive force behind the sixteenth-century rise in prices included other factors besides the discovery of new mines'.

The velocity (V) of the circulation was increased by the development of industry and the expansion of commerce; the sharp rise in speculation in land and in the legalized market for funds; and by the transition of greater sections of society from rural self-sufficieny into urbanized communities dependent on markets (money-supply) for their food.

The volume of the circulating media (M) was increased by successive issues of base and forged coins; by some easement of the shortage of precious metals; by partial legalization of various sorts of bills of sale and exchange, in addition to other concealed means of payment; and the loosening of the legal and moral objections to loans and credits.

The relatively reduced supply of products (Q) was caused by increased demand due to population growth, and the shifting of agents of production from employment with only marginal returns to sectors of the economy which temporarily yielded

---

[1] I. Hammarström, op. cit., *Scandinavian Economic History Review*, vol. v, No. 1 (1957), p. 154.

high profits. The intensified tightness of demand for agricultural products was caused by urbanization which precipitated structural changes in the nature of the markets, and by increased speculative business.

The prices of industrial products and labour rose less sharply than those of victuals. This was due to their greater elasticity of demand; improved methods of production; and relatively reduced labour costs, in the case of industrial products; and to population pressure, migration of labour to towns and of industry into the countryside, in the case of wages.

Short-term fluctuations of prices were mainly caused by civil wars, harvest failures, and the psychological effect the baseness of the coins had on contemporaries.

4 The Price Revolution Reconsidered

J. D. GOULD

This article was first published in the *Economic History Review*, vol. XVII (1964–5)

Until a few years ago historians of the sixteenth and seventeenth centuries knew that one of the major phenomena of their period was a secular decline in the value of money which was so general and so marked as to justify the title 'the Price Revolution'. They knew, further, that this fall in the value of money was very largely caused by an influx of silver from the Spanish colonial acquisitions in the New World to Europe. They also believed, though with a shade more reservation, that these monetary changes were causally linked, through a process of 'profit inflation', with the alleged growth of capitalist enterprises in this period. All of this knowledge they owed, in large part, to the untiring labour and great scholarship of two men, the German Wiebe and the American Hamilton.

Some historians are still satisfied with this 'orthodox' interpretation of the sixteenth and seventeenth centuries, but others have recently been assailed by doubts as to its validity. These doubts have become implanted in their minds chiefly because of the apparent implications of recent work, which has included the re-working of some of the statistical information on prices, seeming to call for new interpretations. A few historians may have been, and more ought to have been, influenced also by developments in economic theory which have thrown into some degree of disrepute the theoretical equipment used to construct the orthodox interpretation of these events.

The chief aim of the present paper is to offer some thoughts on a number of matters, some of an empirical and some of a theoretical character, which are related at one point or another to the major issues of the debate. The comments offered are made from a standpoint which is on the whole more friendly to the new than to the orthodox interpretation of the so-called 'Price Revolution'; but at the same time the distinctive plea of the paper is for a recognition of the extent to which our understanding of the whole problem is still shrouded in doubt and obscurity, and thus, of the present need for moderation and tentativeness in framing hypotheses as to what happened, why, and with what consequences. It was not the wish of the author to summarize the present state of the debate – a task which has already been attempted, with varying degrees of success, by several writers[1] – but to give shape and structure to the paper it seemed necessary somehow to thread together the various rather disparate matters on which it was intended to comment. The obvious method of doing this was to cast the argument into the form of an account, as brief and clearly articulated as possible, of the chief issues currently being reconsidered, those matters on which the author has nothing new to add being referred to in only the most summary fashion.

I

One may first confess to a very strong temptation to question the very concept of a 'Price Revolution'.[2] For what after all was involved? While the measurement of long-term price trends is a statistically difficult and conceptually dubious enterprise, especially when the rate and even the direction of price changes are not uniform for all commodities, and when the 'output-mix' of goods and services is changing fairly substantially, it is probably of the right order of magnitude to suggest that in England, in the 100 years or so before the Civil War, *silver* prices[3] rose about threefold, a geometric rise of about 1·1 per cent annually. This is a tame affair by present-day standards. Wholesale prices in Great Britain, for example, almost doubled

[1] Notably I. Hammarström, 'The "Price Revolution" of the sixteenth century: some Swedish evidence'. See pp. 42–68 of this volume. And Y. S. Brenner, 'The inflation of prices in early sixteenth-century England', *Economic History Review*, 2nd ser., XIV (1961–2), 225–39 (see pp. 69–90 of this volume) and 'The inflation of prices in England, 1551–1650', ibid., XV (1962–3), 266–84.

[2] Cf. C. M. Cipolla, 'La Prétendue Revolution des Prix', *Annales* X (1955), 513–16.

[3] The word *silver* is, however, vitally important, and the restriction it imposes qualifies the validity of the comparison which follows.

between 1935 and 1946, and rose again in similar proportion in the following ten years – an almost fourfold rise in twenty-one years.[1] This represents a geometric increase of over 7 per cent per annum – a far more rapid movement, evidently, than that of the fall in the value of silver during the 'Price Revolution'. It may be objected that to compare modern experience with that of the Tudor and Stuart period is unfair because of the differences of economic and social structure involved. But, then, to accept this modification implies that we should look to the peculiar rigidities of the Tudor and Stuart economy, rather than to the magnitude of the price changes, when we seek to explain the alleged perplexity of our Tudor and Stuart forbears in dealing with the problems to which those changes gave rise.

It is not certain that the Price Revolution was in fact a wholly new phenomenon, even by the standards of preceding centuries. In particular, it is doubtful whether prices in the later sixteenth century rose any more rapidly than in the later twelfth century.[2] It is difficult wholly to share the easy assumption of many modern historians who see in the Price Revolution a process which bewildered and caused hardship to all those who lived through it. The following propositions would, however, command fairly general assent:

(1)   Contemporaries were aware of the secular rise of prices in the later sixteenth and early seventeenth centuries, and of the fact that this was a different experience from that of the fifteenth century, and sought to explain it.

(2)   They were further aware that a rise of prices prejudiced some groups and benefited others (they were also aware, though for obvious reasons they did not feel called upon to assert so often, that exactly the same comment could be made of a fall of prices).

(3)   Particular groups deplored the increased prices of particular commodities: for example, town-dwellers deplored the rise in the price of grain, as did the Crown, to whom it was

[1] The cost of living, of course, rose much less because of price controls, subsidies, rent restriction, etc.

[2] M. Postan, in *Cambridge Economic History of Europe* (Cambridge, 1952), II, 166.

unwelcome because dearth tended to lead to civil unrest, and increased the cost of provisioning the armed services.[1]

(4) The very sharp rise of prices during the debasement of 1543–51 – a very rapid inflation, the only part of the Price Revolution comparable with twentieth-century experience – caused widespread hardship, confusion and discontent (it is significant that most of the literature cited in support of the 'catastrophic' view of sixteenth-century price changes dates from this period).

These propositions, however, whether taken singly or in combination, do not correspond to the assertion that on balance contemporary opinion deplored the secular decline in the value of money, nor do they necessarily justify such modern characterizations of that process as a 'change so sudden and so uncontrolled that to many . . . it brought bewildering hardship and even disaster'.[2] A piece of research designed to elucidate contemporary assessment of the *effects* (rather than of the *causes*) of the Price Revolution would be an interesting project. It would be surprising if the scholar undertaking such a review did not conclude that the monetary experience most favoured by mercantilists, on the whole, and subject to the qualifications listed above, was moderate inflation; and 'moderate inflation' is not an inapt characterization of the period under review.

II

The orthodox view of the causes of the Price Revolution points to the large quantity of the precious metals, at first of gold, but later and principally of silver, shipped from Spanish possessions in the New World to Europe, and links this with the behaviour of prices in European countries in accordance with the teaching of the quantity theory of money.[3] Six major reasons have been put forward for doubting whether this explanation of the fall in the value of money in the sixteenth and seventeenth centuries

---

[1] B. Pearce, 'Elizabethan food policy and the armed forces', *Economic History Review*, xii (1942), 39–46.

[2] G. N. Clark, *The Wealth of England, 1496–1760* (Oxford, 1946), p. 60.

[3] See, especially, Earl J. Hamilton, 'American treasure and the rise of capitalism', *Economica*, xxvii (1929), 338–57.

is completely satisfactory, though not all of these have received equal degrees of attention from those hostile to the orthodox interpretation.

(1)   One might expect that a change in the value of money brought about purely by an expansion in the circulating medium would have similar effects on *all* prices; whereas, in fact, prices of different commodities and services moved at different speeds and, in one or two instances, even in the opposite direction.

(2)   The fall in the value began to be marked, in some instances, several decades *before* the influx from the New World became appreciable.

(3)   There exists an alternative hypothesis, namely a rise in population, for which in the case of several countries at least there is some independent evidence, which might be expected in certain circumstances to have exerted an upward pressure on prices, especially of commodities in inelastic supply, e.g. grain. This alternative hypothesis is attractive because it accords better than the traditional explanation with the common experience that prices of the basic foodstuffs rose relatively rapidly, and that the wages of labour lagged, in some instances at least, behind prices in general.[1] It would also overcome the chronological difficulty mentioned above in (2).

(4)   Recent developments in monetary theory have led to doubts whether changes of the type supposed in the quantity of the circulating medium have any automatic or determinate effect on prices, and have concentrated on other approaches to the investigation of effective demand, especially that associated with the concept of liquidity.

(5)   Even, however, if we retain the theoretical equipment used by Hamilton and other 'orthodox' scholars, the 'Fisher version' of the quantity theory,

$$MV = PT,$$

it is obvious that we can only assert that an increase in M will

---

[1] 'In some instances', but cf. C. Verlinden, 'Mouvement des Prix et des Salaires en Belgique au XVIe siècle', *Annales*, x (1955), 173–98.

lead to a proportionate increase in P if we assume that V and T remain constant. It would be difficult to arrive at an independent estimate of the behaviour of V in this period; but there is considerable reason – for example, the growth of urban populations and of industry, and the large volume of new building, all implying a consequent increase in production for the market – for supposing that T may have increased, perhaps very markedly, in the course of the sixteenth and seventeenth centuries, and this might have been expected to offset the supposed movement in M.

(6) To assert that a net import of precious metals into Spain is equivalent to an increase in the monetary circulation of a considerable number of European countries omits, of course, several logically intermediate steps. It remains to be shown *how* this increase in Spain's stock of the precious metals became dispersed amongst other European countries and incorporated into their media of circulation.

III

In regard to England, the last difficulty mentioned in the preceding section calls for more extended comment. Professor Judges has pointed out that it is *prima facie* difficult to reconcile the hypothesis of an inflow of 'Spanish' bullion into England during the reign of Elizabeth I with current orthodox views regarding the depressed state of commerce for much of that reign.[1] This at once invites us to consider the validity of these views. The evidence most frequently quoted in favour of them is the figures of shortcloth exports from London which Professor Fisher's industry has provided[2] for us. Misgivings as to the reliability of these figures have been voiced on several occasions.[3] Even supposing them, however, to be accurate in

[1] In his review of R. de Roover's study of Gresham, *Economic History Review*, 2nd ser., III (1950), 142.

[2] F. J. Fisher, 'Commercial trends and policy in sixteenth-century England', *Economic History Review*, x (1940), 95–117.

[3] L. Stone, 'State control in sixteenth-century England', *Economic History Review*, XVII (1947), 104–5, 107; J. D. Gould, 'The crisis in the export trade, 1586–1587', *English Historical Review*, LXXII (1956), 220.

themselves, it is surely inadmissible to infer from them that the balance of payments on current account during the reign of Elizabeth was unfavourable. The figures do not relate to the export of commodities other than cloth, or from ports other than London; they take no account of evasion of the customs; they relate only to the volume of exports, not to their value; they tell us nothing as to the volume or value of imports or as to the net balance on invisible items. Hence they cannot be used as a direct indicator of balance of payments trends during the period concerned.[1] There are, in fact, some obvious reasons for thinking that they may tend to paint too gloomy a picture of the commercial conditions of the last third of the reign. For instance, it is highly probable that the activities of 'interlopers' increased during the late sixteenth century. It is also probable that London's share of cloth exports declined somewhat in the later stages of the reign, as certain other trade routes less completely dominated by London – notably the trade of the Eastland Company – became relatively more important.[2]

This is not the end of the matter, however, for two reasons. First, even if we assume that the balance of payments on current account was generally unfavourable, it is possible that there was a more than offsetting inflow of capital. I have suggested elsewhere that the explanation of the otherwise puzzling upsurge in the minting of gold in the early 1620s may lie in this area,[3] and it seems not impossible that such an inflow should have occcurred during the period of religious wars in France and in the Low Countries in the later sixteenth century. Capital flows usually accompany migrations of peoples; and England was a receiver of immigrants from these areas in the later sixteenth century. Secondly, even if we assume both that there was an unfavourable balance of payments on current account, and

---

[1] The present writer does not, of course, intend by these remarks any disparagement of the contribution of Professor Fisher, to whose brilliant pioneer articles every historian of this period owes so much. The warning is only against applying the figures to purposes they cannot, of their nature, serve, and for which Professor Fisher himself gives no warrant.

[2] R. W. K. Hinton, *The Eastland Trade and the Common Weal in the Seventeenth Century* (Cambridge, 1959), Appendix D, pp. 226 ff.

[3] J. D. Gould, 'The Royal Mint in the early seventeenth century', *Economic History Review*, 2nd ser., v (1952–53), 242.

also that there was no offsetting inflow of capital – so that
bullion had to be exported to meet the deficit – it is yet feasible
that there should have been an increase in monetary circulation
in England. This suggestion would cause no surprise if one
were speaking of a gold or silver-producing country: yet while
Britain had no gold or silver deposits worth mentioning, she
did in fact harbour a large reserve of non-monetary gold and
silver in the form of plate and ornament, and possibly to a lesser
extent of hoards of coins. It is possible, therefore, that the active
monetary circulation should have been augmented by the melting down of plate or ornament, and by dehoarding. Again, the
circumstances of the time make this not unlikely on *a priori*
grounds. Whether peers as a class rose, and gentry as a class
declined, or vice versa, the present writer is quite incompetent
to adjudicate. But clearly some well-to-do people rose, and
other well-to-do people declined. Now it is reasonable to suggest that those who were declining would be more likely to
make ends meet by melting down the family plate, than those
who were rising would be to add to the collection. For in the
late sixteenth and early seventeenth centuries gold and silver
were declining in value, while the value of real estate was
appreciating rapidly. Those in financial straits would therefore
have been well advised to melt down plate, and hang on to their
land as long as possible, in the hope that it might yet prove the
salvation of the family fortunes; while those who prospered
would have been inclined to invest in land, the appreciating
asset, rather than in treasure and ornament. One thus suggests
the likelihood of a net movement of gold and silver from plate
and ornament to money.

The burden of the argument of the foregoing paragraphs is to
question the adequacy of the evidence on the basis of which we
have hitherto supposed the commercial history of the reign of
Elizabeth to be largely a story of depression, and secondly, to
suggest that, even if this orthodox view be sustained, it is yet
far from impossible to believe that monetary circulation should
have increased during that period. The argument of itself does
not, of course, afford any reason for supposing that the supply
of money *did* increase: but I have elsewhere suggested that, on

a first inspection, the history of the Mint issues during Elizabeth's reign supports such a view.[1] That view was shared by most if not all of the contemporary opinion on the matter which the writer has had the opportunity to examine. Though this positive evidence is at present very tentative, therefore, and far from proving the case that the supply of money did in fact increase, the effect of the foregoing argument is provisionally to exempt the traditional interpretation of the cause of the Price Revolution (so far as England is concerned) from one of the more obvious and serious criticisms which could be levied against it.

It may seem to readers that the present writer is guilty of some perversity, first in proclaiming his scepticism regarding the traditional interpretation of the Price Revolution, and then in going to some trouble to remove one of the more obvious difficulties standing in the way of that interpretation. On reflection, however, it will be seen that the present position is much less open to criticism than its opposite. It may seem somewhat teasing, but it is certainly perfectly legitimate, to suggest that the supply of money did increase during the reign of Elizabeth, and yet that that increase was not chiefly responsible for the rise of prices in the same period. It is, however, completely unacceptable to maintain both that an increase in the supply of money *was* the cause of the rise of prices, and yet that Elizabethan foreign trade was so depressed that it is impossible that such an increase should have come about. Yet the latter combination of opinions is perhaps only a slight caricature of what, until recently at least, has been orthodox teaching. The foregoing argument may therefore be welcome to those who prefer these 'orthodox' views, since they will in future be able to combine them without the suspicion of self-contradiction which has, or ought to have, troubled them hitherto.

IV

It will by now have become apparent that one of the major difficulties confronting the analyst of the Price Revolution is

[1] J. D. Gould, 'The trade depression of the early 1620s', *Economic History Review*, 2nd ser., VII (1954–55), 86, n. 1.

that we do not know how big, at various periods, the supply of money was. The 'political arithmeticians' of the later seventeenth century, and the debates over the recoinage of the 1690s, threw up quite a number of estimates for that period, and there are also some estimates for earlier dates.[1] But these are only estimates; they do not agree with each other, so that some must be, and all may be, wide of the mark; and in any event they do not permit us to trace with any confidence or in any detail the course of the supply of money during the relevant period, namely the hundred years or so preceding the Civil War.

It might at first sight be thought that records of the Mint output should afford us the evidence we require. It cannot be too strongly stressed that they do nothing of the sort – at least, not in any direct fashion. What the Mint records give is, at best, evidence as to the face value of new coinage struck by the Mint. For several reasons, however, this cannot be taken to be equivalent to net additions to the supply of money. First, the Mint may have re-issued former coins which had been melted down: this would of course notably be the case if the Mint price of one or both of the precious metals had just been raised. Secondly, some coin was exported, either legally (for example, by the East India company), or illegally, for some anticipated gain on the exchanges. Thirdly, if in one country, say England, the 'mint ratio' between the precious metals got out of step with that of neighbouring countries, it might pay to export the undervalued metal in order to import that which was overvalued (these are the so-called 'bimetallic flows', of which a notable example occurred in the second decade of the seventeenth century after James I fixed a new Mint ratio, overvaluing gold and undervaluing silver, in 1611[2]). Finally, a sharp increase in paper money of one sort or another was probably characteristic of the seventeenth century.

To say this, however, is not to deny the possibility of learning something from the Mint records. We may be fairly sure,

---

[1] J. K. Horsefield, *British Monetary Experiments, 1650–1710* (Cambridge, Mass., 1960), Appendix 2, pp. 256–7, and *passim*. See also, for example, B.M. MS. Harleian 1583, fo. 20.

[2] J. D. Gould, 'The Royal Mint', pp. 241–2.

for example, that after a long period of stable 'Mint prices', existing coins would not be melted down in any great quantity to be brought to the Mint: there would be no profit in such a transaction. Again, it is possible to compare Mint ratios in neighbouring countries, and thus form an estimate as to the existence, likely direction, and even perhaps the approximate magnitude of 'bimetallic flows'. Other contemporary records are likely to give some indication on this point, too. It may thus be possible somewhat to narrow the discrepancy which one ought always to suspect – and which at times may be overwhelmingly large – between the records of Mint output and net changes in the supply of money. Other approaches may also help. For example, hoards of coins hidden away during the Civil War troubles have been discovered and their contents enumerated.[1] In so far as we may assume such hoards to constitute a random selection of coins in circulation at the time of their secretion (though this is a big assumption), they afford evidence as to the relative quantities of different coinages in circulation at that time: and this, in connection with a study of Mint output in the past, may offer a useful indication of the extent to which Mint activity has at various periods represented, on the one hand, genuine additions to the supply of money, or on the other merely the reminting of former coins.

V

Discussion of these technical matters connected with the currency leads to an examination of one difficulty of absolutely capital importance besetting analysts of the Price Revolution – a difficulty of which, however, these analysts have been largely if not completely unaware. The evidence as to changing prices, on which all of our conjectures are ultimately based, are contemporary records from which price series have been compiled by later historians. In the case of England, for example, the basic statistics are to be found in the well-known volumes of

[1] e.g. *Numismatic Chronicle*, 5th ser., XIX (1939), 183–4, discussed on pp. 37–8 of my Bristol M.A. thesis (1951), *Economic Thought in England, 1600–1630, with reference to its evolution in the light of economic history.*

Thorold Rogers. When the German historian of the Price Revolution, Wiebe, first tried to examine the price history of the early modern period, he realized that the necessary international comparisons could not be effected unless the various local currencies in which these records were expressed could be reduced to some common denominator. Further, the expression of prices in local currencies makes it impossible to distinguish the effects of debasement of the coinage (the incidence of which varied, of course, from place to place) from that of changes in the value of the precious metals.

Wiebe sought to overcome both of these difficulties by translating the local currency prices into 'silver prices', that is, prices expressed in terms of a given weight of fine silver. To do this, it was necessary to know the changing silver content of each major unit of local or national currency, and this seemed to be provided by Mint records which indicated the 'Mint price' of silver. The 'Mint price' of 5s., for example, which ruled in England from 1560 to 1601, meant that the fine silver content of each shilling minted according to that standard was one fifth of an ounce. The 'Mint price' would thus serve as a 'deflator' to turn local currency prices into an index of silver prices.

This procedure, which the International Committee on Price History and the works issued under its auspices have followed, involves a number of difficulties. One is that the changes in Mint price may not be accurately known. For England, for example, Mint prices have chiefly been derived from the classic work by Ruding, who in turn drew on the writings of the eighteenth-century numismatist, Thomas Snelling; but in his researches into the history of the Mint in the early seventeenth century, the present writer found that Ruding's data on Mint prices were not completely accurate,[1] and such a comment may well apply to other periods and other countries. There is, however, a yet more important objection to the procedures adopted for estimating silver prices.

The belief that reducing local to silver prices in the fashion outlined would serve precisely to offset the degree of inflation ascribable to debasement of the coinage would be justified only

[1] J. D. Gould, 'The Royal Mint', pp. 240, 247.

in so far as both of the following propositions were true: (*a*) that the proportion in which the coinage was debased was at once reflected by a precisely proportional increase in the supply of money, and (*b*) that that increase in the supply of money should equally promptly lead to a proportionate increase in the general level of prices. In fact, neither of these propositions is true. As to the second, it will suffice to indicate that the whole basis on which we are reconsidering the causes of the Price Revolution is the belief that an increase in the supply of money need *not* lead automatically to a commensurate increase in prices.[1] In any event, there would perhaps be quite general agreement that it need not and will not do so *immediately*, since in so far as any elements of the structure of prices respond sluggishly owing to institutional rigidities – wages, for example – the permeation of the whole economic system by the inflationary stimulus would be to that extent delayed. It is this circumstance which has been widely recognized as being responsible for the lag of export prices behind the price of foreign exchange in the period immediately following a major debasement of the coinage – a lag which has been invoked, for example, to explain the stimulus to English exports during the 1540s[2] or, again, when it was *foreign* currencies which were being debased, the declining competitive power of English exports during the early 1620s.[3] Yet, of course, the formula for deriving 'silver prices' from prices in national currencies dictates that the increase in the Mint price of silver should be incorporated into the calculation of silver prices *immediately* that increase is promulgated. The effect, therefore, is to apply too severe a deflator to prices in local currencies, the degree of over-severity being greatest immediately following the debasement, and declining gradually as the inflationary effect of the debasement works its way through the economy. Hence such apparent anomalies as the behaviour of silver prices during the English debasement of the years 1543–51: the Wiebe 'silver price'

---

[1] Though theoretical considerations would lead us to expect a debasement of the coinage to be *more* likely to lead to this result than any other autonomous increase in the supply of money.

[2] F. J. Fisher, op. cit.

[3] J. D. Gould, 'The trade depression', pp. 88–90.

H

index, used also by Hamilton in his researches, shows for the 1540s a sharp *decline* from the level of the 1530s – this at a time when actual prices in the currency of the day were rising more rapidly than at any time during the whole Price Revolution!

The yet more serious objection, however, to the formula for deriving 'silver prices' arises from the invalidity of the first proposition, namely, that a given degree of debasement of the coinage at once leads to an equiproportional increase in the supply of money. Three reasons combine to lead us to assert, with complete assurance, that this will not be so. In the first place, a change in the Mint price of silver, unless indeed it is great enough to induce a 'bimetallic flow', will directly affect only the *silver* coinage. This, however, is but a portion of the whole supply of money: gold, paper money and near-money of various forms are ignored by a deflator which acts as though silver constituted the whole supply of money. If a change in the Mint price of silver *is* great enough to induce a bimetallic flow, it will automatically induce a corresponding decline in the circulation of gold coins. Secondly, the physical capacity of the Mint is naturally limited: and if a debasement is severe, it may take many years to work and re-issue all of the silver which merchants may bring in. During the great debasement of 1543–51, indeed, the English Mint never really caught up with the successive debasements of the silver coinage. Thirdly and most important, however, it is unrealistic to suppose that any given degree of debasement will cause *all* coins already in circulation to be melted down and brought into the Mint. The technical processes of the early modern period were not accurate enough to enable every coin to be issued with completely identical silver or gold content, and in any event, since coins gradually wore away through use, the older coins would generally tend to be lighter than those more recently issued from the Mint.[1] Any

---

[1] From this point of view, one can argue that an occasional gentle debasement of the coinage was advantageous. To withdraw from circulation clipped or worn silver or gold coins, and replace them with coins of correct weight, costs the State more than withdrawing worn banknotes and printing new ones. The currency crisis of the 1690s was largely brought about because Mint prices had remained unchanged for so long that the silver content of newly minted coins was well above the average silver content of old coins already in circulation.

given degree of debasement would naturally tend to lead to the culling out only of those coins whose weight and appearance promised a silver content in excess of the newly promulgated silver content of new coins of similar face value; the greater the debasement, the greater the tendency for the more badly worn coins to be culled also. Only a very severe debasement indeed, however, would bring *all* the old coins into the Mint. Moreover, it cost something, in terms of both time and capital, to cull the weightier coins, melt them, and bring the silver into the Mint; and often enough, the return the merchant bringing in silver actually got did not increase *pari passu* with the increase in Mint price because the prince took the opportunity to increase seignorage at the same time as debasing the coinage.

An index of silver prices calculated in the manner described would therefore be open to the following objections: first, that it would apply too severe a deflator to local currency prices in the period immediately following a debasement (the degree to which the deflator overshot the mark, however, tending to decline as the inflation worked its way through the economy), and secondly that the deflator would progressively become more and more excessive in a permanent sense for a country whose currency suffered successive debasements. Hence an index of silver prices would tend, in any country undergoing debasement of the coinage, to overstate (by implication) the extent to which the rise of prices (in current coinage) was due to the debasement of that coinage, and correspondingly to understate the extent to which it was due to a secular fall in the value of silver. The disturbing thing is, of course, that different countries did not experience the *same degree* of debasement, nor at the *same time*, and the extent to which silver prices constructed as described misrepresent reality would therefore vary from country to country and from time to time. Hence, translation of local currency prices into silver prices serves, in this sense, to obscure that very process of international comparison of price trends which it was intended to facilitate.

To discover *how far* silver price indices misrepresent reality it would be necessary to know (amongst other things) the extent of the divergence between the proportionate increase in

Mint prices and the proportionate increase in the supply of money; and this we do not as yet know, if we ever shall. All that can be offered at present by way of general hypothesis is that the 'silver price' approach to the study of the price history of this period has led historians generally to underestimate the fall in the value of silver; and secondly, that the extent of such underestimation would likely be greater for those countries which suffered repeated debasements of their silver coinage, than for others.[1]

VI

One turns with relief from these somewhat arid technicalities – vitally important to our interpretation of price history though they are – to comment briefly on the reorientation of economic theory which has made the orthodox approach to the Price Revolution somewhat *démodé*. The importance which pre-Keynesian economists attached to the supply of money and to price fluctuations has been replaced, since the publication of the *General Theory*, by a preoccupation with income fluctuations and their causes. In this connection it is the relation between savings and investment which is regarded as the prime mover of short-term fluctuations: an increase in the ratio of investment to savings brings about an inflationary, and the opposite movement a deflationary, impact on the economy. An inflationary pressure will normally express itself in an increase both in employment and in prices, but the distribution of its effect between these two will depend on a number of structural factors. Broadly speaking, we may expect the chief consequence to be an increase in the level of employment, so long as there are plenty of unemployed resources in the economy, whereas once the level of full employment is reached, the chief consequence will be a rise in prices. But such an aggregative way of looking at the matter distorts reality: there may be still a considerable reservoir of unemployed resources in one sector of the economy, while the level of full employment has been reached elsewhere. Labour, for example, is far from completely mobile either

[1] This circumstance may help to explain the relative stability of Swedish *silver* prices during the Price Revolution, a fact which puzzled Dr Hammarström.

occupationally or geographically: the construction industry may be stretched to its limit while there is still much idle capacity in textiles; the South and the Midlands may prosper, with inflationary movements of prices and wages, while relatively high levels of unemployment persist in Northern Ireland and in Scotland.

The Keynesian approach has thus dethroned the supply of money from its erstwhile pre-eminence. The doubt which theory cast on the quantity theory approach to price fluctuations was strengthened by the empirical observation that the supply of money did not necessarily move *pari passu* with fluctuations in incomes and employment during the course of the trade cycle; and, as a practical matter, attempts in several countries to pull the economy out of the great depression of the early 1930s by credit creation were notoriously unsuccessful. Hence economists have felt obliged to go behind the back, so to speak, of the supply of money, and to search for the factors which influence changes in the demand for money. In this connection, the concept of liquidity, and its interdependence with business trends and investment programmes, has been of central importance. The equation $MV = PT$, being a tautology, remains necessarily true, but mere changes in the supply of money (M) can no longer be regarded as determining either prices (P) or the level of economic activity (T), since they may be neutralized, reinforced, or even reversed by changes in the velocity of circulation (V).

It is this line of argument which culminated in the pronouncement of the Radcliffe Committee: 'We cannot find any reason for supposing, or any experience in monetary history indicating, that there is any limit to the velocity of circulation; it is a statistical concept that tells us nothing directly of the motivation that influences the level of total demand. . . .'[1] It is fair to say that, while some economists have expressed their satisfaction at the short shrift which the Radcliffe Committee gave to the quantity theory,[2] this aspect of the *Report* has also

[1] *Report of the Committee on the Working of the Monetary System* (Cmnd. 827, 1959), para. 391.

[2] e.g. C. Kennedy, 'Monetary policy', in *The British Economy in the 1950s*, ed. G. D. N. Worswick and P. H. Ady (Oxford, 1962), pp. 317–18.

been criticized. But a number of recent empirical studies have seemed to confirm that there is no statistical evidence to relate the differing experience of western European countries with regard to inflation in the 1950s to the degree of restraint in the creation of money which they have exercised.[1]

However, the relevance of these ideas for *long-term* price trends is something more of an open question. The strongest argument for supposing them to be relevant to the long run as well as to the short is simply this: that if the velocity of circulation is so elastic in the short run, why should it be more rigid in the long? There seems no obvious reason why long-term changes in the level of economic activity and of prices should be any more straitly determined by the supply of money, than those of the short term. In the long run, too, it is very tempting to suppose that not only the *volume* of investment, but its character, must have a decided relevance for price trends. It is in comformity with such arguments that the price history of the nineteenth century, once written largely in terms of gold,[2] has latterly been re-examined in the light of changing habits of savings and investment.[3] A re-examination of the Price Revolution in the light of such an approach would surely be welcome. Not only would such an exercise be in line with recent trends in economic theory, but it might prove to be less severely hampered by the difficulty of securing adequate empirical evidence.

Yet, despite the cloud under which quantity-theory approaches find themselves at the moment, it is not easy to be wholly convinced that such considerations can be overlooked with impunity in the investigation of long-term price trends. It is placing a considerable strain on credulity to ask one to believe that the upward trend of prices in the second half of the sixteenth century, the third quarter of the nineteenth century, and the first decade of the twentieth, bears no relation other

---

[1] A. E. Holmans, 'The quantity of money, gross national product and the price level', *Scottish Journal of Political Economy*, VIII (1961), 28–44; M. J. Artis, 'Liquidity and the attack on quantity theory', *Bull. Oxf. Inst. Stat.*, 23 (1961), 343–66.

[2] Cf. in particular W. T. Layton and G. Crowther, *An Introduction to the Study of Prices* (1935).

[3] W. W. Rostow, *British Economy of the Nineteenth Century* (Oxford, 1948).

than coincidence to the increased output of the precious metals which characterized all of those periods. In any case, further investigation of monetary phenomena in the early modern period might be expected to yield useful information about, e.g., the balance of payments, even if it did not lead to a satisfactory explanation of price trends.

It therefore seems prudent to keep an open mind for the present, and seek to advance knowledge of the 'Price Revolution' on as broad a front as possible. One advantage of such open-mindedness is that it would allow us to embrace a theory of 'multiple causation', which, for instance, hypothesized a rise in the price of certain important individual commodities – e.g. wheat, timber – brought about by 'real' factors, superimposed upon a generally inflationary situation associated with enlarged credit creation and heavy defence expenditures. Such a hypothesis would more easily overcome the difficulties summarized in Section II of this article, and would moreover permit us to attach differing weights to the various factors in explaining the price history of different countries. In the case of Spain the massive inflow of precious metals failed to serve any progressive economic purpose: instead, it was largely used to finance unproductive military expenditures. It would be carrying scepticism a little far to look much beyond these circumstances for an explanation of Spanish inflation in this period. In some other countries, on the other hand, monetary influences may have had much less importance, and we may prefer to look to other factors such as population trends or the character of investment. Moreover, even in so far as the monetary circulation of a given country *was* increased, the effects of such a change would vary according to the nature of different economies. Such a suggestion ought not to surprise historians, in view of the well-known differences in the reactions (say) of Spain herself, of Holland, and of the East to the influx of precious metal. Such an influx might well act as a catalyst on the economic system; but the nature of the reaction provoked would depend on the properties of the economy in question.

Had economic historians felt the need for any theoretical

warrant for the belief that an increase in the quantity of bullion has no determinate economic effects, they could readily have found it in the comment of the most historically-minded of all the great economists of this century: 'Increase in the supply of monetary metals does not, any more than autonomous increase in the quantity of any other kind of money, produce economically determined effects. It is obvious that these will be entirely contingent upon the uses to which the new quantities are applied, and the way they take through the economic organisms.... In the case of an inflow of precious metals it is perfectly conceivable that they disappear in hoards, or are worked into objects of use and adornment. ... This consideration alone would, even if there were no other, negative all money-quantity theories of the rise of capitalism.'[1] Such a view would have served to counteract the authority which Keynes's untimely and rather uncritical reference seemed to lend to Hamilton's views.[2]

VII

In conclusion, a few comments on the effects of the Price Revolution seem in order. Here again it is to Professor Hamilton that we owe the seminal idea, which is simplicity itself. Under the influence of Spanish treasure, prices rose; wages and rents, held back by 'institutional' rigidities, lagged behind; and entrepreneurs were presented with an undeserved and unexpected increase in profit margins represented by the widening gap between prices of the finished product and costs (equated with wages and rents). This facilitated capital accumulation and the development of capitalist forms of industry.

We may first notice that the likely effect of such a change in the distribution of incomes, according to our usual assumptions regarding the consumption function, would be an increase in the savings ratio of the community as a whole. In the absence of offsetting circumstances this would set in motion compen-

---

[1] J. A. Schumpeter, *Business Cycles* (New York and London, 1939), I, 231–2.

[2] J. M. Keynes, *A Treatise on Money* (1930), II, 148–63.

sating *deflationary* tendencies; and, in the circumstances supposed, the 'profit' gap might be expected to lead to a long-term growth of industry only if one could suppose that there was some simultaneous upward movement in the propensity to invest – associated, for example, with technological innovation. Thus, profit inflation on the Hamiltonian model is in any event an incomplete explanation, on its own, of the growth in largescale industry.

However, Hamilton's thesis was challenged on other grounds. J. U. Nef early questioned the adequacy of the wage data, pointing, for example, to complications introduced by the payment of wages in kind; stressed that costs *other* than wages and rents, for example the price of timber, rose very sharply; indicated that similar circumstances in France did not lead to similar results; and offered an alternative explanation of the growth of capitalist industry.[1] More recently, another support of the Hamiltonian edifice has been weakened by Dr Kerridge's empirical investigations suggesting a rapid rise of rents in the century before the Civil War.[2] Regional studies have tended to support Kerridge's findings.[3] It must, indeed, be said that Hamilton's evidence for a lag of rents was always extremely tenuous: a reference each to Tawney and to Lipson, and a quotation from the *Discourse of the Common Weal* (written in 1549, before the effects, if any, of Spanish silver can have been felt in England) which failed even to note that when this treatise was revised on the occasion of its first publication in 1581, the passage which Hamilton quoted alleging a lag of rents behind prices was omitted and new material substituted, which invoked the *rise* of rents after 1549 as an explanation of the continuation of the upward trend of prices after the 'restoration' of the coinage.[4] It is sobering to recall the insouciance with which fine historians accepted the doctrine of lagging rents, not only as an ingredient of profit inflation, but as support for the hypothesis

---

[1] J. U. Nef, 'Prices and industrial capitalism in France and England, 1540–1640', *Economic History Review*, VII (1937), 155–85.

[2] E. Kerridge, 'The movement of rent, 1540–1640', *Economic History Review*, 2nd ser., VI (1953–4), 16–34.

[3] e.g. A. Simpson, *The Wealth of the Gentry* (Cambridge, 1961), chap. V.

[4] Tawney and Power, *Tudor Economic Documents* (1953), III, 305–10.

that the great landowners were impoverished by the closing of the scissors between rising prices and inelastic rent-rolls.[1]

The significance of recent work on prices in this direction is to deepen suspicion of profit inflation by demonstrating that the 'prices' behind which costs are alleged to have lagged are a statistical figment, combining very rapidly rising food prices and much less rapidly rising prices of manufactures.[2] The 'gap' between prices and costs alleged by Hamilton had already been narrowed by the arguments of Nef and of Kerridge *et al.* that Hamilton underestimated the rise in costs: the new criticism is that he overestimated the *relevant* rise in prices, by using a series which lumped together all prices, including food prices, instead of one confined to the prices of manufactures. Whether there is any 'gap' left, our statistics are too crude to permit us to say. In any event, it is unlikely that production functions would remain unchanged over such a long period. But that the evidence for profit inflation, always extremely inadequate, has been whittled away to the point where it seems best to drop the concept in future discussion of the industrial changes of the period, seems to the present writer a conclusion which it is difficult to avoid. By the same token, the demonstration that food prices rose much more than the average enhances the plausibility of Kerridge's assertions regarding the course of rents: one would naturally expect the price of land to reflect to some extent at least the sharp rise in the price of its products. Broadly speaking, the new view of the Price Revolution directs our scrutiny towards the agricultural rather than the industrial sector of the economy, when we look for the chief beneficiary of the trends of the period. However, the distribution of benefits between landowners and tenants would naturally depend upon the 'institutional' factors which determined rents. It may also be well to recall that in Tudor and Stuart England, as in

[1] Indeed, the whole historiography of the Price Revolution should strengthen the historian's resistance to the seductive charms of oversimplified theory.

[2] This is one of the chief contributions of the series of articles by E. Phelps Brown and S. V. Hopkins. See, especially, 'Seven centuries of the prices of consumables, compared with builders' wage rates', on pp. 18–41 of this volume; and 'Wage rates and prices: evidence for population pressure in the sixteenth century', *Economica*, XXIV (1957), 289–306.

Russia before the days of collective farming, most of the agricultural surplus may well have been provided by only a small proportion of all cultivators, while many small peasants may have depended on earning money, say in domestic industry, and have been *buyers* rather than *sellers* of grain.

Perhaps the most unfortunate consequence of the ready acceptance of Hamilton's views on profit inflation is that they have diverted attention and inquiry away from another possible and perhaps more likely influence of the rise of prices upon profits and capital accumulation. It is widely recognized today that in the mid-twentieth century, the impact of rising prices on industrial profits has come less from any lag of wages behind prices – in most cases there has been no such lag – than from the lag of capital costs behind them.[1] In a period of steadily rising prices, a constant stream of output from a given machine will sell at ever-rising values: but, of course, once the machine has been installed its 'historical cost' is fixed and a fixed annual depreciation charge based upon that historical cost will therefore represent a falling percentage of the gross income derived from the sale of the machine's output. Even, therefore, if other costs including labour costs rise in proportion to the price of the final product, net profits from the work of that machine (which equal gross income less all costs including depreciation) will rise *more than* proportionately with the price level. The apparent rise in the profit margin arises only, of course, where the accounting convention in use fixes depreciation by reference to historical cost rather than replacement cost.[2] In effect, part – an increasing part – of the *apparent* profit is unappropriated depreciation which will have to be made good somehow when the machine ultimately has to be replaced. The day of reckoning does finally come. But if the life of the machine or structure is a long one – and this may well have been the case with a very

---

[1] G. L. Bach, *Inflation* (Providence, R.I., 1958), pp. 33 f., 79 ff.

[2] It would be very surprising if Tudor and Stuart enterprises usually made any provision *at all* for depreciation, let alone in any fashion which took account of the falling value of money. As late as the 1840s even the railway companies frequently made no provision for depreciation: H. Pollins, 'Aspects of railway accounting before 1868', in A. C. Littleton and B. S. Yamey, *Studies in the History of Accounting* (1956).

substantial part of the fixed capital of the Tudor and Stuart periods: waterwheels, salt pans, furnaces, and so on – then high *apparent* profit rates may have been widespread in those centuries.

Secondly, rising prices also lead to higher profits in so far as they reduce the real burden of interest on borrowed capital. Production from a machine installed during a period of prolonged inflation not only *appears* more profitable if the accounting convention of the day relates depreciation on it to its historical rather than its replacement cost, but additionally *is* more profitable since the interest on the capital borrowed to install it represents a falling proportion of the value of the annual output produced by it. In many inflationary periods, of course, rising interest rates have counteracted this tendency for the real burden of interest on borrowed capital to fall. But such a counteracting force did not operate during the Tudor and Stuart periods, which, as is well known, witnessed a great secular fall in interest rates. Professor Cipolla, indeed, has argued – and not without plausibility – that this fall in interest rates, rather than the rise in the price level, is the *true* economic revolution of the sixteenth and seventeenth centuries.[1]

It is not germane to the present argument to seek to explore the reasons for this fall in borrowing rates, though of course it is not impossible that it should have been induced, as many seventeenth-century writers believed, by the same increase in monetary stocks which has been pointed to as the cause of the rise in prices. But it is an important part of the argument of this paper that one theoretically congenial hypothesis which deserves investigation is that there occurred during the Price Revolution (*a*) a *genuine* rise in profits associated both with falling interest rates and with the otherwise falling real burden of interest on already borrowed capital brought about by the rise in the price level, together with (*b*) a further *apparent* rise in profits associated with the well-known lag of depreciation charges based on historical cost in a period of inflation.

In one direction, however, recent work does support Hamil-

---

[1] Carlo M. Cipolla, 'Note sulla storia del saggio d'interesse', *Economia Internazionale*, V (1952), 255–74.

ton, namely in pointing to a very sharp decline in the real income of the wage-earner. Professor Phelps Brown and Miss Hopkins, indeed, have suggested that real wages in the late sixteenth and early seventeenth centuries were no more than two-fifths of what they were in the late fifteenth century.[1] True, the argument of Phelps Brown and Hopkins is also open to the criticisms urged by Professor Nef against Hamilton. Nevertheless, making very large allowances for defective statistics and possibly for doubtful interpretation, the record can afford no satisfaction at all to those who would like to think of the artistic achievements of the Elizabethan period as built upon a solid foundation of widely spread prosperity. And, by implication, such views of fifteenth-century real wages as those put forward by Professor Postan seem to be confirmed: real wages in Elizabethan England were at least not so low as to prevent a notable rise of population, and if the wage-earner of the fifteenth century was anything up to twice as well off, or even more, he must have been uncommonly prosperous for such an underdeveloped country as England then was.

Finally, one may note that recent reinterpretations such as that of Phelps Brown and his collaborator have used prices in current money, rather than silver prices. The latter were intended as a device (*a*) to permit international comparisons, and (*b*) to isolate the effects of debasement from other causes of inflation. The shortcomings of silver prices for these purposes have already been argued. If, however, we have other purposes in mind, e.g. to ascertain changes in real income within a given economy, there can be no reason for using anything but prices in current money. To do this reduces the fall in the value of silver to its proper perspective, and brings into greater prominence the influence on the course of prices and of real wages of debasements of the coinage. In particular, one can restore to its rightful position the debasement of the English coinage in the years following 1543: a piece of history, which, like the great depression nearly four centuries later, must have been a traumatic experience for those who lived through it. While wishing

---

[1] Phelps Brown and Hopkins, 'Seven centuries', Appendix B. See pp. 38–41 of this volume.

5 The Circulating Medium and the Movement of Prices in Mid-Tudor England[1]

C. E. CHALLIS

I

The attempt to explain the movement of prices in the sixteenth century is as old as the event itself, and that it should continue yet is a measure both of the complexity of the problem and our uncertain knowledge of the period. On the one hand we are aware of the need to evaluate the importance of real causes of the inflation, such as population pressure, as opposed to monetary explanations, yet we know that to do this effectively we must discuss many issues about which we are singularly ill informed. It is clear that a great deal of work, particularly of the fact-finding type, still needs to be done before a final solution can be attempted.[2] One line of investigation which seems to call for some attention concerns the circulating medium; not because existing discussions of the inflationary situation have entirely neglected alterations in the volume and quality of the coinage – this they certainly have not – but simply because the sources for coinage production which are still extant have never been used in their entirety. Consequently, our present notions of the circulating medium are based on only a partial survey of the available evidence. It would be idle to suppose that these coinage statistics can unlock all doors, for, as we shall see, they remain at best imperfect. Nevertheless, they do suggest new lines of enquiry and certainly deserve closer attention.

[1] Copyright 1971 C. E. Challis.
[2] For the most recent survey of the whole controversy see R. B. Outhwaite, *Inflation in Tudor and Early Stuart England* (1969).

II

For the period upon which this survey concentrates – the years of the Great Debasement, 1544 to 1551 – we know that the English mints turned out at least £3,970,145 in English coin: £1,298,593 being in gold, and £2,671,552 in silver (Table 1). We also know that, huge though these totals are, they do not

TABLE 1 *Known production of English coin, 1544–1551*

Date	Gold coin			Silver coin			Total		
	£	s.	d.	£	s.	d.	£	s.	d.
1 Jun 1544–31 Mar 1545	165 931	4	0	149 287	4	0	315 218	8	0
1 Apr 1545–31 Mar 1546	372 179	7	6	440 212	16	0a	812 392	3	6
1 Apr 1546–31 Mar 1547	263 165	0	0	453 615	12	0	716 780	12	0
1 Apr 1547–30 Sep 1547	215 725	0	0b	119 113	11	0b	334 838	11	0
1 Oct 1547–30 Sep 1548	174 375	0	0	259 906	0	0	434 281	0	0
1 Oct 1548–30 Sep 1549	69 677	16	8	582 779	4	0c	652 457	0	8
1 Oct 1549–30 Sep 1550	34 762	3	4d	378 338	7	0d	413 100	10	4
1 Oct 1550–31 Jul 1551	2 777	14	0	288 299	6	6	291 077	0	6
Totals	1 298 593	5	6	2 671 552	0	6	3 970 145	6	0

a This figure includes production at Canterbury down to 30 Apr 1546
b These figures include production at Tower II down to 31 Dec 1547
c This figure includes production at Bristol and York down to 31 Oct 1549
d These figures include production at Tower I down to 31 Oct 1550 and at Southwark (gold only) down to 31 Dec 1550.

Source:
The accounts listed in C. E. Challis, 'The debasement of the coinage, 1542–1551', *Economic History Review*, 2nd ser., xx (1967), 457–66, where a breakdown of production, mint by mint, is also given. *Note:* In Table 9 the figure of 17 700 lbs 0½ oz (silver production at Southwark between April and September 1550) should read 17 007 lbs 0½ oz and the calculations in this present article take account of this.

represent total mint production during these years, for after Michaelmas 1547 some of the under-treasurers' accounts, in which coinage production is recorded, have not survived.[1] To arrive at a figure for total gross coin output in the years 1544 to 1551, therefore, it is necessary to supplement the record of actual coin production with estimates for the gaps where the record is incomplete. One basis for establishing such estimates is the accounts of Sir Edmund Pekham, high treasurer of the

[1] For this and subsequent remarks on the mint accounts see C. E. Challis, 'The debasement of the coinage, 1542–1551', *Economic History Review*, 2nd ser., xx (1967), pp. 444–5, 448–53.

mints, to whom most of the profits of debasement were paid. Unlike his subordinates, the under-treasurers, who noted in their accounts the exact amount of coin produced as well as the profit arising from its manufacture, Sir Edmund was simply concerned with the fiscal success of debasement and usually recorded in his accounts only the amount of profit he received from each under-treasurer. Not all the profits of debasement came Sir Edmund's way, it is true, but the vast majority did. And since his accounts cover the entire period from 1544 to 1551 the profit made from coinage at a particular mint is known in broad outline even though the actual record of production may have disappeared. This knowledge of the fiscal success of debasement enables us to guess at the missing production figures in the following way. The figures noted in Pekham's accounts are net profits and, if we assume that the ratio between these profits and the face value of coin produced was the same as that between net profit and face value as shown in the accounts of the under-treasurers, it follows that the £94,419 in profits from the English mints, which Pekham's accounts show to have been made over and above the profits recorded in the under-treasurers' accounts, represented a coin output of about £330,000. Again, assuming that the ratio of gold to silver production (measured at face value) revealed in the reckonings of the under-treasurers is typical of the pattern of production in general, this total of £330,000 may possibly have consisted of £110,000 in gold, and £220,000 in silver. Clearly, these are large assumptions, but if the resulting estimates do not do too much violence to the true course of events, and if we also include here the production of debased coin between 1542 and 1544 (£15,595 in gold, and £52,927 in silver) which was not released until 1544,[1] the total gross output of English coin between June 1544 and July 1551 may have been in the region of £4·3 million, £1,424,000 being in gold and £2,944,000 in silver.[2]

---

[1] Ibid., Table 1 and p. 445.

[2] Some qualification both to these and other figures calculated on the basis of the official accounts is imposed by what we know of coinage on private account. In 1549 Sir William Herbert was licensed, in recompense for his services to the

Now it is clear that these figures of gross coin output aid our enquiry concerning the size of the circulating medium during these years only in so far as it is possible to establish what percentage of the whole constituted a net addition to the existing stock of coin, and here a number of factors must be taken into account. Firstly, to what extent did the output of new coin consist of the reminting of existing coin? Secondly, was there any exportation of English coin and/or importation of foreign coin and, if so, what were the quantities involved? And, thirdly, how far were the issues of legal coin augmented by counterfeiting?

Of all these problems perhaps the last is the most difficult to answer because, although the activities of the hangman and of the Privy Council, the record of the statute book and of the pardon roll, besides practices such as the manufacture of counterfeit English coin in foreign mints,[1] leave us in no doubt that counterfeiting of English coin was an ever-present problem in the sixteenth century, we simply do not know how representative this type of information is of the general course of

---

Crown, to have 2000 lb of fine silver bullion coined at the mint, receiving back all profits once the charges of coinage had been deducted. Similar grants were made to Warwick, Arundle, Southampton, Paget, Dorset, Bedford and Northampton, while Sir Thomas Wentworth and Sir Thomas Darcy were allowed to have 2000 lb coined between them, Huntingdon, Clinton and Cobham 1000 lb each, and Mary Howard, Duchess of Richmond, 500 lb. The total amount of profit diverted to this privileged group, and therefore unrecorded in the official accounts, which were concerned only with profits accruing to the king, was a little short of £70,000 and represented a coinage of about £150,000. Whether this coinage arose simply through the exceptional political circumstances of 1549 or was a continuation of a practice begun in the reign of Henry VIII is far from clear. And in view of this uncertainty the question of coinage on private account has been excluded here as a factor influencing the size of the circulating medium. This has the effect of deflating some totals, especially that for coin output 1549–51, but, since the known sum involved is hardly large when compared either with the total given above for gross coin output (£4·3 million) or that suggested below for the circulating medium in July 1551 (£2·5 million), the general argument is not seriously distorted.

(B.M. Harl. MSS. 660 fos. 67 and 69; J. A. Froude, *The Reign of Edward the Sixth* (Everyman), pp. 150–1. Gerard Malynes remarked that Henry VIII allowed some of his nobles to convert their plate into base coin, but upon what evidence is uncertain. R. Ruding, *Annals of the Coinage* (1840), I, 300–1 n. 6.)

[1] F. B. M. Tangelder, *Muntheer en Muntmeester* (Arnhem, 1955), pp. 169, 257, 311.

events. It may be that the majority of the activities of the counterfeiter went unrecorded, for presumably they were pursued as secretly as possible. But we cannot be sure. And here we come to the crux of the problem. For if we cannot ascertain how representative is the extant information on counterfeiting, we are no nearer to an understanding of how counterfeiting affected the circulating medium quantitatively, which is our main consideration here. At the outset, then, we must acknowledge that we do not really know how issues of legal coin were augmented by counterfeiting.

An examination of the relationship between the output of new coin and the reminting of old is more feasible. As Feavearyear recognized long ago,[1] part of the gold and silver coinage issued during the debasement period was in fact quickly reminted. From January 1546, when the mint price for fine gold was raised to 51s. 0d./oz, it became profitable to recoin the earlier 23 carat issues which had given an ounce of fine gold a denomination of 50s. 1d. Similarly, in the Spring of 1547, when fine gold was enhanced by a commission of 16 March to 58s. 0d./oz, the 22 carat coins of 1545–6, which at issue had rated fine gold at 54s. 6½d./oz, also became vulnerable. Obviously it would be unrealistic to suppose that all undervalued coin did in fact find its way back to the melting pot. For we know through stray references in contemporary accounts, as well as from the survival of the actual coins themselves, that some old coin was preserved intact, and it is no surprise to find that, from time to time, the Government saw fit to revalue old coins so that their face value might once more accord with the current mint price.[2] But for all this, it would seem reasonable to argue that the majority of coins were in fact reminted once it became profitable to do so. Taxation was heavy in incidence and efficiently levied in mid-sixteenth-century England,[3] and this, together with the failure of some incomes to rise at the same

---

[1] A. E. Feavearyear, in *The Pound Sterling*, ed. E. Victor Morgan (Oxford, 1963), p. 60.

[2] *Tudor Royal Proclamations*, ed. P. L. Hughes and J. F. Larkin (New Haven and London, 1964–9), I, No. 326.

[3] R. S. Schofield, *Parliamentary Lay Taxation, 1485–1547*, unpub. Ph.D. thesis (Cambridge, 1963), chap. 7.

speed as prices,[1] would have reduced the possibility of holding cash reserves. At the same time an appreciable rise in mint prices during the debasement period[2] offered a positive inducement to take old coin to be reminted and the assiduity with which some merchants are known to have plied the mints with specie[3] attests to the force of this attraction. Consequently, in the calculations which follow, the totals for withdrawals have been set at the maximum which could have been withdrawn at any given time. Clearly, this will tend to overstate the effect of withdrawals on the circulating medium, the degree of distortion depending on the rate of survival of undervalued coin, and our final estimate of the circulating medium will be to that extent deflated. Bearing this limitation in mind, let us set the amount of gold coin which could have been withdrawn during the debasement as a result of rising mint prices at £554,000 (i.e. all the debased gold at 22 and 23 carat produced between 1542 and 1546) and estimate, in consequence, that the net output of gold coin during the debasement period was of the order of £870,000.

The likely withdrawal of silver during the corresponding period was roughly the same as for gold, totalling, perhaps, £539,000. Part of this figure came, as in the case of gold, in response to a change in mint price, since both the 9 oz issue of 1544–5, which had given an ounce of fine silver a denomination of 5s. 4d., and the 9 oz 2 dwt issue of 1542–4 became vulnerable when the mint price for fine silver rose to 5s. 8d./oz in September 1548.[4] But in addition to the £202,000 which might have been withdrawn in this way the silver coinage also suffered

---

[1] E. H. Phelps Brown and Sheila V. Hopkins, 'Seven centuries of the prices of consumables, compared with builders' wage rates'. See pp. 18–41 of this volume.

[2] Challis, op. cit., p. 446.

[3] In this connection see a number of letters relating to the years 1544 to 1546 amongst the correspondence of John Johnson, merchant of the Staple, and his business associates. These letters were transcribed by Dr Barbara Winchester in an appendix to *The Johnson Letters*, unpub. Ph.D. thesis (London, 1953), where they are numbered 61, 62, 64, 67, 154, 166, 174, 335, 369 and 373.

[4] In theory the raising of the mint price for fine silver to 10s. 0d./oz from October 1550 should also have placed in jeopardy the 6oz silver issue of 1545–6, which at issue had valued fine silver at 8s. 0d./oz (Table 5), but in practice we may doubt if this were so. From the scanty evidence available it seems that Sir John

from the government manipulations of 1548–9, when at least £337,000 in testons was withdrawn for the purposes of re-coinage.[1] When due allowance has been made for all these possible withdrawals, it seems that the silver coinage may still have approached £2,405,000 on the eve of the revaluation in the summer of 1551.[2]

In practice, of course, these net figures for gold and silver –

York, who was engaged in supplying the Crown with silver bullion as well as minting coin, was allowed to claim the rate of 10s 0d./oz, even as he had the rate of 7s. 2d./oz (Challis, op. cit., Tables 9 and 10), as a special favour, to recompense him for the great pains and losses he had sustained while serving the king (*Acts of the Privy Council of England*, ed. J. R. Dasent (1890–1907), III, 316, 332; P.R.O. E159/331 Rec. Trin. 41 m. 15d–16, E351/2079). Precisely what these losses were is not clear, but we do know that Sir John was one of several merchants who had bullion confiscated by the Flemish authorities in March 1551 (*The Chronicle and Political Papers of King Edward VI*, ed. W. K. Jordan (1966), p. 54). It is because it looks as though the rate of 10s. 0d./oz for fine silver was a special concession to York, rather than a public mint price of which anyone could take advantage, that it is ignored here as a factor influencing the withdrawal of current coin.

[1] P.R.O. E101/303/6, E101/302/25, E159/331 Rec. Trin. 41, E351/2078, E101/296/18; Guildhall Library London, Thomas Gresham's Day Book, 4001, 4434, 4542, 4649, 4719. I owe these last references to the editor, Professor Ramsey.

[2] At first sight an estimate of £2·4 million for the debased silver in circulation in July 1551 looks high when it is recalled that at the time of the Elizabethan re-coinage of base money little more than £667,000 was withdrawn; the equivalent of £953,000 before the revaluation of 1561, or about £1,906,000 before that of 1551 (calculated from P.R.O. E351/2185, SP65/6). Between 1551 and 1561, how-ever, several factors combined to reduce the size of the debased coinage in circu-lation and make it possible to reconcile the estimate given above with the figure suggested by the accounts for the recoinage. (1) The revaluations of 1551 reduced the face value of the silver coinage by 50 per cent and in so doing made possible the recoinage on private account of the 6 oz silver issue of 1545–6, which had had a denomination at issue of 96s. 0d. and a total face value of over £440,000 (Tables 1 and 5). It seems reasonable to suppose that by 1560 all but a fraction of this coinage had in fact found its way back to the mint. (2) Between 1555 and 1559 some debased silver was withdrawn from circulation for the purposes of manufacturing Irish coin 3 oz fine. The sum involved is not precisely known be-cause, though the commissions ordering these issues specified the sums to be sent to the mint, they were not always equally explicit as to the proportion to be used (and therefore preserved) for coinage expenses. However, making allow-ance for those sums definitely known to be intended to cover expenses, £68,000 (or £136,000 prior to the 1551 revaluation) seems a reasonable estimate for coin withdrawn under this head (P.R.O. AO1/1670/497; *C.P.R. Philip & Mary*, III, 82, 83, 532, 369; IV, 12, 72, 74; P.R.O. SP65/6). (3) Some base coin seems to have been exported at the time of the Elizabethan recoinage (P.R.O. SP12/14, No. 59, Hughes and Larkin, op. cit., No. 472).

£870,000 and £2,405,000 – were not additions to the existing stock of coins but replacements, since it is clear that the same process which swept away the better debased issues would also have removed the standard coins of both gold and silver produced before major debasement began. The size of this existing stock of coin is again conjectural but, since it seems likely that the reduction of 1526 would have resulted in the disappearance of the bulk of the issues before that date, we may not be too wide of the mark in guessing that it did not exceed the total production of both gold and silver between 1526 and 1544.[1] As can be seen from Tables 2 and 3 the record of mint production during these years, though more full than formerly we have been led to believe, is still far from complete: the gaps in the evidence amounting to about 13 per cent of the entire

TABLE 2 *Known production of English silver coin, 1526–1544**

Date				Weight of coin		Face value		
				lbs	oz	£	s	d
22 Oct	1526–4	Jun	1527	13 703	3½	30 832	8	1½
4 Jun	1527–20 May		1530	94 755	4	213 199	10	0
20 May	1530–1	Mar	1533	40 405	1	90 911	8	9
1 Mar	1533–30 Oct		1534	20 467	11¾	46 052	19	0¾
30 Sep	1536–29 Sep		1537	18 897	6	42 519	7	6
30 Sep	1537–30 Apr		1538	5 783	0	13 011	15	0
22 Apr	1538–21 Apr		1542	69 171	0	155 634	15	0†
30 Sep	1542–29 Sep		1543	2 578	0	5 800	10	0
30 Sep	1543–31 Mar		1544	2 408	0	5 418	0	0
		Totals		268 169	2¼	603 380	13	5¼

*Neither this nor Table 3 takes account of the secret production of debased coin between 1542 and 1544 since this was not disbursed until after debasement had been openly announced in 1544.

†The document which refers to this period of production states that coinage was from the beginning of 30 Henry VIII until the end of 33 Henry VIII and these dates are indicated here. If the exchequer year beginning or ending in each of these regnal years was intended, however, the period of production would have been 30 Sep 1538 to 29 Sep 1541.

Source: P.R.O. E101/303/2, AO1/1595/1, E101/302/20, E101/303/8, AO1/1595/3, B.M. Harl. MSS. 698 fos. 20–21d.

[1] This method of adding together annual coinage output for a number of years in order to obtain some idea of the size of the circulating medium has been used to calculate the size of the circulating medium in eighteenth-century Russia, and in seventeenth-century France. F. Braudel and F. C. Spooner, 'Prices in Europe from 1450 to 1750', *Cambridge Economic History of Europe*, IV (Cambridge, 1967), p. 444.

TABLE 3 *Known production of English gold coin, 1526–1544*

Date		Weight of coin		Face value		
		lbs	oz	£	s	d
1526–	1544*	746	6¾	20 157	3	9†
30 Sep 1526–29 Sep	1530	7 016	4	176 285	7	6
30 Sep 1530–29 Sep	1531	320	3	8 046	5	7½
1 Mar 1533–30 Oct	1534	1 087	0¼	27 311	7	11½
30 Sep 1536–29 Sep	1537*	31	5¼	848	16	3
		1 011	0¾	25 402	18	10½
30 Sep 1537–31 May	1540	3 113	2	78 218	6	3
30 Sep 1540–29 Sep	1541*	28	10	778	10	0
		432	7	10 868	13	1½
30 Sep 1542–29 Sep	1543	275	6	6 921	18	9
30 Sep 1543–31 Mar	1544*	31	6	850	10	0
		181	9	4 566	9	4½
	Totals	* 838	4	22 635	0	0
		13 437	8¼	337 621	7	5½

*Gold 23 carat 3½ gr fine (£27/lb); the rest was crown gold (£25 2s. 6d./lb).

†Undated, but attributed to this period on the grounds that the presence of george nobles in this pyx testifies that the year was not earlier than 1526, when these coins were introduced, and not later than 1544 when coinage at this standard finally gave way to debased issues. Since this production does not seem to belong to the periods covered by the known accounts and records of pyx trials it ought, perhaps, to be attributed to the years for which no evidence seems to have survived. In order to minimize possible distortion through double counting it is assumed that the 400 lb in gold produced from plate sent to the mint in October and November 1536 and yet not included in the warden's account for that year forms part of this larger total.

Cf. H. Symonds, 'The documentary evidence for the English royal coinages of Henry VII and Henry VIII', *British Numismatic Journal*, 1st ser., x, 148. It was in this article that the records of the pyx trials used in the construction of both this and the preceding table were first made generally available. The figures for coinage production between 1537 and 1540 were printed in detail by Miss Nora Milnes in 'Mint records in the reign of Henry VIII', *English Historical Review*, xxxII (1917), 270–3. Other, more general series including the period 1526–44 have been published by G. C. Brooke and Miss E. Stokes, 'Tables of bullion coined from 1377–1550', *Numismatic Chronicle*, 5th ser., IX (1929), and Sir John Craig, *The Mint* (Cambridge, 1953), Appendix I.

Source: B.M. Lans. MSS. 4, fos. 209–210, P.R.O. S.P.1/167 pp. 110–11, E101/ 303/2, AO1/1595/1, E101/302/20, AO1/1595/2, AO1/1595/3, B.M. Harl. MSS. 698, fos. 20–21d.

period in the case of silver, and about 27 per cent in the case of gold. Since production varied a good deal from one year to the next it is difficult to estimate what output might have been during these lacunae, but here a solution has been tentatively reached by calculating from the surviving records for the entire period 1526–44 the average monthly production for gold and silver respectively and then using these figures to establish a total for each gap in the evidence. Altogether, perhaps another £97,000 should be added to the figure for silver production (£603,380), and another £131,000 to that for gold (£360,256), so that the total production of all coin between 1526 and March 1544 may possibly have amounted to £1·19 million.[1] Comparing this total with the one already suggested for July 1551 it is tempting to conclude that one result of the debasement of the coinage between 1544 and 1551 was to increase the size of the circulating medium about two and a half times.

But this pattern of events suggested by a survey of coinage production needs to be modified in the light of gains caused by the importation of foreign coin, and losses due to the drainage of English coin abroad. Throughout the debasement period there are frequent references to the currency of foreign coins in England, and it would be possible to construct from records, such as royal proclamations and cases of confiscation of coin

---

[1] Compare Feavearyear's view that 'in 1542 there was in circulation in England at least £400,000 worth of silver coin'. Feavearyear, op. cit., p. 61. Note also that this figure of £1·19 million takes cognizance neither of additions to the circulating medium – in the form of coin produced abroad or at the English mints in Canterbury, Durham, and York – nor of losses due to an efflux of English coin. The amount of coin involved in each case is unknown but we may guess that not only was the quantity of foreign and 'provincial' coin small in comparison with the output of the London mint, but also that the failure to take account of this in our estimate of the circulating medium will be offset, to some extent at least, by a similar failure to take account of coin which was exported. The accepted view that 'the bishops' privilege of coinage ceased in November 1534 with the passing of Cromwell's famous Act of Supremacy' has been challenged with reference to coinage at Canterbury by the late Professor Reddaway. C. A. Whitton, 'The coinages of Henry VIII and Edward VI in Henry's name', *British Numismatic Journal*, XXVI (1949–51), 58; T. F. Reddaway, 'Two Tudor Notes', *British Numismatic Journal*, XXXIV (1965), 121–5. For examples of the exportation of English coin see T. F. Reddaway, 'The King's Mint and Exchange in London 1343–1543', *English Historical Review*, LXXXII (1967), 21. For foreign coins in circulation in England see Hughes and Larkin, op. cit., I, Nos. 102, 103, 111, 112, 178, 180.

brought before the Exchequer court, a long list of denominations from many lands. That foreign coin should find currency in England is not surprising, for fine gold and silver was, by the very certainty of its value, always likely to be internationally acceptable, and of the bimetallic flows which would account for particularly concentrated movements of coin at certain times something is said below. Here it is necessary to estimate only the quantity of foreign coin in circulation and in this connection an estimate made for the government in 1559 is of some interest.[1] In 1559 the total for Spanish rials and pistolets and French crowns was put at £50,000 and, even if we assume that this was fairly inaccurate – for, after all, it takes account of only some of the foreign coins likely to be in circulation at that time[2] – an error of the magnitude even of, say, 500 per cent still would not result in an estimate for foreign coin which is more than 10 per cent of what seems, as we shall see, to be a reasonable estimate for the circulating medium in July 1551. In other words, it may be that foreign coin was only a small part of the circulating medium at the time of the debasement of the coinage, especially if we are right in concluding that, as a result of the Government's misguided policy of overvaluing foreign coin between 1554 and 1559, and thereby encouraging its importation into England,[3] foreign coin would have been even less plentiful in 1551 than it was to be in 1559. The figure to be added to our estimate of the circulating medium to take account of foreign coin is clearly problematical. But let us tentatively adopt the near-contemporary figure of £50,000.

Finally, we must glance briefly at the way in which the circulating medium was effected by the drainage of coin out of England. And here a number of factors seem to be of particular

---

[1] B.M. Add. MSS. 40,061 fos. 11*v*–12; *Calendar of State Papers, Domestic Series, 1601–03, Addenda (1547–65)*, ed. Mary A. E. Green (1870), Eliz. I, IX, No. 71.

[2] In Mary's reign French crowns, 'all manner of crowns of the Emperor's coin', Spanish ducats and rials, pistolets, and Portuguese crusados had been declared legal tender. It was not until 15 November 1561 that all foreign coins, other than French, Flemish or Burgundian crowns, were demonetized. Hughes and Larkin, op. cit., II, Nos. 408, 412, 487.

[3] Ibid., Nos. 408, 412, 472.

importance: the balance of trade, expenditure on war and bi-metallic flows. About the balance of trade it is difficult to say much because our knowledge of the relative value, and movement, of imports and exports at this time is very unsatisfactory. The boom in cloth exports which characterized these years[1] may mean that the balance was favourable and that there was a movement of coin into England. Such a movement is certainly difficult to reconcile with the trading accounts of Thomas Gresham for 1546 to 1551, which suggest that, far from being able to import any quantity of foreign specie, Gresham was obliged to import goods to sell at no profit or even a slight loss in order to repatriate the proceeds of his cloth sales in Antwerp.[2] It is impossible to say whether Gresham's case was typical but if this were not so the specie which his fellow merchants brought home may possibly be accounted for in the figure for foreign coin discussed above. If the balance of trade was adverse, of course – as indeed one contemporary suggested it might be[3] – we should expect England to lose coin, and our estimate of the circulating medium would have to be deflated accordingly. Whichever possibility obtained it may not be too unrealistic to suppose that the vulnerable element in the coinage would be gold, because gold was attractive by virtue both of its value in relation to bulk and its international acceptability. And the same considerations may also have resulted in gold becoming vulnerable due to the Government's expenditure on war. Between 1544 and 1550 about £3·5 million was poured out on campaigns in France and the borders of England,[4] and from the fact that expenditure on the French territories alone – Boulogne, Calais, Guines and Newhaven – amounted to £1·7 million, it is clear that foreign war could have denuded the circulating medium to a considerable extent. Yet since we know

[1] F. J. Fisher, 'Commercial trends and policy in sixteenth-century England', *Economic History Review*, x (1940), 96.

[2] I owe this information to the editor.

[3] 'We spende and consume with in thys Reme swche sumes and quantytys of forin comodytys that all the wolle, clothe, tyn, lede, lether, and coles, and other mercha[n]dys to be caryyd owte of thys Reme, ys not abyll to contarvayle, paye, or Recompense for the sayde marchandys browghte in to the Reme.' *Tudor Economic Documents*, ed. R. H. Tawney and Eileen Power (1951), II, 184.

[4] P.R.O. SP 10/15, No. 11.

that part of this expenditure went on provisions bought in England, and part too, like £114,484 disbursed by Pekham to Richard Gresham and others,[1] was paid over by exchange, it is doubtful if war was in practice the drain on specie which at first sight it appears. Even so, some coin was certainly shipped overseas, as, for example, £17,600 sent to Henry VIII during his visit to Boulogne and a further £110,721 sent over to Boulogne, Calais and Guines once the king had returned from his triumph,[2] and it seems possible that such movements of specie would have primarily[3] involved gold – the less debased and more acceptable element in the currency.

The suggestion that it was gold which was the more vulnerable part of the currency is supported by what we know of likely bimetallic flows at this time. As contemporaries recognized and Sir Charles Oman had long since demonstrated,[4] the various manipulations during the debasement underrated gold in terms of silver, sometimes to a quite serious extent. In 1546, for example, the English ratio of gold to silver stood at 1:5; whereas in France the écu d'or à la croix rated in terms of the douzain gave a ratio of 1:10·69; in the Netherlands the gold real rated in terms of the silver Karolus florin gave a ratio of 1:10·82; and in Spain the Castilian escudo rated in terms of the silver real gave a ratio of 1:10·61.[5] In such circumstances it was

---

[1] P.R.O. E351/2077. This figure includes £1,666 13s. 4d. not specifically said to have been paid over by exchange.

[2] Ibid.; B.M. Salisbury MSS. M485/1, p. 81, 'A Shorte Abrigement of the Money Sent to Bulloyn, Callys & Guijsnes Sens the coming of the Kings Maj[es]tie from Bulloyn'. The printed version of this (H.M.C. Salisbury, I, No. 188) is inaccurate.

[3] But not entirely. That some English silver crossed the Channel is clear from the fact that in the Low Countries in 1544 English silver coin was either completely unacceptable or taken only at a discount, while in 1546 the English troops there were paid off partly in debased English silver coin. In 1545 the Scots thought so poorly of the debased English silver which had come their way that 'the grote with the braid face' was forbidden. *Letters and Papers . . . of the Reign of Henry VIII*, ed. Brewer, Gairdner and Brodie (1862–1929), XIX, i, Nos. 583, 654, 763, 836, 869; XXI, i, No. 1202; XX, i, No. 1163.

[4] C. W. C. Oman, 'The Tudors and the currency, 1526–1560', *Transactions of the Royal Historical Society*, New Series, IX (1895), 179.

[5] The first ratio is taken from Oman (op. cit.) and the last from E. J. Hamilton, *American Treasure and the Price Revolution in Spain, 1501–1650* (Cambridge, Mass., 1934), p. 71. The others have been calculated from statistics in J. Lafaurie, *Les*

only natural that English gold should be exported to the Continent, there to be exchanged for a larger amount of silver than it had been worth at home. In turn, the silver could then be brought back to England and, after being put into the mint, used to buy more gold. The whole process might then be repeated. The way to such exploitation was far from clear. In England the exportation of coin without licence had long been forbidden, under pain of being judged a felon and forfeiting the goods seized. Details of these confiscations are recorded on the Memoranda rolls and between 1544 and July 1551 we can study twenty-eight such cases, involving sums totalling just short of £800.[1] The extent of this evidence is not great, but, since gold was the exclusive concern in twenty-one cases and part of the issue in three more, it does seem reasonably clear that it was primarily gold which the merchants were anxious to take out of the country. This impression is reinforced by other, scattered evidence. The few surviving rough books of the tellers of the Exchequer, in which were recorded the actual coins received in payment of taxes, suggest that gold gradually disappeared from circulation in England between Michaelmas 1544 and Easter 1551.[2] In 1549, when William Thomas, clerk to the Privy Council, reported the view that there was little gold in circulation,[3] the decision to make the penalty for illegal

---

Monnaies des Rois de France (Paris, 1956), and H. Enno van Gelder and Marcel Hoc, *Les Monnaies des Pays-Bas bourguignons et espagnols 1434–1713* (Amsterdam, 1960). In passing it should be noted that as far as the ordinary citizen was concerned ratios established by comparing the values of gold and silver coins at the time of issue will overstate the degree of disequilibrium since the exaction of seigniorage ensured that the price paid at the mint for bullion was less than the face value of the coin issued. 'The rise of the mint price was at no time commensurate with the degree of debasement, because minting on private account was subject to excessive seigniorage and mint charges. After 1546, these charges even exceeded the mint price, since every pound of fine silver was coined into £7. 4s., of which the government retained as much as £4. 4s. for seigniorage and paid only £3 to those who brought silver to the Mint.' So (with slight exaggeration as to the mint price for fine silver) R. de Roover, *Gresham on Foreign Exchange* (Cambridge, Mass., 1949), p. 53.

[1] P.R.O. E159/323–330 Recorder, *passim*.

[2] P.R.O. E405/483, 491, 494.

[3] *The Works of William Thomas, Clerk of the Privy Council in the Year 1549*, ed. A. D'Aubant (1774), p. 173.

exportation of coin include imprisonment 'at his highness' will and pleasure, over and beside such pains and forfeiture as be in such case by the laws and statutes of the realm appointed', arose directly from the Government's determination to check an efflux of gold.[1] And in January 1551 William Lane gave it as his opinion when writing to Cecil that '. . . in the monthes of June, Julij, and awguste laste . . . was caryyd owte of ynglond not so lyttyll as a hundarthe thowsand powndes of gold; and yette dyd there sylvar cume in to the land as faste, and all for the private gayne in quynynge the sylvar styll, and also was caryyd awaye, for that the pownd of gold ys Rychar than the pownd of whyte mony'.[2] In the last resort the extent to which bimetallic flows did reduce the size of the English circulating medium would depend on the extent to which gold exported to the Continent was replaced by goods other than silver. For only if the English gold passing over to the Continent was '"returned" by the import of goods or the purchase of bills of exchange'[3] instead of in silver coin would it have constituted a net outflow of specie, thus diminishing the quantity of coin in circulation. In the passage already alluded to, Lane suggests that the efflux of gold was in fact matched by an influx of silver but in view of his further statement – 'and also was caryyd awaye' – it does not look as if this gain in silver was permanent. However this may be, if we work on the assumption that none of the gold which was exported from England was replaced by specie – thereby maximizing the effect of the bimetallic flow on the circulating medium – and if we also bear in mind the possibility that an adverse balance of payments, caused either by trade or the demands of war, could also have reduced the amount of gold in England, it is possible to argue that gold virtually disappeared from circulation during the debasement period. If this were so, our estimate of the circulating medium would need to be reduced by £870,000 to £2,455,000. Clearly, since it is unlikely either that every single scrap of gold was drawn out of

---

[1] Hughes and Larkin, op. cit, I, No. 326.

[2] Tawney and Power, op. cit., II, 183.

[3] Professor Supple's phrase in 'Currency and commerce in the early seventeenth century', *Economic History Review*, 2nd ser., x (1957–8), 242.

England or that there was absolutely no compensatory influx of silver,[1] such a conclusion must inevitably involve some exaggeration. Yet it may be near the truth.

The fortunes of the gold component of the circulating medium are thus crucial to an understanding of how the circulating medium was affected by seven years of debasement. And in making our choice between that estimate which does include English gold – £3,325,000, consisting of £2,405,000 in debased silver, £50,000 in foreign coin, and £870,000 in English gold – and that which does not – £2,455,000 – it is useful to consider the contemporary view of events by alluding once more to the estimate made for the Government in 1559. This estimate set the total coinage in circulation at that time at £1,820,000, divided in the following way:

	£
Fine sovereigns, ½ sovereigns, angels, ½ angels, crowns	100 000
Spanish rials, pistolets and French crowns	50 000
Fine gold and sterling silver of Edward VI	100 000
Fine gold and sterling silver of Mary	370 000
Base silver	1 200 000

Clearly, before this figure can be compared with those suggested above for 1551, it is necessary to deduct from it the fine gold and silver produced during the reigns of Edward and Mary – for this was made after July 1551, the terminal date for the estimates discussed here. Then, since silver lost half its value in the late summer of 1551, we must double the 1559 estimate of base English coin in order to make it comparable with the similar estimate for July 1551, which was calculated at pre-revaluation rates. The net result of these adjustments to allow for events which took place after July 1551 is that the 1559 estimate would lead us to believe that in July 1551 the circulating medium stood at £2,550,000 (£100,000 in English

[1] But this factor should not be overstressed. Any silver which came into the country and was subsequently held as plate does not concern us here, while an influx of silver which was either coined at the mint or allowed to circulate in its existing form would be accounted for in the figures for silver production and foreign coin given above.

gold, £50,000 in foreign coin, and £2,400,000 in base silver) – a total which is remarkably similar to the minimum estimate of £2,455,000 discussed above. This similarity, of course, stems from the fact that both the estimate suggested here, which discounts English gold completely, and that established from the 1559 total, which includes only £100,000 of English gold, play down the significance of the yellow metal. Obviously we cannot be sure that such an emphasis is justified. But it does seem a reasonable possibility. Consequently, let us tentatively conclude that by the end of July 1551 the circulating medium had risen to approximately £2·5 million[1] (apportioned roughly as the 1559 estimate would suggest), or about twice the size it may have been before the Great Debasement began, and in so doing came to consist almost entirely of silver.

III

If this analysis of the way in which the debasement of the coinage may have affected the circulating medium has any validity it has significance for the wider discussion on prices, in that it helps us to understand more clearly the behaviour of M – the supply of money – which stands in relation to the other factors in the equation of exchange as follows: $M = \dfrac{PT}{V}$. Naturally, since we do not know the precise composition of the money supply at this time, it may be an oversimplification to infer directly from the fortunes of the gold and silver coinage what was happening to the supply of money in general. But, bearing in mind that in the mid-sixteenth century paper notes, official token money and bank balances transferable by cheque still lay some way in the future, it does look very much as though the supply of money at that time did consist 'overwhelmingly of coins'[2] and, consequently, that alterations in the gold and silver

[1] See above, p. 119, n. 2.
[2] Professor Hamilton's phrase referring to Europe at the end of the fifteenth century. 'History of prices before 1750', XIe Congrès International des Sciences Historiques (Stockholm, 1960), *Rapports*, I, 154.

coinage may not in practice be too untrustworthy a guide to changes in the money supply as a whole.[1]

Proceeding on this basis, let us compare our conclusions concerning changes in the size of the circulating medium with what we know of price movements at this time. According to the indices summarized in Table 4 all prices fluctuated to some extent during the debasement years and all prices showed a

TABLE 4 *Prices in England, 1540–1554 (medians)*

Date	(1)	(2)	(3)	(4)	(5)	(6)
1540–2	7·94	8·46	154	167	171	105
1543–5	9·27	11·26	192	176	191	122
1546–8	8·15	8·19	160	205	214	118
1549–51	18·00	18·48	313	258	276	151
1552–4	10·56	12·66	281	249	270	173

Source: (1) Wheat (s. per qtr) Rogers General Average. Beveridge Price Collection.

(2) Wheat (s. per qtr) Beveridge New General Average. Ibid.

(3) Grains (1450–99 = 100) Bowden Annual Average. Table VI, *Agrarian History of England and Wales*, IV (Cambridge, 1967).

(4) Livestock (1450–99 = 100) Bowden Annual Average. Ibid.

(5) Composite Unit of Consumables (1451–75 = 100) Phelps Brown and Hopkins, op. cit., Appendix B.

(6) Timber (1450–99 = 100) Bowden Annual Average, loc. cit.

marked increase between the beginning of major debasement in 1544 and the revaluation of the coinage late in 1551, the extent of the increase varying from about 25 per cent in the

[1] To argue that gold and silver coins were the most important part of the money supply at this time is not to ignore the possibility that at certain times and in certain places – as, for example, in the London community of international merchants and wholesalers where extensive use was made of the bill of exchange and the obligation – credit instruments could be a supplement to specie. Nevertheless, since such credit instruments were not sufficiently standardized and widely enough known at this time to be generally acceptable, their contribution to the money supply as a whole remains somewhat conjectural. Cf. Outhwaite, op. cit., p. 30 ('. . . the number of instruments which fulfilled the functions of money were extremely limited before the mid-seventeenth century. The growing use of bills of exchange, inland bills, and other securities, sometimes cited in support of a growing *M* is evidence of doubtful validity, since it is arguable that only if such securities are discountable and negotiable can they be stretched so as to fit into the category of money. They had much more important effects on the velocity of circulation than they had on the quantity of money.').

case of timber to about 100 per cent in the case of wheat, according to the Rogers index. This marked rise in prices indicated by the Rogers wheat index is roughly the same as the increase in the circulating medium suggested above (*c.* 100 per cent), but, since the other indices show a smaller, and in some cases a much smaller, increase in prices and we know that wheat prices are particularly susceptible to fluctuations according to the harvest, it hardly seems justifiable on this basis to argue a straightforward correlation between rising prices in general and increases in the circulating medium. This divergence between alterations in the currency and movements in prices is emphasized if we consider the qualitative changes during the debasement (Table 5).

TABLE 5 *Fine gold and silver rated in terms of the coins produced,*
1526–1551

Date	Metal	Fineness of coin		Face value /lb of coin		Rating of fine metal/lb	
1526	Gold	23 c.	3½ gr	£27	0·0s.	£27	2·8s.
		22 c.		£25	2·5s.	£27	8·0s.
	Silver	11 oz	2 dwt		45·0s.		48·6s.
1544	Gold	23 c.		£28	16·0s.	£30	1·0s.
	Silver	9 oz			48·0s.		64·0s.
1545	Gold	22 c.		£30	0·0s.	£32	14.5s.
	Silver	6 oz			48·0s.		96.0s.
1546	Gold	20 c.		£30	0·0s.	£36	0·0s.
	Silver	4 oz			48·0s.		144·0s.
1549	Gold	22 c.		£34	0·0s.	£37	1·8s.
	Silver	8 oz			96·0s.		144·0s.
		6 oz			72·0s.		144·0s.
1551	Gold	23 c.	3½ gr	£28	16·0s.	£28	18·9s.
	Silver	3 oz			72·0s.		288·0s.

Source: Calculated from Tables 2 and 3 above, and Tables 9 and 10 in Challis, op. cit.

Before major debasement began the gold coinage rated fine gold at a little over £27/lb, and the silver coinage rated fine silver at a little over 48s. 0d./lb. At the height of the fraud, on the other hand, these figures stood at a trifle over £37/lb and 288s. 0d./lb, respectively. On this basis we might expect that

K

between June 1544 and July 1551 the effective purchasing power of gold coin was reduced by about one third and that of silver coin by about five-sixths. Consequently, if we are correct in thinking that as debasement wore on the money supply became increasingly dominated by silver, we might also expect the purchasing power of money in general to have fallen roughly in line with that of silver. In practice, however, the increase in prices which the index indicates is much nearer the rise of one third indicated by gold than to the sixfold increase suggested by silver. Even if we assume that the purchasing power of the greater part of the silver currency fell by only two-thirds – which is reasonable in view of the paucity of 3 oz coin produced[1] – we should still expect prices to have tripled if measured entirely by silver standards, and this they manifestly did not.

IV

To conclude that prices did not rise proportionately either to the increase in the volume, or to the decrease in the quality, of the coinage between 1544 and July 1551 is neither new nor particularly surprising. As far back as 1549 observers have doubted if the movement of prices was linked solely and simply with alterations in the currency,[2] and today, when we no longer expect all prices to move simultaneously[3] nor all alterations in

[1] After April 1546 the silver issues at 4, 6 or 8 oz fine, which were all alike in intrinsic value, amounted to over £2 million in coin whereas the known 1551 issue at 3 oz fine, at Southwark and Tower I, was a little short of £173,000. See above, Table 1; Challis, op. cit., Tables 9 and 11. In 1559 the Government estimated that the poorest type of testons was not 'above the sixth part of the number of the whole base testons coined within this realm'. Hughes and Larkin, op. cit., II, No. 471; while another estimate of the same year, referred to above (p. 127), put the figure for the worst sort of testons as high as £300,000.

[2] 'Polices to Reduce this Realme of Englande vnto a prosperus wealthe and estate', Tawney and Power, op. cit., III, 315–6.

[3] 'As Professor W. C. Robinson has clearly explained, all prices would rise or fall together only if there were no differences in the income elasticity of demand for different commodities or in the elasticity of supply. The *a priori* expectation of diverse price movements has been fully borne out by price behavior in all cases of inflation and deflation . . . of which I have any knowledge.' So Hamilton, op. cit., p. 155.

the coinage to be reflected in the price level immediately,[1] we are very much aware that even if we approach inflation through the traditional equation of exchange we shall need to know a great deal more about the velocity of circulation and the level of economic activity before we can begin to understand the impact on the price structure of changes in the supply of money. Obviously in this brief analysis we cannot hope to survey all the factors which might explain the observed disparity between movements in prices and changes in the supply of money but, in conclusion, we may note three factors which on the evidence of the coinage alone would seem to be of some significance.

First of all let us glance at the pattern of specie accumulation between June 1544 and July 1551, which is of interest because the overall increase in the circulating medium at this time does not appear to have been steady and continuous. From 1544 to March 1546 money flowed from the mints in abundance – amounting, if we include the secret issues of 1542–4, to £1,196,133. Consequently, at first glance we might expect the circulating medium, which in 1544 may have stood at £1·19 million, to have risen to about £2·38 million. On the other hand, if we assume that at the same time as this accumulation was taking place withdrawals of standard coin (11 oz 2 dwt, 23 carat 3½ gr, and 22 carat fine) and the first debased issues at 23 carat fine could have denuded the circulating medium of £1·37 million, it is possible to argue that almost two years of feverish mint activity actually reduced the amount of coin in circulation, to approximately £1 million. In practice we may doubt if either an increase to £2·38 million or a reduction to approximately £1 million represents the likely course of events. If we accept that the standard coin which found its way back to the mint in response to increases in the mint price would produce a greater weight of coin when reissued in debased form, it follows that not all of the pre-debasement coin could have been recoined by

---

[1] '. . . prices always betray a pronounced inertia in relation to devaluations and are never automatically adapted to a new parity. The application of gold and silver equivalents, based on the new parity, even when rectified on the basis of free market rates, is for that period of transition purely fictitious'. So H. van der Wee, *The Growth of the Antwerp Market and the European Economy* (The Hague, 1963), I, 121.

the end of March 1546, because to that date the debased coin issued (£1,196,133) scarcely exceeded the £1·19 million which were possibly in circulation on the eve of debasement. Precisely how much of the old coin remained in circulation in March 1546 there is, of course, no accurate way of knowing. But, judging from the fall in the intrinsic value of coin between 1544 and March 1546,[1] we may guess that the debased coin put out in these years would represent the recoinage of, perhaps, only £790,000 in standard coin, so that possibly as much as £401,000 in old coin still remained in circulation. On this basis let us set the circulating medium in March 1546 in the region of £1·41 million.

During the next two and a half years the mints were once again prolific in production, and once again part of this output was counterbalanced by withdrawals of existing coin.[2] Altogether possibly £1·57 million in new coin was produced and £1,366,000 of existing coin – representing the last, save a little gold, of the pre-debasement issues, and all the gold produced since April 1545 – withdrawn, so that by Michaelmas 1548 the circulating medium may have stood at about £1·62 million. In the following year this upward movement of the circulating medium possibly continued. To be sure, the likely withdrawal of the silver produced between 1542 and March 1545, the recall of base testons in general, and the continued drainage away of new gold, which was 'piked out . . . as fast as it came forthe of the minte',[3] almost counterbalanced the production of silver coin at this time, but some of the new silver did in fact represent an addition to the stock of coin which may have risen to £1·71 million. After Michaelmas 1549 silver production was once again sufficient to offset likely losses of gold and still

---

[1] See Table 5 above.

[2] The figures which follow include known production (Table 1) and estimated production (above, p. 119), the latter being apportioned, with an eye both to the profits coming from the mints and, wherever possible, the earlier pattern of production, as follows: Apr 1546–Sep 1548, £90,000; Oct 1548–Sep 1549, £90,000; Oct 1549–July 1551, £150,000. The amount of old gold not withdrawn from circulation has been set at £100,000 in all, as the 1559 estimate would suggest. Since all these figures are only estimates they should be treated as tentative, and thus with caution.

[3] *A Discourse of the Common Weal of this Realm of England*, ed. Elizabeth Lamond (Cambridge, 1954), p. 106.

represent an addition to the circulating medium, but this time the gain was more appreciable, so that by July 1551 there may possibly have been as much as £2·5 million in circulation.[1]

If this analysis is at all near the mark, it seems reasonable to suppose that the most important net additions to the circulating medium came from 1549 onwards and, consequently, if an increased volume of currency did influence the price level it may have done so with significant effect largely in 1550 and 1551. That prices did rise sharply in these years is perfectly clear, but to attribute this rise solely to a marked increase in the circulating medium would almost certainly be too simple an explanation. 1549, 1550 and 1551 are thought of as years of poor harvest[2] and it may well be that it was this deficiency in grain – met to some extent, it is true, by imports from abroad[3] – which pushed up prices so quickly in 1550 and 1551.

Perhaps also contemporaries were not in practice hypersensitive, initially at least, to alterations in the quality of the coinage. For the greater part of the sixteenth century the face value of coin was (allowing for seignorage) tied directly to its intrinsic value and because of this it is possible to assume that contemporaries – who were prevented by the Government from altering the face value of coin – answered each alteration in intrinsic value during the debasement by a corresponding reduction in purchasing power. Thus, if a shilling lost half its intrinsic value and became in effect a piece of sixpence we may be tempted to think that this change would work itself out in practice as a twofold increase in prices with the denomination of the coin remaining constant. But we may doubt if in practice the majority of contemporaries did react to alterations in intrinsic value in this way. Against the much quoted Doctor in the *Discourse*, who was able to discern the 'difference betewne 6 grotes that made [an] oz. of silver, and xij grotes that made an ownce of silver',[4] we must set 'thunlerned and vplandyshe

---

[1] See above, p. 133, n. 2.

[2] W. G. Hoskins, 'Harvest fluctuations and English economic history, 1480–1619', *Agricultural History Review*, XII (1964), 32, 35–6, 45.

[3] C. Wriothesley, *A Chronicle of England*, ed. W. D. Hamilton (1877), II, 30, 37, 45, 47.

[4] Lamond, op. cit., p. 71.

people', who – more numerous than the Doctor then, and certainly less familiar to us now – seem to have found the task of distinguishing a badly debased coin from an even worse one 'no easy thinge'.[1]

In theory, of course, given the weight and fineness of the metal of which a coin was composed, the calculation of intrinsic value was not difficult. And, in practice, for all those with a good touchstone or assaying facilities and an accurate set of balances there was small difficulty either. Mint officials, goldsmiths and other knowledgeable persons such as merchants no doubt fell into this category, but they were few in number and had in any case a private interest in concealing their knowledge, since their whole success in dealing in debased coin depended on their being able to unload it on to an unsuspecting public. The majority of the population cannot have had either the means or the knowledge to calculate intrinsic value accurately and consequently we may surmise that for them the precise value of any given debased coin was unknown. In this situation the physical appearance of a coin must have been all-important, since a good deal about the intrinsic value could be guessed simply from its thickness, colour, circumference and weight. Of these factors the first was probably the least important since it would have been most difficult to measure the actual thickness of a coin – particularly since hammered edges were often imperfect, and natural wear would obscure the true thickness of good coin in any case – and more difficult still to calculate on the basis of a given knowledge of the variation in thickness of a coin how much its intrinsic value was thereby affected. Variations in colour, circumference and weight could be more easily judged. If a coin was ostensibly silver, but billon in fact, no amount of blanching would long conceal the fraud, because the more prominent parts of the design on the coin would wear away to reveal the redness of the alloy beneath. It was the very redness of the Henrician testons which in fact caused so much contemporary comment[2] and which helped to bring

---

[1] P.R.O. SP 12/13 No. 48.

[2] See the extracts from Heywood's epigrams printed in R. Ruding, *Annals of the Coinage* (1840), I, 313 n. 1.

about the improvement in fineness – from 4 oz to 8 oz, or 6 oz fine – under Edward VI. Then, too, if a coin of a high denomination were given a flan and weight which differed but little from that of a much lower denomination, it would be difficult indeed to prevent people from confusing the two and accepting the coin of the higher denomination at the lower value. It will be recalled that it was precisely because the 8 oz silver issue of 1549 gave a shilling a weight of 60 gr, which compared more nearly to the weight of an old sterling groat (42·6 gr) than to that of the earlier shilling piece (or teston, 120 gr), that the issue had been denounced even before the king,[1] and subsequently discontinued. The failure of this 'prety litle shilling', as Latimer called it, seems to have been an object lesson for the future. In January 1551 Sir John York, who was by then the most important under-treasurer at the mint, experimented with a new type of coin, preparatory to the restoration of the coinage later in the year. He planned to strike eleven shillings from every ounce of fine silver, thus giving a shilling a fine silver content of approximately 44 gr. As he rightly argued, this would make the new coin 'rychar than the other mony late made, or now amakynge' since a shilling of the 1549–50 standard – whether 8oz or 6 oz fine – had contained only 40 gr of fine silver. On the other hand, since his new coinage was to be almost sterling, a shilling piece would weigh, even with the admixture of alloy, less than 50 gr, which was less than either the present 6 oz issue (shilling = 80 gr) or the ill-received piece of 1549 (60 gr). It seems likely that it was precisely because Sir John feared that the lightness of his new coin would seriously jeopardize its acceptability that he planned to issue it in pieces of 2s. 0d.[2]

This surmise that coin was acceptable so long as it did not differ too radically in appearance from the older, accepted varieties is supported by the success of the 6 oz silver issue, which was first put out in 1549. In theory this issue had no more to recommend it than its predecessors, since at 72s. 0d./ lb it was of exactly the same intrinsic value as the issues at 4 oz fine (48s. 0d./lb) and 8 oz fine (96s. 0d./lb). However, while the

[1] H. Latimer, *Seven Sermons before Edward VI*, ed. E. Arber (1869), pp. 34–5.
[2] Tawney and Power, op. cit., II, 182–3.

new coin was not as pleasing to look upon as the 8 oz issue, it did avoid the coarseness of the 4 oz coins and partly disguised within its flans, which roughly equalled in size those of the earlier 4 oz issues,[1] not only that it was lighter than the testons put out after 1544, but also that it was not so very much heavier than the coin of the 8 oz issue. The result was an acceptable silver standard in which the larger silver coins were struck, with the exception of the 3 oz shillings of 1551, right down to the restoration of the coinage in 1551. Probably the appearance of the 3 oz issue – the worst coin of the entire debasement – undermined yet again the willingness of some people to accept coin turned out by the English mints. Nevertheless, if the events of the Elizabethan recoinage are any guide, we should guard once more against overstating the degree of panic which the new coins caused. In 1560 the Government decided to re-value the coinage preparatory to recoining it and, consequently, fixed the values of the coins according, or almost according, to their intrinsic value. So uncertain did it seem, however, that people really could distinguish between one coin and another – even though the 3 oz coin was at best only half the value of the other coins in circulation, and could be distinguished from the rest by the slightly different portrait of the king which it bore[2] – that the Government went to considerable pains and expense to have all the base testons counterstamped – the better sort bearing the sign of the portcullis, and the poorer that of the greyhound.[3] For those set in authority, at any rate – and perhaps they were better placed to judge their fellows than we – there was small doubt that the common man could distinguish

[1] C. W. C. Oman, *The Coinage of England* (Oxford, 1931), plates XXVII (4), XXVIII (1, 3).

[2] In the better shilling the image of the king had a short neck and a round face, compared with a long neck and a lean face in the poorer sort. P.R.O. SP 12/14 No. 14. A further distinguishing feature of the poorer teston was that it was 'marked in the uppermost part of the said teston in the border thereof on both sides the teston with one of these four kinds of marks: that is, either of a lion, a rose, a harp, or a *fleur-de-lis*'. The utility of these marks was not necessarily great, however, since they were 'but small and may be partly worn out'. Hughes and Larkin, op. cit., II, No. 471.

[3] For a general account of the countermarking of base testons see W. Cunningham, *The Growth of English Industry and Commerce in Modern Times* (Cambridge, 1903), I, 131 ff.

one debased coin from another only in the crudest of pictorial terms.

It is possible, then, that although contemporaries were well aware of coinage manipulations they could not judge their true extent, and this would certainly help to explain why prices were forced up neither as fast nor as far as the course of debasement might lead one to expect. Between 1544 and 1551 there was undoubtedly alarm over the adulteration of the coinage. But it may be that it was not the reduction in standard and weight of 1544, nor the further reduction in standard of the following year, so much as the issuing of the coarse billon coinage between 1546 and 1549 which really shook confidence and had an appreciable impact on the price level. How great was this impact, and whether it accelerated a trend noticeable from the first alarums in 1544, it is difficult to say. But it seems possible that the withdrawal of Henrician testons – first put out when major debasement began and, therefore, a symbol of all the evils which debasement was thought to have caused – and their replacement by other coins, some of which were shillings of a new stamp at the 6 oz or 8 oz standards, meant that from 1549 until early 1551 confidence in the coinage was to some extent restored and the incentive to increase prices correspondingly reduced. Between April and July 1551, when the silver standard was slashed by half, debasement could have directly influenced prices once more – although the paucity of 3 oz coins actually produced, the revaluation of testons later in the same year,[1] and the production of fine coin from October 1551, must have done much to deaden the impact; but then, during the last ten years of their life, the debased coins gave less cause for alarm. True, the debased currency of the 1550s was a managed currency,[2] circulating above its intrinsic value, and for this very reason likely to cause short-term losses in confidence when it was rumoured that coins were to be called to their intrinsic worth. In 1553, for example, one of the Earl of Shrewsbury's receivers

[1] In the long run the revaluation of the currency so that face value accorded more nearly to intrinsic value would have helped to increase confidence, but in the short run it seems to have caused some price increases. Hughes and Larkin, op. cit., I, Nos. 373, 376, 378, 379.
[2] De Roover, op. cit., p. 68.

paid his money into the mint at York 'bycause there was such a Rumo[ur] here that testons shulde be grots. So that he dare kepe non in his handes.'[1] But in general the debased coin did prove reasonably acceptable and continued to circulate side by side with coins of the finer issues.

To these tentative suggestions of why prices were not rising as fast as the course of debasement might at first lead us to suppose let us add, equally tentatively, a third: namely, that coin was accepted, debased though it was, because it was necessary to the economy. Weighing the possibility recently discussed by Professor Braudel that 'the stock of metal [in the economy] has to be increased regularly for the price level *merely to be maintained*'[2] with our knowledge that bullion remained in short supply in Europe, despite increased supplies – thereby causing bullion prices to rise and coin weights to be reduced[3] – it seems possible that demand for precious metals in early sixteenth-century England outpaced supply, and that when debasement in the 1540s greatly increased the amount of coin in circulation it met a real need. Just how scarce was coined money in pre-debasement England is most difficult to judge, although there are a few indications of shortage. In 1523 the Commons opposed Wolsey's proposed tax on the grounds that if it were levied the stock of coin in England would be exhausted and the economy reduced to a state of barter.[4] In the following year the expedient of allowing payment in plate arose solely from anxiety that stocks of coin were insufficient to meet the Government's demands.[5] In 1524, 1540, 1543 and 1545 the subsidy acts allowed payment in English coins, were they never so cracked or clipped, and in foreign coins, too, for precisely the same reason.[6] And in 1536 part of the argument of the northern rebels against the Act of Annates was that

[1] College of Arms, Talbot MSS., vol. P, fo. 215.

[2] Braudel and Spooner, op. cit., p. 384.

[3] Hence the reduction of coin weights in the early sixteenth century of which the 1526 English reduction was but one example. For a graphic illustration of this see Fig. 4. 'Moneys of account in Europe', Braudel and Spooner, op. cit., p. 458.

[4] E. Hall, *Henry VIII*, ed. C. Whibley (1904), I, 285.

[5] Schofield, op. cit., p. 289.

[6] *Statutes of the Realm* (1810–28), III, 239, 823, 949–50, 1030–1.

'money was sent out of the north, where there was too little coin already'.[1] This problem of scarcity can be posed another way: supposing a population of 3·2 million in 1545[2] and supposing that the total circulating medium at that time was in the region of £1·3 million, the average sum *per capita* – 8s. 1½d. – would be miserably small indeed.[3] An average figure of this kind hardly carries much weight, for between the two extremes of having no coin at all – and to judge from probate inventories this was not exceptional – and holding a large cash fortune must come every degree of liquidity. But the general impression seems to be one of a little money having to go a long, long way. By creating an increased supply of money the debasement could have temporarily eased this situation – reducing the amount of truck or book-credit, or even, perhaps, the use of commodities, as furs were used in sixteenth-century Russia[4] – and in so doing the impact on the price structure of the increased supply of money must necessarily have been reduced.

V

In suggesting that between June 1544 and July 1551 the circulating medium in England may have doubled, and in so doing come to consist almost entirely of silver, this analysis has emphasized the apparent disparity between movements in prices on the one hand, and the increase in the volume, and the decrease in the quality, of the coinage on the other. It has then gone on to suggest three possible explanations for this: namely, that the most important increases in the circulating medium may have come only towards the end of the debasement period; that most contemporaries may not in fact have been very

[1] Madeleine H. and Ruth Dodds, *The Pilgrimage of Grace* (Cambridge, 1915), I, 351.

[2] J. C. Russell, *British Medieval Population* (Albuquerque, 1948), pp. 270–2. Clearly, if the population was less than this figure in 1545 then the sum *per capita* which follows would be greater; if larger, smaller.

[3] 8s. 1½d. in silver, rated at 48s. 0d./lb troy, would weigh 975 gr or 63·18 grammes. By comparison the sum *per capita* in France in 1660 was 141·22 grammes. Braudel and Spooner, op. cit., p. 444.

[4] J. Blum, *Lord and Peasant in Russia* (New York, 1964), p. 131.

sensitive to alterations in the quality of the coinage; and that the economy may have been sufficiently short of specie to enable appreciable additions to be absorbed without affecting the price level directly. Bearing in mind the limitations of the evidence, which at times have given rise to the broadest of generalizations, there is certainly cause to treat these estimates with some caution. And, in view of the many non-monetary influences which could have affected prices at this time, it would be unjustifiable to suppose that these hypotheses alone can explain why alterations in the coinage did not affect prices more directly. As it stands, however, this analysis does help to make sense of a good deal of puzzling contemporary evidence, and serves to increase our curiosity as to the way in which other factors were affecting prices at this time. Especially when we reflect that, on the basis of the estimates put forward here, the circulating medium may have been reduced late in 1551, as a result of the revaluation of the coinage in that year, by almost half – thereby returning to roughly its pre-debasement level; and yet once more there does not seem to have been a direct link between alterations in the coinage and the movement of prices in general.[1] Not until we know a great deal more about the Tudor economy as a whole shall we be able to assess accurately the role which currency manipulations did play in the Tudor inflation.

[1] True, the price of wheat does seem to have been almost as low immediately after the revaluation of 1551 as it had been in 1543–5, but the pattern suggested by the other, more general, indices is very different (Table 4). On this basis it seems more reasonable to conclude that wheat prices fell as they did, not because the circulating medium was greatly reduced in 1551, but simply because 1552 and 1553 were years of good harvest.

6 American Treasure and Andalusian Prices, 1503–1660:

A STUDY IN THE SPANISH PRICE REVOLUTION

EARL J. HAMILTON

This article was first published in the *Journal of Economic and Business History*, vol. I, No. 1 (November 1928)

The extreme variations of prices issuing from the currency disorders occasioned by the World War have focused attention anew upon the facts that changing prices quicken or retard the production of wealth, that they alter the distribution of income, and that in an unpredictable fashion they multiply or devour reserves against contingencies. It is less obvious but none the less true that over long periods of time unstable price relationships play a significant role in the transformation of institutions and in the realignment of classes. For reasons both practical and theoretical it is essential that our knowledge of price changes, both past and present, be as extensive and complete as possible. A thorough investigation of sixteenth-century prices in Spain, which first and foremost felt the full impact of the greatest price revolution in history, is therefore amply justified.

The upheaval of European prices during the sixteenth and seventeenth centuries has long attracted the attention of scholars, and elaborate studies have been made of the phenomenon in England,[1] France[2] and Germany.[3] But it is strikingly

[1] J. E. Thorold Rogers, *A History of Agriculture and Prices in England*, vols. III–VI (1882–1887).

[2] Vicomte d'Avenel, *Histoire Économique de la Propriété, des Salaires, des Denrées, et de Tous Prix en Général*, vols. I–VII (1894–1926).

[3] Georg Wiebe, *Zur Geschichte der Preisrevolution des XVI und XVII Jahrhundert* (1895).

anomalous that nothing worthy of the name of an investigation of Spanish prices has yet been carried out, that Spain, the direct recipient of the treasure imports from the Indies, has hitherto been neglected. Contemporaries were content to make observations concerning the dearness of necessaries – much as men have always complained of the weather and of the high cost of living. Not many of them, however, bothered to state actual prices in an effort to substantiate their contentions, and those who did adduced very few.[1] Among the recent writers on Spanish prices Don Cristóbal Espejo is worthy of mention. In his work as an archivist he has run across a modicum of material, but his method of presentation, that of the archivist or historian, not of the economist or statistician, has deprived his studies of much of their usefulness. He has made no index numbers, but has been content merely to collect the prices of a miscellaneous list of commodities and throw them together without order or any apparent plan.[2] The dearth of information concerning Spanish prices in the sixteenth and seventeenth centuries is attested by the eagerness with which writers have accepted the meagre data of Clemencín, Colmeiro and Haebler, whose work combined can muster a total of twenty-seven prices, derived from secondary sources or from ordinances fixing legal prices, in a list of ten commodities for nine years.[3]

It is also anomalous that the index number, the modern device for measuring price changes, which was invented by Carli for the purpose of investigating the rise in Italian prices caused by the discovery of the rich American mines, and elaborated by Jevons for use in studying the mid-nineteenth-century price fluctuations precipitated by the output of the recently opened Californian and Australian gold fields,[4] has not

---

[1] Cf. for example, Alonso de Carranza, *El Ajustamiento i Proporción de las Monedas de Oro, Plata, i Cobre, i la Reducción destos Metales a Su Debida Estimación* (1629), p. 180; Sancho de Moncada, *Restauración Política de España* (1746. First ed. 1619), p. 54.

[2] Cristóbal Espejo, *La Carestía de la Vida en el Siglo, XVI* (1925).

[3] Cf. Georg Wiebe, op. cit., p. 367.

[4] W. C. Mitchell, 'The making and using of index numbers', *Bulletin of the United States Bureau of Labor Statistics*, No. 284 (1921), p. 7.

hitherto been used in the study of prices in the country where perhaps as never before or since the influence of an increasing supply of gold and silver upon prices stands in clear relief.

As will be shown presently, Spain was unique among the countries of Europe in that her price structure was most affected by American treasure. Andalusia probably towered above the rest of Spain in the same respect. The prevailing mercantilist illusion that treasure is wealth *par excellence* and the corollary that it should be accumulated and impounded within a country at all costs, together with the desire to facilitate the collection of royal dues, led to decrees which required all public and private imports of treasure to be brought up the Guadalquivir to Seville,[1] where most of it was coined and placed in circulation. Hence presumably prices rose in Seville, as well as in the whole of Andalusia, its hinterland, more suddenly and violently than in the rest of Spain, whither, for the most part, gold and silver percolated only through irregular channels of trade.

One of the chief defects of historical price studies in the past has been the failure adequately to distinguish regional or local price areas, and, with the paucity of material available, the national averages are often distorted by the lack of homogeneity in the data. It has therefore seemed desirable to attack the problem of prices in Spain not for the country as a whole but for more limited areas. Because of its pivotal position Andalusia has been selected for the initial study.

To determine the effect of American treasure upon Andalusian prices, it was necessary to have accurate information as to the amounts of gold and silver arriving from the Indies – information which could be obtained only from the original records, for all past accounts of American treasure not based on sheer guesswork have been chiefly concerned with the volume of production in the Indies,[2] which is quite distinct from the amount reaching the motherland.

[1] José de Veitia, *Norte de la Contratación de las Indias Occidentales*, bk II (1672), pp. 74–5; *Recopilación de Leyes de Indias*, lib. ix, tit. xxxiii, ley xxxvii (1681); lib. ix, tit. xxxiv, ley xxx.

[2] Francisco de Laiglesia's 'Los Caudales de Indias en la Primera Mitad del Siglo XVI', *Estudios Históricos* (1908), pp. 299–321, contains an account of the

The gold and silver which came to Spain from her trans-marine possessions – before 1520 from Hispaniola, Cuba, Puerto Rico and Central America, but after, say, 1535 chiefly from Mexico and Colombia and the then Peru – may be roughly classified as public and private. The public treasure consisted largely of receipts from the quint, or fifth,[1] a severance tax on mining; but the crown also received gold and silver from such miscellaneous sources as the sale of papal indulgences, tribute levied upon Indian tribes, and the sale of prayer books. Private treasure was made up of emigrants' remittances, the savings of individuals returning from Spain and the payments due merchants on account of the favourable balance of Spanish trade with the Indies. The last-named item comprised the bulk of the imports; for the colonists, finding themselves in a position to tap the El Dorados in the lands of the Aztecs and Incas, did not care to fritter away their time in such prosaic and unremunerative undertakings as growing crops, tending livestock or manufacturing goods. It was more profitable to mine gold and with it buy other things.

In an effort to promote imports of gold and silver and to secure revenue for an ever-depleted treasury, the crown controlled the movement of bullion from the mouth of the colonial mine to the door of the Castilian mint. The law required all bullion to be carried to royal assay offices, where it was assayed cast in bars or plate and stamped with an official seal.[2] Bullion

---

public treasure reaching Spain during the reign of the Emperor, but private treasure is neglected. Laiglesia's work is based on the records of the treasurer of the House of Trade (Casa de la Contratación). All sums debited in these accounts were considered receipts of treasure from the Indies. Consequently we find that his figures include such extraneous items as the sale in Spain of caravels and of licenses to carry slaves to the Indies.

The resources of the Archive of the Indies have not been utilized in arriving at the production of metals after 1557. Cf. C. H. Haring, 'American gold and silver production in the first half of the sixteenth century', *Quarterly Journal of Economics*, vol. XXIX, pp. 433–79. In the near future I expect to extend Professor Haring's work by a century.

[1] The quint was not uniform. At certain times and places it was as low as a tenth.

[2] Antonio Ulloa, *Noticias Americanas* (1792), p. 215; *Recopilación de Leyes de Indias*, lib. iv, tit. xix, ley ii.

bearing this seal might be shipped to Spain by entering it in the register of mines and in the books of the royal officials at the American port.[1] Treasure had to be listed in the registers of vessels, which registers, upon arrival at Seville, were delivered to the officials of the House of Trade.[2] No matter what unusual circumstances intervened, the House of Trade was the goal of all Indian treasure. The pragmatic of 1529 authorizing sailings to the Indies from diverse ports provided a penalty of death and the confiscation of all of his goods for the captain of the ship failing to return to Seville.[3] Whenever vessels were forced by storms, unseaworthiness, attacks by pirates or aggression by enemies to put in at other ports, the gold and silver had to be sent post-haste to the House of Trade. The responsible officials were enjoined to avail themselves of the safest and fastest means of transportation obtainable.[4]

Royal supervision of every phase of mining and transporting the precious metals and the restriction of imports to a single port facilitated the collection and preservation of data which enable us to determine with precision the volume of treasure imported during most of the period under investigation.

Table 1, compiled entirely from data obtained from documents deposited in the Archive of the Indies at Seville, shows the amounts of treasure received from the Indies between the years 1503 and 1660, the receipts of the crown and those of private individuals being listed separately. The data were secured from the records of the treasurer of the House of Trade, who received the crown treasure; from the annual summaries of the arrivals of public and private treasure, which were compiled by the comptroller of the House of Trade from the registers of ships reaching Spain; from the reports on receipts of gold and silver submitted to the Council of the Indies and the Council of the Treasury by the officials of the House of Trade; and, where better sources were lacking, from the registers of

---

[1] *Recopilación de Leyes de Indias*, lib. iv. tit. xxii, ley i.

[2] Ibid., lib. ix, tit. xxxiii, leyes xxvi-xxvii.

[3] Manuel Colmeiro, *Historia de la Economía Política en España*, vol. ii (1863), p. 402; José de Veitia, op. cit., bk ii, p. 136.

[4] José de Veitia, op. cit., bk ii, pp. 74-5; *Recopilación de Leyes de Indias*, lib. ix, tit. xlii, ley xxvii.

L

treasure ships. In most cases no single source, unchecked by comparison with others, has been relied upon.

Before the conquest of Mexico all of the receipts of treasure

TABLE I *Average yearly treasure imports: five-year periods (in silver maravedís)*

	Public	Private	Total
1503–5	14 582 495	No records	
1506–10	19 246 848	do.	
1511–15	28 191 145	do.	
1516–20	23 419 572	do.	
1521–5	3 163 717	do.	
1526–30	24 486 329	do.	
1531–5	38 912 475	do.	
1536–40	121 579 635	232 830 652	354 410 287
1541–5	68 200 956	377 659 472	445 860 428
1546–50	143 340 441	352 443 547	495 783 988
1551–5	326 565 593	561 332 224	887 897 817
1556–60	141 164 609	578 745 262	719 909 871
1561–5	163 757 969	844 920 233	1 008 678 102
1566–70	340 626 866	932 082 539	1 272 709 405
1571–5	296 879 446	774 715 381	1 071 594 827
1576–80	598 471 066	954 203 622	1 552 674 689
1581–5	679 554 365	1 964 160 726	2 643 715 091
1586–90	723 889 112	1 421 047 635	2 144 936 746
1591–5	902 101 378	2 264 536 250	3 166 637 628
1596–1600	987 688 615	2 110 876 441	3 098 565 056
1601–5	586 789 679	1 609 509 844	2 196 299 523
1606–10	769 471 096	2 056 997 538	2 826 468 634
1611–15	649 162 963	1 558 367 904	2 207 530 867
1616–20	391 300 935	2 318 820 468	2 710 121 403
1621–5	440 204 052	1 990 757 020	2 430 961 072
1626–30	415 692 062	1 830 215 310	2 245 907 373
1631–5	426 044 219	1 113 932 634	1 539 976 853
1636–40	422 217 252	1 046 096 931	1 468 314 183
1641–5	417 929 569	820 812 648	1 238 742 217
1646–50	149 860 132	909 489 115	1 059 349 247
1651–5	201 499 037	454 940 011	656 439 048
1656–60	54 587 172	247 913 248	302 500 420

were in gold. The first silver that could be regarded as more than a sample was the sixty-two marks reaching Seville on 5 November 1519, in the first shipment of Aztec spoils, which Cortés sent by Alonso Fernandez Portocarrero and Francisco de Montejo as a gift to the Emperor. Of this shipment, if we neglect works of art, only 45 per cent by weight was silver.[1] Of the crown treasure sold at auction during the decade 1521–30 about 97 per cent by weight was gold; but with the opening of silver mines in Mexico and Peru in the following decade crown silver was in weight six times as great as gold and in the last decade of the century 187 times as great.

Since the principal purpose of this study is to investigate the influence of Indian treasure upon Andalusian prices, the receipts of gold and silver in Table 1 are, for convenience, stated in terms of the value, expressed in silver maravedís, of the two taken together. To economize space, only yearly averages for five-year periods are given here.

Chart 1 presents the above data in graphic form.

The amounts of private treasure are not stated here for the years prior to 1535 because of a lack of data. In the early years of the House of Trade (founded in 1503) the machinery for keeping accounts was not perfected, and the first receipts of private treasure, naturally not of so much concern to the crown officials as those of the king, may have been so small that it was considered useless to conserve the records after the metals had been delivered to their owners. Furthermore, the accounts of private gold, if kept, may have been destroyed in the fire which consumed the priceless correspondence between the officials of the House of Trade and the Council of the Indies up to the year 1558. After the middle of the sixteenth century, when the treasure ships commenced regularly to sail in convoyed fleets, the records of private gold and silver were just as carefully kept as were those of crown treasure.

Chart 1 shows that commencing with the period 1503–5 there was an upward trend in the arrivals of treasure which persisted

---

[1] Archive of the Indies, *Contratación*, 39–2–2/9 (1). Again neglecting the works of art, which were of little value as bullion, this shipment of treasure was worth only 1,847,020 maravedís – an insignificant sum in comparison with the bullion which the crown had been regularly receiving from Cuba, Puerto Rico and Hispaniola. When Professor Merriman (*The Rise of the Spanish Empire*, vol. III, 1925, p. 45) remarked that this shipment was 'the first real indication of the wealth of the Indies', he overlooked the far greater imports of treasure of earlier years. Cf. Table 1 above.

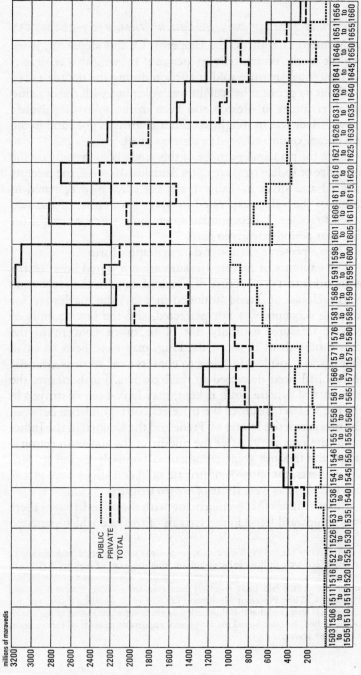

CHART I. Average yearly treasure imports: five-year periods.

through 1591-5.[1] After 1600 there was a significant decline in the receipts of gold and silver. Lacking space for argument, I can but indicate some of the probable causes of this phenomenon. It may be suggested, however, that the decrease in the production of the mines at Potosí toward the close of the sixteenth century; the constant increase in the cost of the labour and materials for mining in conjunction with the fixed prices of the precious metals; the accession of weak monarchs unable to maintain efficient administrations, which, in view of the prevailing paternalism, was a serious impediment to the efficient conduct of business; the growth of population and the expansion of trade in the colonies, which absorbed more of the metals for monetary use; the activity of interlopers, who commenced to supply the colonies with large amounts of manufactured goods and to carry an equal value of specie to countries other than Castile; and the laxness of public administration, which caused the avería, or convoy tax, to rise and thus encouraged smuggling, were among the outstanding causes of the decrease in the amounts of gold and silver reaching the motherland. But, whatever may have been the causes of the decline of treasure imports after 1600, the fact remains that a precipitous decline occurred.

It is not to be inferred from what has been said that all imports of gold and silver were registered. From the very first, smuggling was a matter of concern to the Government, and vigorous measures were taken to suppress it.[2] With the lapse of

[1] The paucity of receipts of crown treasure from 1521 to 1525 may be explained on the ground that the colonial officials were reluctant to remit treasure to Castile while she was, and while they believed her to be, in the throes of domestic turmoil.

It is striking that the largest receipts of precious metals between 1503 and 1660 came in the period 1591-5, the five-year period – as divisions are made in this study – immediately following the destruction, in 1588, of the so-called Invincible Armada. Obviously the opinion that Spain, unable to furnish adequate protection to treasure fleets, received a greatly diminished supply of gold from the Indies after this catastrophe has no foundation in fact.

[2] Unregistered treasure found on board a vessel was confiscated, and the man in charge of it was fined four times its value. *Recopilación de Leyes de Indias*, lib. ix, tit. xxiii, ley xlvi. Royal officials in America and on treasure fleets were exhorted to be vigilant in searching for unregistered gold and silver, and the captains general of armadas were instructed to make every possible effort to ferret out the

time the severity of these measures was enhanced. An ordinance of 1593 provided a penalty of four years' suspension from office for any captain or minister carrying goods out of register and a sentence of a like number of years in the galleys for any one of lower rank committing the same offence. In March 1634, these penalties were superseded by others still more severe. For smuggling, masters, mates and guards of vessels, and men of a low station in life were subject to the loss of the treasure together with all of their goods, to a sentence of ten years as galley slaves, to perpetual exile from the Indies and to permanent loss of the privilege of engaging in the India trade. All of the above penalties except the ten-year sentence in the galleys were also applicable to men of a high station in life.[1] The fact that it was necessary to repeat the interdictions of smuggling and to increase the sanctions with each new decree indicates that the evil was not imaginary.

It cannot be said, however, that the figures for legal imports of gold and silver do not accurately show the trend of the actual volume of imports, for the extent of smuggling probably did not vary a great deal from decade to decade, at any rate not until after the close of the sixteenth century. After the death of Philip II (1598) there was probably an increase in this evil, which attained great proportions at the close of the reign of Philip IV (1621–5); but Chart 2, showing the movement of Andalusian prices, indicates that the figures do not seem to be seriously vitiated by the fact that there were surreptitious imports of the precious metals.[2]

All of the prices used in this study were collected from docu-

---

men who embarked as soldiers, sailors, or passengers for the purpose of smuggling treasure. Ibid., lib. viii, tit. xvii, ley l; lib ix, tit. xxxiii, ley lxii.

[1] José de Veitia, op. cit., bk II, p. 196.

[2] The records of the Seville mint would aid greatly in determining the extent of smuggling. They would also shed light upon the amount of treasure produced in the Indies, since bullion intended for smuggling doubtless did not pay the quint. To guard against impelling its owners to export unregistered treasure instead of coining it within the kingdom, smuggled bullion that once reached the mint was accorded the full status of registered treasure. The notaries of the mints kept records of the amount of bullion delivered each day. Cf. José de Veitia, op. cit., bk I, pp. 253–4, 265. Although past efforts have proved futile, it is hoped that these records may be found.

ments in one of the following Spanish archives: Archive of the
Indies, Municipal Archive and Cathedral Archive, all of Seville,
and the General Archive of Simancas. By far the greater part
of the prices were found in the Archive of the Indies, the reposi-
tory of the official papers of the House of Trade.[1]

All of the institutions – the city and the Cathedral of Seville
and the House of Trade, of which the accounts have been
examined – purchased commodities on a large scale. Since the
House of Trade bought goods to supply colonists and to outfit
vessels for exploration and for convoys of treasure fleets, it

---

[1] Most of the prices were found in the following series of documents in the
Archive of the Indies:

(1) *Accounts of Armadas of the Indies and Coast Guard Galleons of Tierra Firme*,
1553–1741, 31 'legajos.' A recent fire damaged many of these documents.

(2) *Inventory of the Papers Pertaining to the Armadas of the Guard of the Indies and
Others Sailing under the Direction of the House of Trade of Seville*, 1519–1611, 123
legajos. These documents have also been damaged by fire.

(3) *Records of Accountants of Supplies* (Cuentas de Tenedores de Bastimentos),
1565–1671, 97 legajos. The accountants were more interested in the quantities of
the various commodities than in their prices. Complete inventories of supplies
for vessels are tantalizingly abundant, but prices are seldom stated.

(4) *Papers Pertaining to the House of Trade of Seville*, 1503–1750, 142 legajos. The
only prices found in this miscellaneous series were in the accounts of the factor
and comptroller.

(5) *Papers Pertaining to Armadas* (Papeles de Armadas), 1538–1750, 324 legajos.
This group furnished prices for several years between 1538 and 1588, but practically no data were found in a sample of twenty-three legajos bearing dates later
than 1588. The prices obtained were taken chiefly from factors' accounts.

(6) *Accounts of Factors*, 1542–1705, 20 legajos. Between 1542–57 and 1562–1615,
when the Francisco Duartes – father and son – served as factor, this series is fairly
rich in prices; but for other years it contains almost nothing. As compared with
the aimless, slovenly book-keeping of other men of their epoch in the employ of
the crown, the accounts of the Duartes are clear and well kept.

(7) *Books of Receipts and Disbursements of the Treasurer of the House of Trade*, 1503–
1717, 30 legajos. This series supplied most of the prices for the early years, but
none for the later ones.

In *Libros de Mayordomazgo* of the Municipal Archive – which, unfortunately, are
not catalogued and arranged beyond 1554 – and *Cuentas de Fábrica* of the Cathedral Archive of Seville prices were found which proved valuable in filling gaps.
Perhaps a half dozen prices found in the General Archive of Simancas were also
used for this purpose.

Because of less extraneous material, the *Cuentas de Fábrica* of the Cathedral
Archive of Seville were the easiest documents to handle that I made use of. But
the archive was made available only one hour a day during a short period. In the
future I hope to secure from this source prices of bricks, lime, and plaster (yeso)
to complete a series collected up to 1554 in the Sevillan Municipal Archive.

bought in extremely large quantities. It is evident from the sources that this is a study of wholesale prices.

Inasmuch as most of the prices come from records of the House of Trade, a brief statement of its purchasing methods may not be amiss. Methods employed during the experimental stage, say, before the middle of the sixteenth century, can be neglected.

After the officials of the House of Trade and the Council of the Indies had agreed, through correspondence, upon the number of vessels to be used in convoying the treasure fleets, and the vessels were selected, the prior and consuls of the Corporation of Merchants met with officials of the House of Trade to draw up a budget. The amounts of supplies and provisions needed were estimated, and the factor,[1] apparently with the advice of the others present, estimated the cost of each item. Then funds were placed at the disposal of the factor or of the purveyor, as the case might be, who, assisted by numerous subordinates, bought the commodities.[2] According to Veitia,[3] the factor acted as purchasing agent until 1588, after which time he was superseded by the purveyor, for whom the factor substituted when for any reason he could not perform his duties or when the office was vacant. But the plethora of prices in factors' accounts after 1588 suggests that the factor had more than a casual connection with the buying of goods.

It may be questioned whether inefficient purchasing by bureaucrats does not impair the reliability of these prices. Alonso de Carranza, who was thoroughly familiar with every phase of the India trade, writing in 1629, said that the impractical and inexperienced buyers of the House of Trade ordinarily purchased the worst grades of the least suitable goods at the highest prices and that the goods passed through

---

[1] The factor, one of the three judge-officials who controlled the House of Trade, exercised general supervision over the purchasing and storing of supplies and the outfitting of the fleets. He was a sort of combination of port agent and purchasing agent.

[2] As will be shown presently, goods were sometimes bought on credit. This practice became common in the closing years of the reign of Philip IV. For an example of the arrangements made for buying supplies, see Archive of the Indies, *Contratación*, 30-3-9.

[3] Op. cit., pp. 165, 178.

'numberless hands in which there ordinarily remains a great part of the price which in name only is for the supplies and armaments.'[1] The buyers, selected because of political considerations, were probably at the outset not competent; but, considering the long average term of office of the officials and employees of the House of Trade, one cannot say that they were inexperienced. The present prices are those paid dealers, exclusive of the expenses complained of by Carranza. The costs of handling goods, such as transportation and the salaries and expenses of buyers, which were listed separately in the accounts, were not included in the prices contained in this study. The supplies were inspected and the accounts checked, first by the overseer and later by the official who dispatched the armada.[2] This official scrutiny possibly made the buyer a little more careful than if his actions had not been investigated, though it could not make an expert purchaser out of a poor one, nor could it altogether preclude fraud and collusion. Furthermore, the allegations of Carranza are discredited by the fact that prices paid by the House of Trade were not higher than those paid by the city and Cathedral of Seville and by the army in Málaga. It is not probable that inefficiency and extravagance were more prevalent in the buying of all of these institutions at one time than at another, except possibly in the closing years of the reign of Philip IV, when laxness of administration became rife.

Much of the buying was done in and around Seville, but the territory was not limited to that immediate neighbourhood. An effort seems to have been made to purchase where it proved most economical. With the estimates of supplies for 1581 orders were found directing that they be bought as follows: white bread, olive oil, 'tollos' (a kind of fish), medicines, raisins, almonds, sugar, iron hoops (for pipes), tallow candles, shields, lances, bullets and naval cables in Seville; wine and vinegar in Xarafe, Cacalla and vicinity; beef in Xerez and vicinity; tuna fish in Rota (coast town near Cadiz); beans and chick peas in Osuna, Medina, Vexer, Cabra and Montilla; rice in Seville and Cadiz; garlic in Cabra; pork in Ronda and Aracena; cheese in

---

[1] Op. cit., p. 323.
[2] José de Veitia, op. cit., bk 1, pp. 57, 159.

Osuna and Cabra; pipes, plates and cups in Seville, Cadiz and San Lucar de Barrameda; and lead in Cadiz and San Lucar de Barrameda.[1] The buying territory for this year may be taken as typical.

In the beginning I intended to collect prices for every year from 1503 to 1660, but the work proved so slow and tedious that it seemed wiser to spend the time in collecting them for alternate years. It would have been more satisfactory to have a complete series; but, in fact, it is doubtful whether for the present purpose much would be gained by having prices for every year, since the influx of the precious metals worked out its effect in the trend of prices, not in the year to year fluctuations.

Obviously it would be desirable to have prices for the same season of the year, but this was not always possible. However, a certain degree of uniformity was attainable because of the fact that most of the vessels or fleets either sailed in the late spring or prepared then to sail in the summer. For all years spring prices were secured when possible, or perhaps they might better be classified as winter and spring prices. The desideratum was to obtain prices before the new harvest came on the market. In the vicinity of Seville at the present time the harvesting of wheat and chick peas – and I believe of beans – begins about the middle of June or a little earlier; it is probable that the seasons have not changed a great deal in the last four centuries. By far the greater part of the prices collected are for dates earlier than 1 June. March, April and May prices are most numerous and next to them come January and February prices; but for summer and fall there is only a sprinkling of prices – taken when more acceptable ones were not forthcoming.

In the inclusion and exclusion of commodities for the index numbers little was left to choice, for selection was limited to the range of commodities used in outfitting, provisioning and arming vessels. The provisions of seafarers in those days were necessarily made up of food which could be preserved without refrigeration for an indefinite period. This was one limiting

[1] Archive of the Indies, *Contratación*, 30-3-9.

factor in the selection. Doubtless expense was another. Supposing that the scale of living of working-class Spaniards was used as a model in providing for the seamen, one would expect none other than a meagre fare. Fortunately for our purpose, however, the higher officials and men ill at sea were supplied with a greater variety of food,[1] thus providing prices for a few more commodities. Seventeen of the twenty-four commodities used in making index numbers are of the food group.[2] Of these seventeen, four and sometimes five – namely, almonds, white bread, raisins, sugar and at times rice – were provided only for officers and for men who became ill at sea. The remaining thirteen commodities of the food group composed the sailors' diet.

There was little elimination from the list of provisions for ordinary seamen on account of insufficient data. Sardines were supplied regularly in the first half of the sixteenth century and occasionally thereafter; but, when they were listed frequently, codfish seldom appeared. Hence sardines were spliced with codfish – or, perhaps more properly speaking, codfish prices were derived from those of sardines – for the early years. Price quotations were found for both of these commodities in the years 1505, 1539, 1549, 1567, 1572 and 1581. On the average the price of codfish per quintal was 222 per cent of that of sardines per thousand. Up to 1557 the prices of sardines per thousand multiplied by 2·22 were taken as the prices of codfish per quintal.

Sporadic prices of other kinds of fishes, especially of tuna, were found, but prices for no other variety appeared often enough to justify its inclusion in the index numbers.

Many commodities had to be eliminated from the group making up the diet of the aristocrats. Immediately before sailing, fresh eggs and live hens, and often a few sheep, yearlings and pigs were bought in Cadiz or San Lucar de Barrameda, all of which, together with old wine, were supplied 'for the table of the captain general and other high officials.'[3]

---

[1] Cf. Archive of the Indies, *Contratación*, 41–1–1/12.

[2] Tallow was used in bread-making. Cf. Archive of the Indies, *Contratación*, 39–2–2/9 (2). Since both tallow candles and tallow in bulk were always bought, it seems logical to conclude that the latter was used in the preparation of food.

[3] Archive of the Indies, *Contratación*, 39–2–2/9, 41–1–1/12.

Since the collection of egg prices at approximately the same date for each year was impossible, the wide seasonal fluctuations characterizing their prices was in itself sufficient to bar them. Furthermore, on account of their being last-minute purchases, hens and eggs were seldom included in the accounts containing other prices. Hens were bought in sufficient numbers – usually from fifty to four hundred – to be considered 'average hens' and used along with the other commodities, had their quotations been more abundant. Too much variety in old wine eliminated it from the list. The wine for sailors was usually bought at the same, or about the same, price at any one time; but there were often many different prices, at times varying widely, for old wine. Because sufficient description to permit of certain classification was not given, several frequently quoted heterogeneous commodities, such as tacks, nails and various kinds of cloth, were omitted. Salt prices were abundant, but the multiplicity of taxes on salt rendered impossible the use of these prices. At times the prices apparently included all of the taxes, sometimes only a part of them, and at other times none at all.

Sail cloth was listed with the supplies fairly regularly during the seventeenth century, but practically never before 1601. Sulphur appeared frequently in the accounts, though not quite often enough to be included in the index numbers. Prices of cannon powder and of iron hoops for wine and vinegar pipes were found in sufficient numbers to be seriously considered, but they were finally rejected. Barley and wheat were listed for most of the early years, though practically never after the first half of the sixteenth century.

Since prices of white bread did not regularly appear before 1532, they were derived from wheat prices. On account of the seasonal fluctuations in the prices of wheat and bread and of the influence upon them of good and bad crops, comparisons were made only when quotations for both were found at approximately the same date. Consequently ratios were obtained for only three years: 1530, 1611 and 1617. Since on the average the price of white bread per quintal was 352·7 per cent of that of wheat per fanega, wheat prices before 1532 were multiplied by 3·53 and the results used as white bread prices. The cases are few, but the fact that the ratios vary little is encouraging.

When more than one quotation was found for a commodity, a spring price, if available, was chosen. In the case of divergent quotations for the same date, the clearly predominant one, if such existed, was selected; in the absence of such a price an arithmetic average weighted by the respective quantities purchased at each figure was struck.

Inasmuch as all prices used in making index numbers were reduced to silver maravedís, very small units of account,[1] quotations are made only to the nearest half maravedí.

After the first quarter of the seventeenth century vellon[2] money was at a discount in terms of silver, and depletion of the public treasury often forced the crown to buy supplies on credit or to borrow money to pay for them. Beginning with 1626 many of the prices were stated in vellon, and more than half of the quotations from 1645 to 1660 were credit prices to be paid in silver upon the return of the flotas.[3]

Economy of space does not permit the publication here of a table of premiums on silver from 1624 to 1660 – compiled from contemporary documents – by the use of which vellon prices were converted into silver prices. When more than one premium was quoted for the same year, the discount on each price varied according to the date of purchase, that is, according to the premium which seemed to prevail when the purchase was made. Unfortunately premiums were not found for all years, though many were encountered for most of them. For

[1] The silver maravedí was an imaginary thirty-fourth part of the silver real. The real contained 49½ grains of pure silver until 23 December 1642, when its silver content was reduced to thirty-seven grains. An allowance for this change is made in subsequent prices so that throughout the period under investigation they are stated in terms of 1·45 grains of pure silver – the content of a 'silver maravedí'.

[2] Vellon was originally a mixture of silver and copper used in subsidiary coinage. The silver content progressively became smaller until 1599, when it disappeared entirely. After this time several attempts were made to restore the silver, but all of them proved ineffectual.

[3] The mediums in which prices were stated for the years employed between 1626 and 1660 were about as follows: 1626 and 1644, all vellon; 1628, 1637 and 1639, all vellon except from one to four prices; 1647, about half vellon and half silver credit; 1648, 1651 and 1653, all silver credit except from one to four prices; 1655, 1657 and 1660, predominantly silver credit; 1658, cash in silver.

example, no quotation is listed for 1637. But, since the table indicates a steady rise at that time, 25 per cent, about the figure the premium would have reached in a perfectly uniform increase from 24 per cent in 1636 to 28 per cent in 1639, was used in the reductions. Other cases of missing premiums were similarly handled.

Since up to 1648 silver credit prices closely paralleled vellon prices, they were reduced to silver cash by means of the prevailing discount on vellon. The premiums on cash in later years were arrived at by comparing simultaneous cash and credit prices for the same commodities. For example, in 1653 both cash and credit prices were available for four commodities, the latter exceeding the former by the following percentages: for large wax candles 52 per cent, for tallow candles 39 per cent, for iron hoops 50 per cent, for cheese 36 per cent, and on the average for the four commodities 44 per cent. Silver credit prices for this year were reduced to silver cash by allowing a premium of 44 per cent on the latter. In some years both cash and credit prices were found for a greater number of commodities and in other years for fewer. The premiums arrived at for cash payment in silver instead of payment in silver upon the return of the treasure fleets were $61\frac{1}{3}$ per cent in 1655 and 1657 and $109\frac{1}{2}$ per cent in 1660. It is almost incredible that credit prices were so exorbitant when the Government was the debtor. However, Manuel Colmeiro[1] tells us that Philip IV, finding himself in need of money to equip the treasure fleets leaving Seville in 1639, could find no one in the Sevillan money market willing to advance him funds at less than 70 per cent interest.

The above figures illustrate the depths to which the public credit, which was symptomatic of the general economic debility of the country, sank in the closing years of the reign of Philip IV. They suggest that the historians who have sought evidences of decay in the reign of Philip II might have done better had they moved down by two Philips.

In Table 2, which lists prices for the whole collection of commodities – henceforward termed 'general prices' – all

[1] Op. cit., vol. II, p. 581.

TABLE 2 *General prices (in silver maravedís)*

	1503	*1505*	*1507*	*1511*	*1513*	*1515*
Almonds	203·5	—	—	340·0	223·0	—
Bacon	600·0	—	450·0	400·0	350·0	—
Beans	104·0	125·0	125·0	—	85·0	100·0
Beef	—	6·0	7·0	—	7·0	—
Bread, brown	—	365·0	500·0	170·0	195·0	170·0
Bread, white	388·0	388·0	1079·0	211·5	324·5	—
Cables, naval	600·0	780·0	1000·0	—	800·0	1075·0
Candles, wax	34·0	36·0	44·0	—	—	40·0
Candles, tallow	800·0	800·0	—	1000·0	800·0	1200·0
Cheese	160·0	165·0	—	125·0	140·0	—
Chick peas	104·0	—	350·0	163·0	119·0	136·0
Codfish	—	339·5	—	—	226·5	135·5
Garlic	9·0	12·0	—	—	7·0	12·5
Lead	—	—	450·0	600·0	500·0	550·0
Olive oil	90·0	80·0	110·0	—	85·0	100·0
Pipes	290·0	300·0	375·0	—	306·0	—
Powder	2500·0	—	2000·0	2000·0	2000·0	2800·0
Raisins	—	—	—	250·0	—	—
Rice	—	—	—	550·0	550·0	—
Sheepskins	—	—	34·0	—	40·0	36·0
Sugar	310·0	—	—	265·0	—	—
Tallow	790·0	750·0	750·0	800·0	800·0	1000·0
Vinegar	23·0	12·0	20·0	16·0	24·0	17·0
Wine	40·0	32·0	51·0	—	20·0	—

	1517	*1519*	*1530*	*1532*	*1537*	*1539*
Almonds	238·0	395·5	400·0	—	306·0	442·0
Bacon	730·0	900·0	—	1150·0	1125·0	1100·0
Beans	136·0	129·0	263·5	166·0	272·0	246·5
Beef	7·0	—	9·5	13·0	12·0	11·0
Bread, brown	250·0	250·0	569·0	544·0	306·0	527·0
Bread, white	370·5	441·0	959·5	882·0	—	816·0
Cables, naval	—	710·0	1350·0	820·0	1425·0	1100·0
Candles, wax	—	52·0	44·0	40·0	—	50·0
Candles, tallow	—	1000·0	1100·0	1500·0	1500·0	1360·0
Cheese	165·0	—	250·0	225·0	225·0	238·0
Chick peas	153·0	150·5	230·0	161·5	263·5	340·0
Codfish	113·0	—	377·5	364·0	453·0	333·0
Garlic	13·0	8·5	34·0	8·5	17·0	15·0
Lead	485·0	640·0	562·0	750·0	680·0	680·0
Olive oil	153·0	112·0	170·0	204·0	134·0	238·0
Pipes	—	—	408·0	408·0	408·0	375·0
Powder	1806·0	2000·0	3375·0	2300·0	3750·0	3750·0
Raisins	408·0	—	500·0	375·0	612·0	850·0
Rice	—	—	600·0	—	—	816·0
Sheepskins	—	25·0	55·0	60·0	—	72·0
Sugar	400·0	784·0	750·0	—	561·0	782·0
Tallow	1000·0	—	1000·0	1100·0	1250·0	1200·0
Vinegar	17·0	—	45·0	45·0	41·0	86·5
Wine	55·0	68·0	85·0	60·0	102·0	70·0

TABLE 2 (*continued*) *General prices* (*in silver maravedís*)

	1542	1548	1549	1552	1553	1555
Almonds	612·0	—	680·0	816·0	816·0	918·0
Bacon	1700·0	2750·0	1585·0	1250·0	2000·0	1800·0
Beans	306·0	218·0	306·0	357·0	375·0	272·0
Beef	15·0	—	15·0	16·0	19·0	18·0
Bread, brown	612·0	671·5	340·0	442·0	544·0	816·0
Bread, white	—	935·0	850·0	544·0	816·0	816·0
Cables, naval	1250·0	—	—	1874·0	1666·0	1564·0
Candles, wax	—	—	68·0	—	85·0	68·0
Candles, tallow	1200·0	—	1450·0	1632·0	1768·0	2400·0
Cheese	272·0	375·0	255·0	375·0	375·0	442·0
Chick peas	375·0	383·0	306·0	289·0	375·0	272·0
Codfish	604·0	604·0	528·5	604·0	453·0	655·0
Garlic	20·0	10·0	10·0	30·0	25·0	15·0
Lead	—	700·0	680·0	850·0	782·0	650·0
Olive oil	153·0	255·0	238·0	255·0	221·0	229·0
Pipes	493·0	—	—	816·0	—	683·0
Powder	3750·0	—	4500·0	8000·0	7500·0	7500·0
Raisins	884·0	—	867·0	816·0	—	683·0
Rice	750·0	850·0	800·0	900·0	900·0	1300·0
Sheepskins	—	—	—	85·0	102·0	55·0
Sugar	—	—	937·5	1156·0	1300·0	1190·0
Tallow	1632·0	1700·0	1394·0	1700·0	1700·0	1875·0
Vinegar	34·0	54·0	64·0	79·0	85·0	57·0
Wine	97·5	97·0	151·0	120·0	150·5	128·0

	1557	1559	1561	1563	1565	1567
Almonds	952·0	442·0	—	1020·0	1020·0	680·0
Bacon	1700·0	1938·0	2300·0	2100·0	2300·0	2300·0
Beans	578·0	527·0	340·0	476·0	306·0	442·0
Beef	16·0	18·0	19·0	32·0	24·0	20·0
Bread, brown	1836·0	340·0	629·0	748·0	408·0	562·5
Bread, white	2448·0	595·0	918·0	952·0	731·0	937·5
Cables, naval	—	1870·0	1500·0	—	1700·0	2812·0
Candles, wax	65·0	78·0	77·0	70·0	76·5	92·0
Candles, tallow	1900·0	2400·0	2720·0	2200·0	3264·0	2720·0
Cheese	375·0	527·0	680·0	578·0	646·0	340·0
Chick peas	1020·0	408·0	442·0	459·0	272·0	633·0
Codfish	631·5	750·0	1020·0	—	680·0	696·0
Garlic	29·0	26·0	25·0	24·0	13·0	30·0
Lead	1125·0	937·5	986·0	1156·0	1125·0	1000·0
Olive oil	204·0	167·5	225·0	306·0	324·0	388·0
Pipes	952·0	—	867·0	850·0	918·0	935·0
Powder	6750·0	5062·5	5625·0	5250·0	5250·0	5600·0
Raisins	1020·0	680·0	—	1156·0	1360·0	2040·0
Rice	1876·0	1088·0	1156·0	1292·0	1360·0	1500·0
Sheepskins	55·0	102·0	102·0	119·0	136·0	136·0
Sugar	1054·0	1326·0	—	1564·0	1360·0	1496·0
Tallow	2000·0	2176·0	—	1768·0	—	—
Vinegar	36·0	51·0	102·0	136·0	136·0	68·0
Wine	110·5	88·0	100·0	130·0	153·0	153·0

TABLE 2 (*continued*) *General prices* (*in silver maravedís*)

	1569	1572	1573	1575	1577	1579
Almonds	1156·0	1632·0	1224·0	1870·0	1020·0	1292·0
Bacon	2250·0	3000·0	3000·0	2516·0	1875·0	3162·0
Beans	306·0	527·0	340·0	306·0	562·5	612·0
Beef	19·5	28·0	23·0	25·0	20·0	26·0
Bread, brown	544·0	750·0	510·0	510·0	1122·0	952·0
Bread, white	850·0	1125·0	884·0	884·0	1530·0	1632·0
Cables, naval	2625·0	2625·0	2625·0	2437·0	2040·0	3187·5
Candles, wax	80·0	101·0	102·0	102·0	100·0	100·0
Candles, tallow	2700·0	3000·0	2380·0	2800·0	2500·0	2992·0
Cheese	510·0	656·0	562·5	612·0	510·0	510·0
Chick peas	408·0	714·0	493·0	442·0	782·0	850·0
Codfish	818·0	816·0	840·0	816·0	758·0	918·0
Garlic	15·0	30·0	24·0	34·0	26·0	42·5
Lead	1020·0	1125·0	1156·0	1222·0	884·0	1088·0
Olive oil	310·0	255·5	266·5	319·0	442·0	452·0
Pipes	918·0	833·0	850·0	1500·0	850·0	1088·0
Powder	6375·0	5250·0	5250·0	5250·0	6125·0	6375·0
Raisins	1462·0	1360·0	1500·0	1904·0	1054·0	1360·0
Rice	1088·0	1500·0	1768·0	1462·0	1224·0	1360·0
Sheepskins	68·0	—	144·5	102·0	—	93·5
Sugar	1428·0	1802·0	1836·0	1875·0	1700·0	2125·0
Tallow	3060·0	—	2040·0	—	—	—
Vinegar	85·0	102·5	102·0	259·0	90·0	85·0
Wine	127·5	143·0	187·0	245·5	136·0	153·0

	1581	1585	1588	1589	1591	1593
Almonds	—	1020·0	850·0	1020·0	952·0	1360·0
Bacon	2250·0	3604·0	2244·0	1768·0	2108·0	3200·0
Beans	544·0	544·0	—	612·0	612·0	646·0
Beef	30·5	28·0	30·0	—	29·0	24·0
Bread, brown	1122·0	1156·0	1020·0	1122·0	969·0	1088·0
Bread, white	1700·0	2040·0	1870·0	1875·0	2176·0	2176·0
Cables, naval	2380·0	1598·0	2244·0	2142·0	4125·0	4125·0
Candles, wax	102·0	102·0	100·0	102·0	102·0	102·0
Candles, tallow	3375·0	2933·0	3000·0	2992·0	3000·0	3000·0
Cheese	714·0	527·0	467·5	818·0	748·0	850·0
Chick peas	816·0	612·0	612·0	884·0	952·0	918·0
Codfish	952·0	952·0	952·0	1156·0	1020·0	969·0
Garlic	34·0	20·0	24·0	51·0	51·0	51·0
Lead	1088·0	1020·0	1122·0	1190·0	1500·0	1000·0
Olive oil	360·0	340·0	340·0	432·0	313·0	425·0
Pipes	1258·0	—	1190·0	1428·0	1224·0	1224·0
Powder	6375·0	5250·0	5250·0	5250·0	6000·0	5250·0
Raisins	—	—	952·0	1360·0	1768·0	1564·0
Rice	2250·0	1020·0	1428·0	1875·0	1598·0	2176·0
Sheepskins	102·0	68·0	85·0	110·5	119·0	102·0
Sugar	2250·0	—	2550·0	1904·0	2040·0	1836·0
Tallow	3128·0	2933·0	2720·0	2805·0	2805·0	3000·0
Vinegar	119·0	136·0	119·0	136·0	85·0	119·0
Wine	153·0	170·0	209·5	153·0	129·0	195·0

M

TABLE 2 (*continued*) General prices (*in silver maravedís*)

	1595	1597	1599	1601	1603	1605
Almonds	1020·0	—	—	884·0	1020·0	1500·0
Bacon	2850·0	2822·0	3162·0	2830·5	2252·0	2250·0
Beans	476·0	884·0	612·0	544·0	—	612·0
Beef	27·0			32·0	32·0	28·0
Bread, brown	952·0	1598·0	1326·0	748·0	1054·0	1394·0
Bread, white	1700·0	3196·0	2584·0	1564·0	2448·0	—
Cables, naval	4125·0	2584·0	—	2720·0	3000·0	3000·0
Candles, wax	112·5	120·0	118·0	120·0	129·5	136·0
Candles, tallow	—	3196·0	3200·0	2550·0	2900·0	3400·0
Cheese	816·0	816·0	748·0	799·0	748·0	1036·0
Chick peas	612·0	1190·0	1020·0	578·0	697·0	1020·0
Codfish	1224·0	1258·0	1700·0	850·0	884·0	918·0
Garlic	34·0	51·0	34·0	54·0	51·0	
Lead	1224·0	—	816·0	850·0	680·0	702·0
Olive oil	321·5	500·0	442·0	433·5	306·0	800·0
Pipes	1494·0	1209·0	1176·0	—	1020·0	1122·0
Powder	6750·0	8625·0	7875·0	6800·0	7500·0	—
Raisins	1394·0	1700·0	1479·0	1904·0	2380·0	2550·0
Rice	1700·0	2250·0	1836·0	1870·0	1870·0	—
Sheepskins	136·0	153·0	119·0	153·0	136·0	102·0
Sugar	2040·0	—	—	3000·0	4250·0	3400·0
Tallow	3000·0	3400·0	3128·0	2040·0	2482·0	3000·0
Vinegar	93·5	127·5	136·0	102·0	144·5	170·0
Wine	155·0	—	196·0	198·0	153·0	306·0

	1609	1611	1613	1615	1617	1619
Almonds	1500·0	1125·0	637·5	654·5	714·0	1156·0
Bacon	2448·0	2720·0	2584·0	2822·0	2380·0	2550·0
Beans	714·0	476·0	510·0	544·0	629·0	382·5
Beef	—	30·0	32·0	34·0	35·0	43·0
Bread, brown	1003·0	816·0	884·0	884·0	1751·0	952·0
Bread, white	1989·0	1700·0	1700·0	1479·0	2856·0	1870·0
Cables, naval	4125·0	3400·0	2244·0	2176·0	2244·0	2660·5
Candles, wax	112·5	112·5	113·5	92·0	94·5	112·5
Candles, tallow	2584·0	3570·0	2788·0	2653·0	3009·0	3060·0
Cheese	578·0	493·0	595·0	510·0	680·0	714·0
Chick peas	714·0	476·0	680·0	1020·0	1156·0	510·0
Codfish	561·0	782·0	748·0	816·0	892·5	748·0
Garlic	38·0	34·0	42·0	34·0	42·5	26·0
Lead	1156·0	1156·0	1326·0	1054·0	1054·0	1003·0
Olive oil	442·0	529·0	444·0	408·0	461·0	478·0
Powder	—	986·0	901·0	1292·0	—	969·0
Pipes	6075·0	7990·0	6387·0	—		7650·0
Raisins	1972·0	1564·0	2312·0	1632·0	1190·0	2108·0
Rice	1139·0	1088·0	1360·0	1496·0	1326·0	1700·0
Sheepskins	119·0	93·5	136·0	136·0	102·0	136·0
Sugar	2040·0	2108·0	1836·0	1632·0	1802·0	1904·0
Tallow	2584·0	3570·0	2380·0	1870·0	3009·0	2822·0
Vinegar	128·0	155·0	172·0	200·0	143·0	85·0
Wine	223·0	255·0	272·0	209·0	136·0	184·0

TABLE 2 (*continued*) General prices (*in silver maravedís*)

	1621	1626	1628	1637	1639
Almonds	1700·0	1031·5	999·0	1132·0	763·5
Bacon	2992·0	3142·0	4488·0	2584·0	3187·5
Beans	646·0	—	637·5	979·0	504·5
Beef	—	47·0	—	54·5	31·5
Bread, brown	1037·0	750·5	956·5	2094·5	797·0
Bread, white	2074·0	1431·5	1912·5	3114·5	1183·0
Cables, naval	3060·0	—	—	2856·0	3506·0
Candles, wax	119·0	138·5	—	97·5	95·0
Candles, tallow	2720·0	4385·0	—	3046·5	3254·0
Cheese	714·0	820·5	—	870·5	850·0
Chick peas	646·0	837·0	637·5	2013·0	504·5
Codfish	—	1590·5	—	1632·0	1420·5
Garlic	51·0	23·5	21·5	81·5	60·5
Lead	960·5	—	1594·0	1421·0	1155·5
Olive oil	410·0	391·0	446·5	435·0	493·0
Pipes	1428·0	914·5	—	1088·0	1115·5
Powder	11900·0	—	11900·0	—	—
Raisins	1870·0	1454·0	1020·0	1686·5	1633·5
Rice	2142·0	1572·5	2040·0	2312·0	1665·0
Sheepskins	136·0	—	—	109·0	—
Sugar	1802·0	1454·0	1211·5	1632·0	2421·0
Tallow	2720·0	—	—	2720·0	2231·5
Vinegar	136·0	108·5	111·5	80·0	119·5
Wine	306·0	226·0	120·5	200·0	147·5

	1642	1644	1645	1647	1648
Almonds	1167·5	1308·0	1389·0	1232·0	1205·5
Bacon	2539·0	3021·0	5037·5	3695·5	3713·5
Beans	—	758·5	957·0	1577·0	1688·0
Beef	—	36·0	—	—	—
Bread, brown	880·5	1046·0	856·5	1577·0	1688·0
Bread, white	1156·0	2092·0	1662·0	2710·0	2411·5
Cables, naval	2493·5	—	2687·5	3196·0	—
Candles, wax	102·0	97·0	108·0	108·5	—
Candles, tallow	2965·0	2615·5	2561·5	3695·5	3617·5
Cheese	680·0	837·0	785·5	739·0	603·0
Chick peas	408·0	536·0	957·0	1232·0	1447·0
Codfish	1451·0	1987·5	1763·5	1872·5	1688·0
Garlic	34·0	26·0	38·0	49·5	—
Lead	1624·0	1122·0	1700·0	1575·5	1509·0
Olive oil	468·0	392·5	503·7	443·5	583·0
Pipes	—	1203·0	1246·5	1084·0	970·0
Powder	12920·0	—	—	10880·0	—
Raisins	1226·0	1464·5	2115·5	2008·0	1603·0
Rice	1394·0	2328·0	1763·0	1577·0	1447·0
Sheepskins	126·0	—	100·5	123·0	—
Sugar	1190·0	1726·0	1763·0	2168·0	1929·0
Tallow	2414·0	2092·0	2015·0	3055·0	2411·5
Vinegar	105·5	124·0	138·0	135·0	150·0
Wine	146·0	187·0	239·0	311·0	194·5

TABLE 2 (*concluded*) General prices (*in silver maravedís*)

	1651	1653	1655	1657	1658	1660
Almonds	1634·5	1953·0	816·0	1870·0	1632·0	931·0
Bacon	3378·0	4250·0	3400·0	3582·5	2040·0	3497·0
Beans	1307·5	1180·5	544·0	1011·5	816·0	—
Beef	—	—	—	—	—	—
Bread, brown	2070·5	1889·0	748·0	566·5	1020·0	1295·0
Bread, white	3596·0	3778·0	1496·0	1133·5	—	2590·5
Cables, naval	3132·5	—	3400·0	—	3400·0	3400·0
Candles, wax	102·5	108·5	105·5	104·5	—	136·0
Candles, tallow	4533·5	5666·5	3400·0	6322·5	—	6800·0
Cheese	817·5	1416·5	850·0	843·0	816·0	1524·0
Chick peas	2179·5	1180·5	544·0	1264·5	816·0	1619·0
Codfish	1351·5	2125·0	1904·0	1813·5	1020·0	1632·0
Garlic	—	—	—	—	—	—
Lead	1632·0	—	2334·5	1768·0	1714·5	2652·0
Olive oil	392·5	330·5	510·0	569·0	442·0	476·0
Pipes	—	816·0	833·0	—	—	909·5
Powder	—	—	—	—	6800·0	—
Raisins	2179·5	2361·0	2176·0	2318·0	—	1619·0
Rice	2551·0	1889·0	1224·0	1586·5	1088·0	1360·0
Sheepskins	83·5	—	—	—	136·0	119·0
Sugar	2179·5	2656·0	2176·0	2266·5	1632·0	1619·0
Tallow	3400·0	5666·5	3400·0	—	3264·0	3400·0
Vinegar	127·0	121·0	141·0	191·5	204·0	151·0
Wine	340·5	473·0	348·5	368·0	—	280·5

quotations are in 'silver maravedís', with a pure silver content of 1·45 grains. The prices are for units as follows: almonds, cheese, sugar, olive oil, vinegar and wine by the arroba;[1] beans and chick peas by the fanega (1·58 bushels); pipes by the pipe; sheepskins by the sheepskin; wax candles by the pound; garlic by the string (ristra); beef by the pound 'carnicera' (thirty-two ounces); and the other eleven commodities by the quintal (101·5 pounds avoirdupois).

Powder prices are for the grade used in harquebuses. The wax candles were very large ones, sometimes weighing a quintal, used for illumination on the treasure ships.

What has been said about the absence of data for private treasure in the early years is equally applicable to the first two

[1] The arroba was both a weight and a liquid measure. As a weight it was equivalent to 25·36 pounds avoirdupois. As a liquid measure it varied according to the substance measured, being 4·26 U.S. gallons for wine and vinegar and 3·32 for olive oil.

significant gaps – 1519–30 and 1542–8 – in the table above. The
dearth of price data from 1621 to 1637 may be ascribed to the
fact that during the greater part, if not all, of this period the
House of Trade contracted with the Corporation of Merchants
of Seville to outfit and provision the treasure fleets.[1]

From the figures in Table 2 index numbers were made, with
an average for the years 1573, 1575, 1577, 1579 and 1581 as a
base. The reasons for selecting this decade were two: first, it
falls about midway of the period under investigation; and,
second, only six prices are missing for the five years. Since the
main purpose of the index numbers is to measure the effect on
prices of the influx of precious metals, the unweighted arithmetic mean was used in their construction.[2] The index numbers
are listed in Table 3.

To convey a clearer idea of the price movement, the figures
of Table 3 are presented in graphic form in Chart 2.

This chart clearly shows a constant, though zigzag, upward
trend in prices until about 1597, after which there is a drop
followed by a series of wild gyrations with a horizontal

TABLE 3 *Index numbers of general prices*

Year	Index number	Year	Index number	Year	Index number	Year	Index number
1503	24·8	1553	72·3	1588	97·0	1621	124·4
1505	28·2	1555	68·3	1589	110·0	1626	114·2
1507	36·5	1557	88·5	1591	112·0	1628	112·4
1511	25·4	1559	69·5	1593	117·0	1637	145·3
1513	25·2	1561	80·1	1595	109·1	1639	110·9
1515	32·2	1563	85·0	1597	141·3	1642	106·4
1517	28·6	1565	81·2	1599	124·6	1644	92·9
1519	34·0	1567	87·3	1601	111·0	1645	101·3
1530	47·5	1569	80·2	1603	117·6	1647	115·5
1532	43·1	1572	96·0	1605	132·0	1648	106·1
1537	45·1	1573	90·0	1609	111·6	1651	129·1
1539	49·9	1575	101·7	1611	107·8	1653	141·7
1542	54·1	1577	90·2	1613	108·0	1655	100·2
1548	62·5	1579	104·6	1615	104·0	1657	120·7
1549	56·8	1581	109·3	1617	114·7	1658	97·9
1552	66·5	1585	98·7	1619	106·5	1660	119·2

[1] Alonso de Carranza, op. cit., p. 323; José de Veitia, op. cit., bk I, pp. 153–6.
[2] For a justification of this method, see Wesley C. Mitchell, op. cit., pp. 63, 71,
76–8.

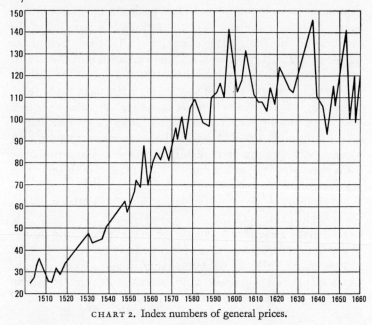

CHART 2. Index numbers of general prices.

tendency at a point somewhat below the 1597 mark. The horizontal tendency indicates that prices were fluctuating about a level at almost five times what they were at the beginning of the sixteenth century.[1]

Since agricultural crops are well represented in the index numbers, much of the year-to-year fluctuation can be ascribed to good and bad crop years.

[1] Though the following estimates were for Castile or the whole of Spain, it is interesting to compare them with the above figures for Andalusia. Sancho de Moncada, writing in 1619, said that things which cost a fourth real when America was discovered cost six reals in his day, op. cit., p. 54. In 1629, Alonso de Carranza stated that in 1497 a mark of silver would buy twenty fanegas of wheat or an equal number of sheep, while at the time he was writing it would not buy four fanegas of wheat nor two sheep, op. cit., p. 180. In his work published in 1687–88, Miguel Alvárez Osorio said that before the discovery of America one mark of silver was worth as much as three marks later – presumably at the time he was writing. 'Extensión Económica y Política', *Educación Popular*, p. 407. Vicente Vázquez y Queipo, writing in 1861, argued that the rise in prices did not begin until the middle of the sixteenth century and that during the ensuing century the increase was very gradual. *La Cuestión del Oro Reducida a Sus Justos y Naturales Límites.*

For purposes of comparison the commodities may be roughly divided into two groups – agricultural and non-agricultural. Group A which purports to include those commodities of which the prices are directly influenced by good and bad crops is made up of the following: almonds, beans, brown bread, white bread, chick peas, garlic, olive oil, raisins, rice and sugar. The other fourteen commodities compose Group B.[1] Index numbers for these two groups made by the same method as the general price index numbers, are shown in graphic form in Chart 3.

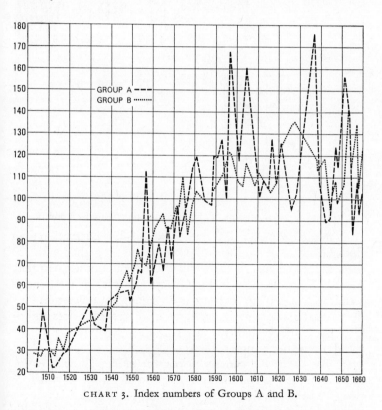

CHART 3. Index numbers of Groups A and B.

[1] Wine and vinegar are included in Group B instead of Group A because presumably the prices were not affected so quickly, so directly, nor to such an extent by good and bad crop years as were those of the commodities in Group A.

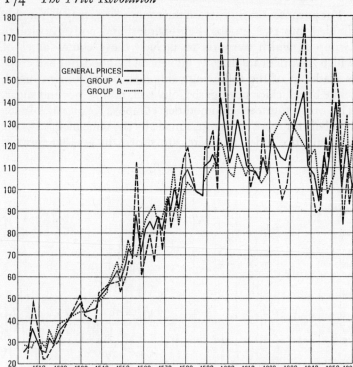

CHART 4. Index numbers of general prices and of Groups A and B.

As might be expected, Group B exhibits less fluctuation than does Group A. Good and bad crop years, together with the inelasticity of demand for several of the commodities, naturally caused abrupt changes in the Group A curve. In the general trends of the two curves there is no significant difference. Nor does Chart 4, showing index numbers of general prices and of Groups A and B, indicate any considerable difference in the trends of the three curves.

In the search for general prices, the money allowances for rations granted to common sailors assembled a few days before taking up their duties on the fleets, and to unskilled labourers working away from home were found for many years. To facilitate comparison of the movement of the cost of rations with the course of general prices, price relatives were made from the figures obtained for the former, with 42·5 maravedís, the average for the years 1580 and 1581, as a base. A graph of these relatives is shown with a graph of index numbers of general prices in Chart 5.

Since these graphs agree very closely, each confirms the other. The agreement also indicates that the unweighted index numbers furnish a fairly accurate measure of the cost of living for the labouring class. The price relatives of rations run slightly lower than the price index numbers up to the base period. A plausible explanation for this discrepancy is that the base price of rations is abnormally high.[1] No quotations for rations after 1623 were found; so it was impossible to carry the comparison up to 1660.

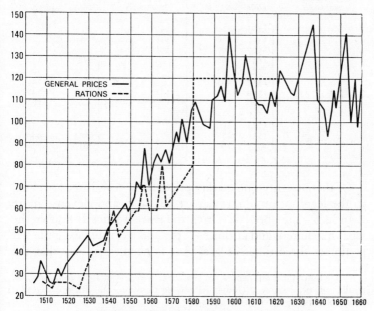

CHART 5. Index numbers of general prices and price relatives
of sailors' rations.

[1] Unfortunately only two quotations for rations are available for the decade used as a base period for general prices, and these are for the last two years of the decade. The figures indicate that the average cost of sailors' rations from 1572 to 1581 was probably considerably lower than 42·5 maravedís.

Repeated efforts were made by legal enactment to control prices, especially those of grains. In view of the unhesitating acceptance by many writers of statutory prices as indices of market prices it is well to inquire how far the former were effective in practice. Assuming that each of the price-fixing ordinances[1] remained in effect until superseded by the next one listed, Table 4 shows simultaneous legal and market prices.

TABLE 4 *Legal maximum and actual market prices of wheat*

Legal price: Date of ordinance and price per fanega in maravedís		Market price		Legal price: Date of ordinance and price per fanega in maravedís		Market price	
		Date	Price per fanega in maravedís			Date	Price per fanega in maravedís
		1503	110	1539	240		
		1505	110	1558	310		
		1507	306	1571	374		
		1511	60			1585	272
		1513	92			1589	765
		1517	105			1603	782
1502	110	1519	125	1582	476	1605	748
		1520	102			1607	765
		1530	272			1609	476
		1531	306			1611	442
		1532	250			1615	442
		1533	160	1615	612	1617	850

Of these twenty-one market prices for wheat, three are equal to the legal maximum, seven are below it, and eleven – more than half – are above it. Often the market price is double the legal maximum, and at times – 1507 and 1531, for example – it is almost three times as great.[2] It is needless to say that the

[1] For a list of these ordinances, see *Novísima Recopilación de Leyes de España*, vol. II, lib. vii, tit. xix, ley v (1805); Alonso de Carranza, op. cit., pp. 185–186; Manuel Colmeira, op. cit., vol. II, p. 232.

[2] In a pragmatic of 20 April 1503, it was alleged that the ordinance of 23 December 1502, fixing the price of wheat at 110 maravedís a fanega, had been circumvented by dealers' selling wheat together with some commodity not subject to the maximum laws, putting an extra price on the latter, or by the exaction of gifts as a condition of sale. Diego Pérez, *Pragmáticas y Leyes* (1549), fols. 131–2. Thus it may be seen that the market price did not always conform to the legal one even when it appeared to do so.

ordinances which supposedly regulated prices for Spain cannot
be considered as a reliable guide, although the measure they
yield of the general rise of prices for the whole period, 1502–
1615, happens not to be far different from the index for general
prices in Andalusia presented above.

Although, as is shown by the preceding graphs, silver prices
did not rise in the seventeenth century, it cannot be said that the
contemporary complaints of soaring prices were without foundation. What has been said about the reduction of vellon prices
to silver prices by means of a table of premiums constructed
for that purpose from primary sources indicates that after 1624
vellon prices rose because of scandalous debasement and overrating of the vellon coinage – which Philip III commenced in
1599 and Philip IV extended, intensified and systematized. For
instance, when the premium on vellon mounted to 205 per cent
in August, 1642, vellon prices rose accordingly.[1] Since few
contemporary writers on economics differentiated between a
rise in silver and in vellon prices, laymen could hardly be
expected to make such a distinction. In fact, all the evil effects
of rising prices were produced by the increase in vellon prices;
a distinction between them and silver prices is purely an
academic one.

The trend of French prices during the period under investigation seems to be similar to that of Andalusian silver prices.
In France during the first quarter of the sixteenth century prices
began to rise,[2] reaching their highest point in the last quarter of
the century, after which there was a downward movement.[3] It
will be recalled that Andalusian prices commenced to rise in
the first decade of the sixteenth century and that the zenith was
reached in 1597, after which there was a slight downward trend
until 1660. But the rise in French prices was less than half as
great as that which occurred in Andalusia. At the close of the
sixteenth century French prices were not two and a half times
as high as at the beginning of the century, whereas Andalusian

[1] Archive of the Indies, *Contratación*, 41–1–3/14, 40–6–2/19, 35–6–63/26.
[2] According to d'Avenel, French prices turned upward during the reign of
Louis XII (1498–1515), op. cit., vol. i, p. 15.
[3] Cf. Georg Wiebe, op. cit., pp. 377–9.

prices were almost five times as high. The similarity in the dating of the price movement between France and Andalusia can be ascribed to the close commercial contacts between Spain and France. Obviously a similar close relationship must have influenced the price movement in Flanders. D'Avenel tells us[1] that on account of higher living costs Spanish officials in the Low Countries were granted increases in pay in 1527.

Although French prices stopped rising by the end of the sixteenth century, the upward movement in other countries of northern Europe continued into the seventeenth century. English prices showed no upward tendency until 1551–70; but from that time to 1643–52, when the highest point – 3·31 times as high as in 1451–1500 – was reached, there was a steady increase.[2] The course of Alsatian prices was similar to that of English. Prices commenced to rise in the period 1526–50 and reached their zenith in 1626–50, when they were 3·41 times as high as in 1451–1500.[3] We have no data for Italy after 1600; but, on the basis of scanty data, it has been estimated that in the sixteenth century the prices of north Italy rose by about a third as much as those of Andalusia.[4]

The fact that prices in other countries did not rise so quickly nor to so great an extent as in Andalusia can be ascribed to the time required for American treasure to make its way thither and to the dilution it underwent in the process.

The question as to whether the sixteenth-century price revolution in Andalusia was the greatest occurring on a specie basis in modern times naturally arises. It has already been shown that by 1597 Andalusian prices rose by approximately twice as much as those of France, Alsace or England up to 1650. Since, with the exception of Mexican silver production from 1780 to 1800, no significant increase in the production of the precious metals

[1] Op. cit., vol. 1, p. 15.
[2] Cf. Georg Wiebe, op. cit., pp. 374–6. When Adam Smith, with the scanty material at his command, concluded that English prices did not commence to rise before 1570, that the price revolution ran its course by 1636, and that silver declined in value by two-thirds, he exercised uncanny powers of penetration. Cf. *Wealth of Nations* (Cannan Edition), vol. 1, p. 192.
[3] Cf. Georg Wiebe, op. cit., pp. 372–3.
[4] Cf. ibid., p. 380.

occurred in the eighteenth century,[1] we may turn our attention to the nineteenth century, in which productive gold and silver mining districts were opened and new processes and improved techniques came into use. Yet if we take the period 1820–1920, in order to include the peak of our war prices, prices in the United States rose considerably less than 100 per cent, or not one third as much proportionally as did those of Andalusia in the sixteenth century.

Among the causes of the price revolution in Andalusia there can be no doubt that the greatest was the influx of American treasure.[2] But many other factors, such as the decline in agricultural production, the decay of industry, the heavy emigration of men at their most productive age and the demand of the colonies for Andalusian goods – to mention only a few – also played a part in bringing about the price revolution.

To present a vivid picture of the correlation between the imports of treasure and the rise of prices, the figures for the former have been brought together with the index numbers of general prices in Chart 6.

An examination of Chart 6 will reveal that throughout the period under investigation there was a close connection between the imports of American gold and silver and Andalusian prices.

---

[1] Cf. Adolph Soetbeer, *Edelmetall-Produktion*, (1879) pp. 14–141.

[2] In the nature of the case, priority in observing the connection between the influx of metals and the rise in prices cannot be settled. Professor Merriman, in his *Gómara's Annals of Charles V* (1912), has pointed out that at least as early as 1558 Gómara expressed the opinion that the rise in Castilian prices was due to the heavy imports of American gold and silver (pp. lii–liii, 2, 162). But Gómara dismissed the matter with a single sentence; he did not take the trouble to elaborate his conclusion or to offer any evidence in support of it. It is altogether possible that a similar statement was made before 1558. So far as I know, Jean Bodin, in his *Reponse aux Paradoxes de Malestroit Touchant l'Encherissement de Toutes Choses*, published in 1568, was the first to demonstrate by careful analysis that the price revolution was caused by American treasure, to amplify his conclusion, and to refute other explanations. Bodin's claim of priority indicates that he arrived at the conclusion independently. Acceptance of this theory was impeded by its incompatibility with prevailing mercantilist preconceptions, though it finally gained credence. Adam Smith attributed the price revolution to American treasure, but erroneously remarked, 'it is accounted for accordingly in the same manner by everybody; and there never has been any dispute either about the fact or about the cause of it.' Op. cit., vol. 1, p. 191. As Wiebe pointed out (op. cit., p. 184.), there were disputes both before and after the time of Adam Smith over the causes, as well as the fact, of the price revolution.

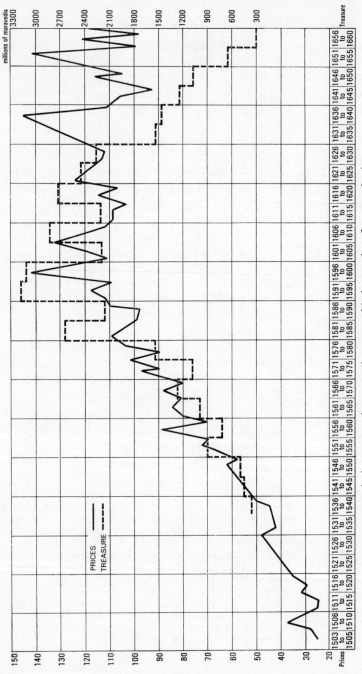

CHART 6. Average yearly treasure imports and index numbers for general prices.

From 1503, crown and presumably private gold coming from the Indies was coined and placed in circulation in Seville.[1] The imports of gold probably exerted some influence after the first arrivals. It may be objected that the receipts in the early years were too small to have any perceptible effect upon prices; but, however valid this argument may be for all of Europe or even for Spain herself, it cannot be said that the treasure, being concentrated in Seville and spreading thence to the rest of Andalusia, was not sufficient to make itself felt in a narrowly circumscribed area. Commencing with the period 1503–5 there was an upward trend in the arrivals of treasure until 1595, while from 1503 to 1597 there was a continuous rise in Andalusian prices. The greatest rises in prices coincide with the greatest increases in the imports of gold and silver.

The correlation between imports of treasure and prices persists after 1600, when both are on the decline. Obviously a corresponding fall in prices could not be expected after 1630, when the enormous drop in treasure imports occurred.[2] Even a constant influx of metals would have caused a progressively smaller percentage increase in prices, for each year's imports would have added a smaller increment to the total stock of precious metals. Hence with smaller imports of gold and silver, which were probably more than offset by surreptitious exports, some decline in prices was inevitable. A severer drop in prices was prevented by a decrease in the quantity of commodities offered for sale, caused by the marked decadence of Andalusian agriculture and industry.

The rise in vellon prices after 1624, which has already been mentioned, was due to scandalous debasement and gross overrating of the vellon coinage.

[1] Archive of the Indies, *Contratación*, 39–3–3/1.
[2] As Chart 3 shows, the disastrous harvest of 1636 (Cf. José de Veitia, op. cit., bk 1, p. 165) caused the peak in prices in 1637. The low prices of 1643–4 can be explained by the fact that prices had not become adjusted to the 25 per cent reduction, on 23 December 1642, in the silver content of the real.

Select Bibliography

The following works, in addition to those reprinted in this volume, deal directly with aspects of the Tudor price rise. Works dealing with parallel developments in sixteenth-century Europe are not listed here. A good general survey, with an extensive bibliography, is that of F. P. Braudel and F. Spooner, 'Prices in Europe from 1450 to 1750' in *Cambridge Economic History of Europe, Vol. IV, The Economy of Expanding Europe in the 16th and 17th Centuries*, ed. E. E. Rich (Cambridge, 1967).

BOWDEN, P. 'Agricultural prices, farm profits, and rents' in *The Agrarian History of England and Wales, Vol. IV, 1500–1640*, ed. Joan Thirsk (Cambridge, 1967).

BRENNER, Y. S. 'The inflation of prices in England, 1551–1650', *Economic History Review*, 2nd ser., XV (1962).

CHALLIS, C. E. 'The debasement of the coinage, 1542–1551', *Economic History Review*, 2nd ser., XX (1967).

CORNWALL, J. 'English population in the early sixteenth century', *Economic History Review*, 2nd ser., XXIII (1970).

CRAIG, J. *The Mint* (Cambridge, 1953).

A Discourse of the Common Weal, ed. E. Lamond (Cambridge, 1893); see also MARY DEWAR, 'The authorship of the *Discourse of the Commonweal*', *Economic History Review*, 2nd ser., XIX (1966).

FISHER, F. J. 'Commercial trends and policy in sixteenth century England', *Economic History Review*, X (1940).

FISHER, F. J. 'Inflation and influenza in Tudor England', *Economic History Review*, 2nd ser., XVIII (1965).

GOULD, J. D. *The Great Debasement: Currency and the Economy in Mid-Tudor England* (Oxford, 1970).

HELLEINER, K. F. 'The population of Europe from the Black Death to the eve of the Vital Revolution', *Cambridge Economic History of Europe, Vol. IV*, ed. E. E. Rich (Cambridge, 1967).

OUTHWAITE, R. B. *Inflation in Tudor and Early Stuart England* (London, 1969).

STONE, L. 'State control in sixteenth-century England', *Economic History Review*, XVII (1947).